UFO
Are we in danger?
The black book of ufology

Egon Kragel

UFO
ARE WE IN DANGER?
THE BLACK BOOK OF UFOLOGY

Max Milo, Paris, 2023
www.maxmilo.com
ISBN : 9782315010936

To Marie-Laure.
To my father, all the way over there, in his sky, gone.

"Our world is saturated with mysteries. It seems that we live surrounded by question marks. (...) The individual of our species has been endowed with the grace to know that he is terribly ignorant."
Bernard Heuvelmans, Ph.D. in zoological sciences

"One cannot, I believe, know anything by simple science; it is too exact and too hard an instrument. The world has a thousand tendencies into which one must bend to understand them before knowing what their sum represents."
Jean Giono, *The Living Water*

"It is good to plan and remember, with one eye in the past, and the other toward the future."
Publilius Syrus, *Sentences and Adages*

Contents

By way of introduction

One is tempted to believe it: something has changed. The ambient air, endowed with an unprecedented lift, suddenly seems lighter. These UFOs, once taxed as impossible and obscure fables, are now in demand. From now on, they strut from newspapers to Internet sites without losing an ounce of their stealth.

Until then, these UFOs of mystery - quick to evade, to reject, to question - were of interest only to a few enthusiasts. Since the 1940s, only a few privileged people have been interested in their strangeness. Not surprising, after all, when one knows that the word "mystery" comes from the Greek μυστήριον (*mustêrion*) which means "initiated".

A revelation that stains

Recently, UFOs have become official. Serious magazines are putting them on the cover. Journalists, until then ovniphobic, are caressing them in the sense of a news *shot* on steroids. What has happened?

It all started on December 16, 2017. On that day, the *New York Times* daily newspaper dropped a stain-inducing article. Reporters Helene Cooper, Ralph Blumenthal and Leslie Kean reveal that, between 2007 and 2012, the Pentagon investigated, in a covert manner, the UAPs (*Unidentified Aerospace Phenomena*, otherwise known as UFOs). This secret program was directed by a military intelligence officer, Luis Elizondo, on the fifth floor of the Pentagon's Annex C, in the heart of the building's labyrinthine network. The article "*Glowing* Auras *and ‹Black* Money': *The Pentagon's Mysterious UFO Program*" goes further: "Of the $600 billion annual budget allocated to the Department of Defense, the $22 million spent on this program is virtually untraceable. And this is of course what the Pentagon wanted.

Nevertheless, thanks to the *Times*' research, we learn that most of the budget for this program went to an aerospace research company headed by a billionaire entrepreneur, Robert Bigelow, a company that is currently working with NASA to produce expandable spacecraft.

This secret program, called AATIP (*Advanced Aerospace Threat Identification Program*), was largely funded at the behest of former Nevada Democratic Senator Harry Reid, then Senate Majority Leader. And the tone is set when he says on his Twitter account, "We don't have the answers, but we have plenty of evidence to warrant questioning. This is a scientific and national security issue."

Thanks to the daily's pugnacious inquiries, Pentagon officials eventually confirmed the existence of the program, stating that it ended in 2017. Allegation denied by investigators who say that UFO research still continues behind the scenes.

What should we learn from this? Mainly the about-face of the high North American authorities towards the phenomenon. Let us summarize: the last commission that officially studied UFOs was called *Project Blue Book*. It investigated from March 1952 to December 1969. The conclusions of this investigation, led by the US Air Force, were lapidary: "Sleep easy, these UFO sightings are nothing but misunderstandings. For decades, this announcement by *Project Blue Book* had the value of gospel and a dissuasive reminder for all those curious who sought to know more about the phenomenon. Today, we discover that the high authorities lied to us. They have never stopped studying these UAPs which, obviously, concern them. In a very official way, we have gone from: "UFOs are only bad interpretations of natural phenomena, and therefore do not exist" to: "UFOs are a serious national security concern because they are REAL!

Beyond the surprise or amazement, it is necessary to ask ourselves why this radical change of attitude occurred. What are the stakes, the motivations, the potential benefits? Who benefits from the crime?

Three essential videos

The general public is like that, we can't help it, they want proof. Let it be! In the wake of its revelations, the *New York Times* published, in December 2017, two videos supposedly shot by sworn military pilots. These documents, in black and white, answer to the sweet names of "Flir" and "Gimbal". Not to be outdone, the *Washington Post* daily newspaper drew a third one entitled "Go Fast", witnessing a similar encounter.

On these documents, we can see strange objects tracked by infrared cameras aboard Navy *jets*. The image quality is snowy; the sound, scrambled. The recordings are then the subject of feverish speculation by UFO enthusiasts who never stop wondering: real or fake? In September 2019, astonishment: the Great Mute becomes loquacious. Susan Gough, Pentagon spokeswoman, confirms that these videos are authentic. They were indeed captured by Navy pilots during their training. And she added that the U.S. Navy "has always considered the phenomena observed in these videos as 'unidentified' and that, in recent years, the increasing number of incursions of this type of object during military training poses a real problem!" The Pentagon then confirms that it has photos of unknown objects, described as "spheres", "cups" or "metallic airships". One could not hope for better. Conclusion: UFOs are here, real and among us!

On April 27, 2020, the Pentagon officially recognized the authenticity of the three videos and authorized their release (*Statement by the Department of Defense on the Release of Historical Navy Videos*). This makes one smile as they had been massively shared on the Net for three years. In addition, we learn that "Flir", the first video, was shot on November 14, 2004 off the coast of San Diego (California). This event is also known as the *USS Nimitz Encounter* (we will discuss this case in detail in the next chapter). The other two videos, "Gimbal" and "Go Fast," are from January 2015. Few details are provided to us, but unlike "Flir", the pilots' comments are audible in them. One exclaims:

- There is a whole swarm of them! Holy cow, they're going against the wind, a 120-knot west wind!

Another yells happily:

- Wow, I got it!

Then:

- What's that thing?

It was also discovered that the consumer versions were poor copies. Having viewed the original documents before they were confiscated by their superiors, several military personnel claim that these originals were quite clean and of longer duration.

Obviously, these documents do not leave anyone indifferent. Many attempts at explanation are made. For the most pragmatic, it is obviously a malfunction of an instrument or a software of the plane. For the science writer Mick West, it could be a natural atmospheric phenomenon or mirages "coming from defects of the radar systems". For Adam Frank, professor of astrophysics at the University of Rochester, these UAPs could be "drones deployed by rivals such as Russia and China to examine our defenses. Astronomer Thomas Bania agrees, suggesting "electronic warfare by China or Russia to gain intelligence on U.S. weapons systems," but British astronaut Timothy Peake, famous for his six-month stay on the International Space Station, says it looks like it came from "somewhere else." "I don't think this technology is designed by any of our nations," he says. These videos are remarkable. What these machines are capable of doing is extraordinary!" Ditto for Alain Juillet, former director of intelligence at the General Directorate of External Security (DGSE): "If any country in the world had made such a discovery, we would know about it. No progress of this magnitude can remain secret. One way or another, there would have been leaks, an indiscretion of the scientists who work on it... Since there has been absolutely nothing, it is that it is something else and that it escapes the terrestrial dimension."

In the end, the Department of Defense classified these phenomena as "unidentified". And the three videos are now downloadable on the official website of the American administration (NAVAIR-FOIA).

A report that causes confusion

These revelations caused a great stir in the corridors of power in Washington. On June 25, 2021, following an insistent request from the Senate, the ODNI (the Office of the Director of National Intelligence) submitted a preliminary report acknowledging the reality of the phenomenon. This 9-page report, entitled *Preliminary Assessment: Unidentified Aerial Phenomena,* is primarily intended for the leaders of the American army (Land, Air and Sea).

Military and intelligence experts have based themselves on 144 cases recorded between 2004 and 2021. 80 of the encounters with mysterious flying objects have been confirmed by several means of detection: radar, infrared and electro-optical equipment. Most of these incidents involve physical *objects, which is* corroborated by the detectors in question. The majority of these phenomena, we are told, have interrupted military maneuvers or activities.

Newspapers and television news outlets everywhere are reporting the incredible news. The *Washington Post* notes, "What once guaranteed you a one-way ticket to the loony bin has left the screens of Hollywood and the pages of science fiction novels to enter the public debate." *Der Spiegel* asks on its cover, "Are we still alone?" On July 1er 2021, *Courrier International* devotes 7 pages to the subject, with the cover headline: "Should we be (slightly) afraid of UFOs?"In short, if the nature of these astonishing phenomena remains unknown (an enemy government experimenting with hypersonic technology? visitors from beyond space?), they are no longer fiction and perplex defense and intelligence analysts.

Former government officials then made some very interesting statements. In particular, ex-president Barack Obama, guest on *CBS* on May 17, 2021, who said:

- What is true is that there are images and records of objects in the sky that we don't know exactly what they are. We can't explain how they move, and their trajectory.

NASA wants in

No time to catch your breath! Since this 9-page report, official announcements have been pouring in.

In June 2021, Bill Nelson, former astronaut and senator from Florida, current NASA boss, admits that the space agency is looking into the phenomenon. This follows a series of strange encounters between these mysterious objects and American military pilots. The NASA chief's comments confirm the seriousness with which the UFO issue is taken at all levels of the U.S. administration. Interviewed on *CNN*, Nelson states:

- I have spoken with these pilots. They are certain that they saw something very real. And, of course, we have seen the videos taken from their planes.

In October 2021, Bill Nelson spoke to an audience of North American students at the University of Virginia. He admits that there is a strong probability that extraterrestrial life exists. This contrasts drastically with the assertions of Steve Jurczyk, his predecessor. He specifies that this is one of the reasons why NASA proposes to examine the phenomenon very closely according to a strict "scientific protocol". A first!

In front of the same students, Bill Nelson mentioned again the numerous UFO sightings made by military pilots:

- These men know they have seen something. Their radars are locked onto it. But they don't know what it is... and neither do we.

Bill Nelson did not exclude that these UFOs could be of extraterrestrial origin.

- There are even theories that there may be other universes, he added. If that's the case, who am I to say that planet Earth is the only one with a civilized and organized life form?

Once again, UFOs are moving from fringe conspiracy theories to a national security issue.

UFOs: beware, danger!

Indeed, the same warning runs from lip to lip: "Beware, danger! This phenomenon is a potential threat." Experts of all kinds are pounding away. Not an *interview*, not an article where the term "national security" is not mentioned.

On April 5, 2022, the alert reached its peak. The news has the effect of a bomb. Following a request from the British magazine *The Sun*, made on December 18, 2017, an astonishing report is released by the Pentagon under the Freedom of Information Act. Its 1574 pages, in which the reality of UFOs is once again recognized, greatly sow the seeds of trouble. They were handed over by the *Defense Intelligence Agency* (DIA), the main manager and producer of military intelligence for the National Defense Service. The service required that certain information remain "partially undisclosed" because of protection and confidentiality issues. The document made public does not hide it: "Regarding the subject of this study, there is confidential information that is very relevant. Only a small portion of this classified literature has been published."

One of the appendices of the report, dated March 11, 2010, is entitled "*Anomalous Acute and* Subacute *Field Effects on Human Biological Tissues.* It presents a "useful database" that lists the physiological and biological effects experienced by people who have been in contact with a UFO, and their frequency. These effects, 57 in number, are classified and listed according to a list compiled in 1996 by John F. Schuessler, former director of MUFON, a civilian research agency dedicated to the study of the phenomenon. The list gathers cases recorded between 1873 and 1994. It lists deleterious events linked to UFOs, such as "alien abductions", "unexplained pregnancies", sexual encounters, telepathy and teleportation experiences. There are also reports of brain and nerve damage, paralysis, "radiation burns", all caused by "advanced technology". *Poltergeists, crop circles* and apparitions of strange beings are also listed. Close encounters are classified according to a specific code:

UFO. Are we in danger? The black book of ufology

CE1: means that the witness was standing at less than 150 meters from the UFO.

CE2: the encounter left traces on the ground or injured the witness.

CE3 : entities were seen inside or near the UFO.

CE4: the witness was abducted (or kidnapped).

CE5: concerns a close encounter that caused permanent psychological injury or death to the witness.

This report examined 42 cases from authenticated medical records. 300 similar cases remain "unpublished. All of the examples involve humans who, during contact with a UFO, suffered injuries that were sometimes irreversible and lethal. There is little antidote to this since, throughout these pages, North American officials declare that UFOs are of unknown origin!

This time, it is official. This phenomenon, considered until now as marginal and unworthy of interest, is becoming a serious national security concern discussed by legislators, sky experts and the military staff.

The main interest of this report is to show the extent to which government agencies rely on sources published by the general press and by the ufological community. Conversely, it highlights the lack of apparent results from the million-dollar contract with billionaire Robert Bigelow. To try to understand this phenomenon, we are asked, without any ambiguity, to go back in time, to look at old newspapers and magazines, and to scrutinize their chronicles.

Conclusion of this thick document: "There is probably something real and disturbing in all this, but we do not know what it is. The technique used by these objects is undoubtedly electromagnetic propulsion," which enthusiasts and civil investigators have long suspected.

A new office at the Department of Defense

So the hunt for UFOs is on. And we learn that American citizens have had their say. They voted for the National Defense *Authorization* Act. It gives the federal government the right to set the budget for U.S. defense spending. An important new amendment to this law now requires the military to create a permanent UFO research office! This is not a fiction. Along with the Pentagon's secret projects and clandestine programs, the follow-up to this report is thus the first major incentive to investigate the UFO phenomenon since the Air Force ended *Project Blue Book in* 1969.

The author of this amendment (which is named after him) is Democrat Ruben Gallego, chairman of the Subcommittee on Intelligence and Special Operations. In a press release, he states:

> It is in the national security interest of the United States to know what is flying in our skies, whether it is emerging technologies from competitors and strategic adversaries or aerial phenomena of unknown origin. My amendment therefore creates a permanent office in the Department of Defense to comprehensively assess these unidentified flying objects.

Reading between the lines, it is clear that the "phenomena of unknown origin" put on the table nothing less than the extraterrestrial hypothesis.

At the heart of its mission, the new office will have to submit an annual report, listing the number of UFOs reported in U.S. airspace as well as all related information: radar, satellite and electromagnetic data. This report should also contain information on international efforts with allied governments "to track, understand and address unidentified aerial phenomena. However, there is a surprising directive. It states that the office's annual report must include "an update on any efforts to capture or exploit potentially recoverable unidentified aerial phenomena." This could imply that such efforts are already underway. An admission? The bureau's first report is due December 31, 2022.

In the meantime, the Assistant Secretary of Defense, Kathleen Hicks, issued a memorandum concerning the creation of the AOIMSG (Aircraft Identification and Management Synchronization Group). This group is the successor to the U.S. Navy's Unidentified Aerial Phenomena *Task Force.* The specific mission of this task force is of course to investigate the UFO phenomenon. "The AOIMSG will synchronize efforts across the Department of Defense and the entire U.S. government to detect these objects in the airspace, identify them, and assess and mitigate any associated threats to flight safety and national security," a press release states.

Alas, a news item that quickly went viral on the Net dampened this enthusiasm. In May 2022, during an *interview* granted to the media *Politico* (a powerful source of information on the White House, the United States Congress and American government policy), government officials - under cover of anonymity - declared that, within

UFO. Are we in danger? The black book of ufology

the Pentagon itself, certain members "prevented very interesting information" concerning UFOs from being disclosed to the public. This hinders the action of those who, inside and outside the Department of Defense, are trying to shed light on this phenomenon. And this in spite of the growing interest of the citizens for the subject.

The Navy confides

The concern is temporary. When some members of the Pentagon balk, the U.S. Navy takes over.

On May 17, 2022, during a public hearing, Scott W. Bray, Deputy Director of Intelligence for the U.S. Navy, admitted that the U.S. military staff had unresolved files on "400 unidentified aerial phenomena" (or UFOs). Questioned by the House of Representatives' Counterterrorism, Counterintelligence and Counterproliferation (C3) subcommittee chaired by Democrat André Carson, Bray added that an "ever-increasing number" of mysterious objects have been reported "since the early 2000s. He said the increase is due in part to "the tremendous effort" by the U.S. military to allow its soldiers to report these sightings without being stigmatized.

In front of the C3 members, Bray also projected a video in which a green pyramid-shaped UFO was seen. Immediately, the legislators present expressed concern that these unexplained phenomena could pose a threat to national security. For Rick Crawford, a Republican from Arkansas, a failure to identify this potential threat would be "tantamount to an intelligence failure. Obviously to be avoided!"

National threat: the *leitmotiv* no longer surprises. Only one novelty challenges. Indeed, for 50 years, it is the first time that the American Congress has held a public hearing dedicated to UFOs... before the committee closed its doors for a confidential "information session".

Scott W. Bray concludes that the United States "is not aware" of any adversaries with such technologies. At the present stage of research, there is no evidence to "suggest a non-terrestrial origin" of the phenomenon. However, there is no evidence to exclude it.

NASA persists and signs

On June 9, 2022, NASA announced the launch of a UFO investigation in the fall of 2022. This investigation will be conducted by eminent scientists and aeronautical experts over a period of 9 months. It will be conducted independently of the Pentagon and should result in a report to the public. Behind this initiative, Thomas Zurbuchen, associate administrator at NASA, states:

> Anyone who asks me if there is irrefutable evidence of intelligent life in any of these phenomena, I will give a perfectly acceptable answer - for a scientist - which is that I don't know.

Three objectives are already announced:
- Gathering the collected data;
- Determine which ones are missing and how best to collect them;
- Decide with which tools to analyze them in the future.

The budget for this investigation is not expected to exceed $100,000. This is very little, and it raises questions. It is still strange that the UFO subject suddenly becomes of capital importance for the American agency. "It is because it concerns both national security and air traffic security," reply those concerned. However, such phenomena have been reported around the world for decades by credible pilots and astronauts. Thousands of testimonies have been transmitted to high authorities. It is unreasonable to think that the phenomenon has been ignored or even disdained for so long by the Federal Aviation and Space Agency. And it is therefore legitimate to ask again what stakes and interests motivate this sudden "awakening" of the North American officials.

UFO alert?

What is it really? Are these mysterious objects really hostile, dispensing, with cruel intent, paralysis, burns and irreversible harm? If we refer to the profuse literature concerning them, it is undeniable that some of their encounters have been very harmful. We will, and this is sometimes violent, deal with them in the course of this work. However, let us specify that out of the thousands (millions?) of confrontations recorded, these cases remain marginal. Many of these witnesses say that they found themselves "at the wrong time and in the wrong place".

Concerning national defense, it is certain that these "objects" violate our airspace with impunity. That they strut about in the face of our supersonic fighters, humiliating them with far superior prowess. And that they have been flying over

---

classified sites, most of them related to nuclear energy, since our fission bomb tests. It is therefore understandable that they can baffle and irritate many staffs, unchanging guarantors of our security.

On the other hand, we know of almost no case where this phenomenon has been deliberately hostile, firing on our armies, our aircraft, our civilian or military buildings. Since the Second World War, we have often sent missiles and rockets at these "objects", without triggering any response from them.

In conclusion, we know almost nothing about these celestial intruders. Following the Pentagon's announcements, I particularly like the line from the *Baltimore Sun* editorial board:

> It is certainly very pleasant to sit together around a campfire to watch the various clips of stunned pilots, read eyewitness accounts or imagine objects traveling at lightning speeds, negotiating turns in a flash. It is important to put all this in context and understand that we are dealing with a real mystery, not a science fiction TV show from the 1960s.

UFOs, a heretical experiment

We can then call UFOs a heretical experience because this phenomenon, both global and possibly ancient, crosses our history with a perennial stealth that has earned it many enmities. Excluded from the commercial society, hated by the sciences, breaking with a *doxa that is out* of breath, UFOs dynamite everything in their path. Epiphany for some, digressive mystery for others, promises of new engineering for the most advanced, they do not care about the rampart of incredulity, intellectual inertia and covetousness erected against them. For officials and experts, this crime is unforgivable.

"Let us respect the form in which reality speaks to us," recommends the philosopher and man of faith Jean-Yves Leloup. Let us not sin by pride. Let us curb, even if only for a moment, our predictable predatory appetites, our dreams of conquest, our thirst for control.

What are these UFOs? For North American officials, the answer is binary, always obtuse: either a threat, or a potential technology that the arms industry and energy experts covet. But should we simply reduce them to that?

Return to the original stories

Since, in order to approach it, the American Defense Intelligence Agency sends us back to the past, let us not hesitate. It is true that it is time to think (or rethink) these UFOs. And not to judge them. They deserve our full attention. To do this, let's make a distinction between the "reality" of the phenomenon and its "truth". Its "reality" coming from sensitive experiences, hence the stories. And its "truth" being, I am afraid, only the result of a subjective process of thought.

These founding stories are unique. The wonder, horror and fantasy that run through them are infinitely rich. Most of the time, everything speaks for itself. Let us rehabilitate them, let us dust them off. Let's knead again this rich raw material, a journalistic manna which, for the general public, has suffered for too long from a hard work of depreciation.

For this, let us keep intact our capacity for wonder. Let's rediscover this enthusiastic welcome, this availability of children to storytellers. With their wildly inventive narratives, these miscellaneous events speak of us. The UFOs that we meet there release our poetic possibilities and open, page after page, a breach in our unifying conception of reality. We might as well say it, this phenomenon does us good. It scolds our forms of thought - supposedly modern - which, under their altruistic airs, do not admit the differences. It rightly questions us about the universal behavior of complexity. On life which, playing with chance and non-determinism, is exuberantly creative. And, with a flick of the wrist, it sends us back to the prose of the world, far from a tectonics of our beliefs and our *preconceptions*.

The stories that follow are a healthy demonstration of this. Some have judged them fascinating; others, totally inadmissible. Each one will choose, but a constant haunts these stories: the UFO, this scientific counterpart, always unknowable and potentially unfortunate, does not cease to question us on what we are, on our world, on this real which escapes us and which we fear because violent, terribly complex, but always ambitious in its projects.

I. What is a UFO?

A Tic-Tac and a translucent sphere

Talking about UFOs is not without risk. What are they? Where do they come from? What do they look like? During the last few decades, when witnesses confided that they had seen inconceivable devices of various shapes, they were laughed at and scorned. Certainly, the American government has recognized the reality of the phenomenon. We have just seen it, its preliminary report of 9 pages, dated June 25, 2021, attests it. However, there are some strange whispers behind the scenes. It is claimed that this report is truncated. As a bone to pick, the Pentagon would have thrown only a handful of innocuous information to impatient citizens.

The investigator John Greenewald, from the American website *The Black Vault*, managed, somehow, to obtain a 17-page version of this famous report. Big disappointment at the end. Regarding this promising surplus, most of the information and graphics, including an inventory classifying these UFOs according to their shapes, are redacted. Comment by Adam Goldsack, from the British website *UAP Media UK*:

> If one of these objects or devices belongs to an opposing nation, we would not want those enemies to know that we know they exist. Now, if these flying objects are something non-terrestrial, then we might not want another nation to know that this technology exists, and then attempt to replicate it. Finally, if they really are from somewhere else, and they appear as "disks," "cubes," "Tic-Tacs," "triangles," "pyramids," etc., so they are not aerodynamic, then that is a very difficult conversation to have with the American public.

The first convincing clue to the strangeness of the phenomenon was provided to us, in December 2017, by the *New York Times*, in the form of a video that now has historical value. In 1'17, this document, named "Flir", totally changed the deal and offered UFOs an unexpected thickness, consistency and relief. Not to mention a very official recognition from the highest authorities. It is clear that, without the *Nimitz* affair and these brief black and white images, the elite of the media and of our governments would still classify UFOs in the shelves of an esoteric fair. But what really happened on that autumn day off the coast of California?

Off the coast of San Diego

Date: November 14, 2004.
Location: along the Pacific coast of California, off San Diego, USA.

Between November 10 and 16, 2004, the *Nimitz*, a U.S. nuclear-powered multi-purpose aircraft carrier, and its Air Strike Group (ASG) were scheduled to operate off the west coast of the United States in preparation for their future deployment to the Arabian Sea. But on November 14, 2004, an unusual event caused panic among these seasoned men, who were ready to face the most extreme situations. That day, the *USS Princeton*, a missile cruiser, was about to start a training exercise, in duo with the *Nimitz*. Suddenly, the ship's operators repeatedly detected the presence of a dozen abnormal air vehicles operating in the nearby sky. These singular "objects", close to the military vessels, moved "at dizzying speeds". From an altitude of 18,000 meters, they fall, in a few seconds, to stabilize at 15 meters from the surface of the sea! On the radar screens, the operators see them moving or remaining stationary. After a brief pause, these "objects" fly at lightning speeds while negotiating improbable turns. For almost two weeks, the operators have been spotting these strange invaders.

The *USS Princeton* decided to cancel its training and brought back a flight of two F/A-18F Super Hornet fighters. One of these aircraft is piloted by Commander David Fravor. The *Princeton*'s operator asks him if he is carrying weapons.

- Yes," says Fravor, "two CATM-9s [*dummy missiles that cannot be fired*].

- Well, this time we have a real target for you!

The order is immediately given to intercept this intruder. As they gradually approached their target, the pilots - then at an altitude of 6000 meters - saw nothing. Their radars either. But, looking down, Fravor saw a disturbance on the surface of the water, "as if the water was boiling". He has the feeling that a large submerged object is causing this disturbance. Fravor then spots an oval, white, Tic-Tac shaped craft moving erratically, 15 meters above the waves. Almost the size of his fighter, the object performs maneuvers defying all logic. According to our pilot, the UFO is "white, of uniform color, smooth, without edges, without nacelles, without wings nor propulsion mechanism". It is about 12 meters long. This was immediately confirmed by Commander Jim Slaight, pilot of the second fighter.

To better examine this strange machine, Fravor begins a circular descent to approach it, but the UFO goes up at once towards him, "as if it came to meet him". Then the object carries out a maneuver of avoidance before disappearing in a wink.

- He produced an acceleration like I've never seen before!

The Princeton's operations officer asks the planes to join the *heading point,* their rendezvous point in military jargon. As they complied, they received a new radio message. The radar on board the cruiser has again picked up the intruder.

- Gentlemen, you won't believe this, says the operator, but your target is already at your meeting point!

Fravor would later recount:

- We were about sixty kilometers from our final destination, and in less than a minute, this thing was there before us...

By the time our two fighters reach their rally point, the object has disappeared. With the UFO no longer in sight, the pilots returned to the *Nimitz to* land. Fravor remembers that day when one of his colleagues asked him what he thought he saw.

- No idea," he replied. This thing had no plume, no wings, no rotor, and was almost as big as our F-18s. I'd love to fly one!

A few moments later, everything starts again. The *Princeton's* radio controller warned that the target had just reappeared on his radar, about 96 kilometers away. Two Super Hornets, this time led by Lieutenant Commander Chad Underwood and Lieutenant Alex Dietrich, took off from the *Nimitz* for another intercept attempt. Unlike Fravor, Underwood's aircraft is equipped with FLIR equipment, using a thermal camera that detects infrared radiation. When the pilots spot the object, this one scrambles their radar. Underwood then triggers his FLIR camera and succeeds in locking it on the object. He can thus make a video of the phenomenon. According to the data of the *Princeton* radar, this Tic-Tac would have reached an acceleration of 74 000 km/h, that is Mach 60, 60 times the speed of sound! It is logical that this document is a milestone in the history of aeronautics.

The pilots returned to the carrier. Barely out of their flight suits, they are summoned to a secure room on the ship for an immediate debriefing that concludes with a peremptory:

- Let's be clear, this event never took place!

Despite this strict warning, a brief excerpt of Underwood's video circulated under the radar and was finally made public by *New York Times* reporters in 2017. What happened next, we know. Thanks to the hype and pressure from citizens, thanks also to the investment of the Senate, the Pentagon is forced to authenticate it. From this official recognition, our pilots are free to speak in the press and on prime time TV shows.

As soon as the revelations were made in the *New York Times*, David Fravor became a national hero. Retired after 18 years of service, he is presented as "the witness of one of the most credible UFO sightings in history".

- Four of us observed this machine for five minutes," he says. It was fully aware of our maneuvers. I don't know who designed this, who has this technology and knowledge. But something is really there, far superior to our planes. I've never seen anything like it.

In the very serious American investigative *show 60 Minutes*, it is Alex Dietrich's turn to speak. Without giving up a disarming smile, she confesses :

- No offense, but I never wanted to appear on national TV. I accept today because, at the time, I was on duty, flying a government plane. So I have a responsibility to share what I saw, now that this case has been declassified.

Upon spotting the strange Tic-Tac, she describes:

- At that moment, your mind tries to rationalize what you see. I thought to myself: maybe it's a helicopter or a drone, but it suddenly disappeared. Just like that... Luckily my co-pilot saw the same thing I did because if I had been alone, I think I would not have reported it when I got home. Reporting all this would have made me look like a crazy person.

More discreet, Chad Underwood ends up coming on the sets. The one who is now presented as the man who shot "the video that changes everything" confides :

- This object had a behavior that I would describe as impossible and that my current physical knowledge does not allow me to describe.

Ten years later, a second observation will only confirm the presence and the strangeness of these UFOs...

Off the coast of Virginia

Date: year 2014.

Location: along the Atlantic coast, off the state of Virginia, USA.

From the summer of 2014 to March 2015, these incredible flying objects kept flying over and disrupting North American military training. According to Lieutenant Ryan Graves, "for almost two years, pilots training on the Atlantic coast saw them daily". The statement of this soldier is shocking, especially since these sightings took place in the middle of the sea, barely 80 kilometers from Washington, the country's capital. Ryan Graves was able to provide the *New York Times* with some details: either the objects were stationary, at high altitude, or they were moving at fairly constant speeds (from 0.6 to 1.2 mach). At first, the military thought that these were anomalies produced by their radars. But they quickly changed their mind and ended up tracking these machines. Using their FLIR cameras, they obtained interesting thermal signatures, which confirmed the presence of physical objects that were colder than the surrounding air. On several occasions, the pilots attempted to intercept them, but once the UFOs were in sight, they magically disappeared. Lieutenant Graves believes that they had to change altitude quickly.

In late 2014, back at Virginia Beach AFB, Lieutenant Graves runs into a fellow squadron member just back from a mission. The distraught pilot confides in him that he almost collided with one of these mysterious craft. He was flying in tandem over the Atlantic, east of Virginia Beach, about 30 meters from his partner, when a UFO flew between them. Terrified, the two men had the opportunity to observe the intruder in detail. According to them, it had the shape of a translucent sphere. Inside the sphere, they could clearly make out a dark cube whose sides touched the edges of the sphere. Interesting detail: at the time of this incident, the F/A-18F fighters had not activated their onboard radars. This could explain why the UFO did not perform its usual evasive maneuver. The incident so frightened the squadron that a flight safety report was filed.

In March 2015, the *Theodore Roosevelt* - one of the US Navy's 11 giant aircraft carriers - sailed from the coast of Florida to the Persian Gulf. Also according to Lieutenant Graves, that's when the UFOs reappeared.

Sources

Tic Tac UFO Executive Report - *New York Times,* December 16, 2017 - *The Nimitz Encounters,* documentary by Dave Beaty, 2019 - *SUFOI Årsrapport 2019,* Denmark,

January 2019, pp. 27-35 - *UFO Truth* #36, March-April 2019, pp. 28-33 - *New York Times,* May 26, 2019 - *Unidentified,* season 1, episode 1, *History Channel* series, May 31, 2019 - *The Joe Rogan experience,* podcast #1361, October 5, 2019 - *The Kevin Rose Show,* December 3, *2019 podcast* - Jim Breslo's *Hidden Truth Show, podcasts* #6, 9, 12, 13, 14, and 15, 2019 and 2020 - *The Man Who Filmed The Tic Tac UFO, interview with Lieutenant Commander* Chad Underwood by Jeremy Corbell, 2020 - *Interview with pilot David Fravor by Lix Fridman, podcast* #122, September 8, 2020 - *Fortean Times* #403, March 2021, pp. 40-47 - *60 Minutes,* North American TV show, May 16, 2021 - *Moustique,* Belgium, July 3-9, 2021, pp. 17-19 - *GQ,* article by Charlie Burton, November 9, 2021 - *Under Investigation: The Unidentified,* episode 2, season 3, presented by Liz Hayes, February 16, 2022, Australia.

The UFO shaped like a Tic-Tac candy (left)
and the strange translucent sphere (right)

A protean phenomenon

A colossal Tic-Tac candy, a sphere equipped with a light-reflecting cube... Enough to disconcert more than one. A question arises: in the end, what is a UFO? The informed know it, *UFO* is the literal translation of the Anglo-Saxon *UFO* (*Unidentified Flying Object*). This acronym means: Unidentified Flying Object. For the investigator, this poses a first problem because this term is almost absurd. Indeed, how to determine the nature of an object without identity?

UFO. Are we in danger? The black book of ufology

According to the Oxford dictionary, the term dates back to the 1950s. It is admitted that it was invented by a certain Edward J. Ruppelt, an American officer in the US Air Force. It is also mentioned in a book written by the North American aviator and investigator Donald Keyhoe in 1953.

Since then, too often used wrongly and knowingly distorted, *UFO* is a tired word. Other terms, just as ambiguous, have come to its rescue, attempting to enrich the lexical field of the phenomenon. Today, some prefer to speak of UAP (*Unidentified Aerial Phenomena*) or PAN (Phénomènes aérospatiaux non identifiés). Not more enlightening because, by way of interpretative analysis, these acronyms ask a question without answering it. So let's push our curiosity a step further.

In 1939, Igor Ivanovitch Sikorsky developed the first aircraft with a main rotor. He became one of the world's first helicopter builders, but met with strong resistance. The opposition screamed foul, arguing that, according to clever calculations, such an aircraft was inoperable and unable to fly. Pugnacious, Sikorsky retorted without breaking stride:

- According to mathematics, the cockchafer can't fly. But the cockchafer ignores mathematics, doesn't care... and flies!

Let us attribute this repartee to the astonishing aeronautical capacities of UFOs. Indeed, for many, it is difficult to conceive that such objects without tailplane or visible means of propulsion defy the laws of gravitation and cross our skies at subsonic speeds. And yet... Even more frightening is the range of this phenomenon which adopts - pilots testify to this - the most improbable forms, the most heterogeneous.

The popular press spoke to us of a trio composed of saucers, cigars or triangles. The rest would have been only misunderstandings or hallucinations. In reality, the phenomenon is more complex. By consulting the historical study of these proud intruders, we discover a celestial hardware which leaves literally stunned. The ufological chronicle delivers us a catalog in which we can find - as J. Allen Hynek, father of scientific ufology, said - "a stunted gherkin, submarines, boilers, prehistoric birds, rugby balls, mushrooms, soup tureens, sandwiches...". And many other oddities.

Here is a brief selection of this airborne bric-a-brac.

A huge pyramid in the sky

Date: October 5, 1996.

Location: Pelotas, in the southeast of the state of Rio Grande do Sul, Brazil.

Haroldo Westendorff was born in 1958. Married with a 9 year old son, he owns a large rice field in the Brazilian state of Rio Grande do Sul and also runs a transportation company. He obtained his flight license at the age of 19, and became an aerobatic champion.

On October 5, 1996, at 9 am, he left the airport of Pelotas on board his single-engine plane, a Tupi EMB 712. The weather was somewhat cloudy. Haroldo first flew over the *Cage a Pesca* club (a hunting and fishing reserve) and then reached the shore of Laranjal beach, near the Lagoa dos Patos. At 10:30 he decided to turn back. He flies at an altitude of 1800 meters when he sees on his left a strange flying object. This "ship" has the shape of a huge pyramid. Haroldo cannot believe his eyes. The UFO - totally silent - turns silently on its axis and heads towards the Atlantic Ocean at a speed of about 100 km/h. Intrigued, our pilot decides to go and observe this phenomenon more closely.

- This object was huge, totally gigantic! Haroldo later confided to the investigators of the GPCU, a Brazilian ufology group. It had the shape of a pyramid with eight faces. On each of its faces, we could see three protuberances in line, probably portholes.

Our pilot estimates the height of this machine between 50 and 60 meters. And its base measures nearly 100 meters in diameter, the length of a soccer field.

Haroldo immediately contacts the control tower of Pelotas.

- Do you see what I see?" he asks.

Airton Mendes da Silva, the agent on duty, grabs his binoculars, points them at the sky and locates the craft. After 11 years of service, this 40-year-old had never seen anything like it. His colleagues Gilberto Martins dos Santos (50 years old) and Jorge Renato S. Dutra (31 years old), informed, also notice the presence of the unusual object. However, when Haroldo contacted the radar center of Curitiba, the operator declared that no aircraft or plane was visible within a radius of 200 kilometers around the single-engine plane. Haroldo then asked for permission to switch to a special radio frequency in order to provide a very precise description of the UFO. Refused. Too bad!

- For twelve minutes, he says, I flew in circles around the UFO, at a distance of about 100 meters. I went around the craft three times in a row. I was able to observe it

UFO. Are we in danger? The black book of ufology

in detail. It seemed to be made of metal, more precisely of aged brass, and its bottom was smooth... As I circled around it, I did not notice any hostile movement on its part. Then, suddenly, the top of the craft opened just at its tip, and a flying saucer emerged vertically. It then tilted at a 45-degree angle and rose at breakneck speed. I thought of positioning my plane over the opening of the UFO to see what was inside, but I quickly gave up when a column of reddish, waving rays shot out of it. I was really scared, I moved away and stood about 200 meters away from this thing. At that moment, the huge object rose vertically, at an incredible speed, without air displacement, without noise or explosion. I once saw an F-16 fighter jet flying at 2400 km/h. In comparison, I would say that this object flew at more than 12,000 km/h in a few seconds.

After landing, our pilot confided in his relatives. This is how the famous Brazilian magazine *Istoé* got wind of the case. At the same time, the journalist André Jockyman published a long paper indicating that the Ministry of Aeronautics (absorbed by the Ministry of Defense in 1999) was conducting a secret investigation on the sighting. The journalist also collected the testimony of the operators of the airport of Pelotas. Gilberto Martins dos Santos told the magazine that the object seen through his binoculars was "the size of a high voltage tower". Jorge Renato S. Dutra added:

- As far as I know, no aircraft on our planet moves vertically. However, the object in question went straight up to the sky before disappearing in the clouds...

The flying pyramid seen by Haroldo Westendorff

Sources

Istoé, November 27, 1996, pp. 19-21 and 78-80 - this case illustrates the cover - *The Brazilian UFO Report,* vol. 2, n°9, March-April 1997, pp. 3-9 - Timothy Good, *Contacts extraterrestres,* Presses du Châtelet, 1999, pp. 311-314 - *The Australian UFO Bulletin,* December 1999, pp. 12-15 - *Historias extraordinárias, Mistério no céu de Pelotas,* Brazilian *RBS* TV program - *Close Encounters of the Brazilian Kind* n°2, Liquid Press, 2000, pp. 10-16.

A three-story room

Date: August 25, 1987.
Location: Broadford, Victoria, 88 kilometers north of Melbourne, Australia.

22 h. Trevor (32) and Cheryl Kerslake (28) were driving home from a friend's house for dinner with their two daughters. They were driving quietly toward Reedy Creek, their home just outside of Broadford. As the Kerslakes were leaving Elliott's Road, a bright light appeared on top of a nearby hill, overlooking a hundred-yard enclosure.

- Look at this house, it's lit up with hundreds of lights!" says Cheryl.

- What if it's a spaceship instead of a house?" Trevor jokes.

The Kerslakes burst out laughing, but not for long. As they approach, they see that the light phenomenon is indeed a kind of spacecraft suspended in the sky. No doubt about it: a huge, dark shape, covered with several rows of lights, hovers in the night sky. Stubby arms seem to move at its top.

- It was three layers, like a wedding cake! Cheryl later told investigators. It looked like a huge three-tiered wedding cake. The object didn't seem to touch the ground, but was hovering right above it.

Shocked, the family decided to go immediately to the Broadford police station, which was unfortunately closed that evening. Trevor then contacted a Seymour police officer. The officer quickly went to the scene, but there was nothing to be seen. However, upon investigation, more witnesses were located. At least six residents said they had seen the UFO in question around 10:00 p.m. Contacted, the army affirms that the observation cannot be in any case related to a defense operation.

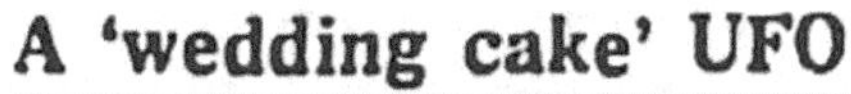

A 'wedding cake' UFO
proves an eye opener for Broadford
Flying in
the face of fiction

Illustration from the Melbourne Herald, August 27, 1987

- We did not conduct any training at Puckapunyal that would match the descriptions people provided," said a staff spokesman. We had some tanks on our range with searchlights, but they were about 20 kilometers from the observation area, so their lights could not be seen.

Even though the UFO left no trace behind, the Seymour police officer told the press that he believed the stories to be true.

- The witnesses all seem exceptionally sincere, he said. These are not people who are talking nonsense... These people are really upset by what they saw.

Sources

Herald, Melbourne, August 26 and 27, 1987 - *Telegraph,* Seymour, September 1, 1987 - *Tasmanian UFO Investigation Centre* n°53, 1988, p. 10.

A large starfish

Date: September 10, 1973.

Location : Outreau, suburb of Boulogne-sur-Mer, Pas-de-Calais department, in the Hauts-de-France region.

The Hanocq family lives in Outreau, at 23 rue Jules-Guesde. 9:15 p.m.: the father (56), the mother (53), the son (19), the daughter (21) and her gendarme husband (23) are all together in front of the TV. The autumn evening looks quiet when a strange incident comes to disturb this family truce.

- It all starts," says the head of the family, "when my son says to me, 'Dad, quick, there's red in the yard! His eyes had just been drawn to a bright orange-red glow over the garden. At first we thought it was a fire. I thought the house was on fire. My daughter thought it was fireworks. My son-in-law went out into the garden to see what was going on, and I followed him. That's when we saw the object from which the glow was coming. It was stationary, about 20 meters above the ground. And 15 meters away from us. It must have had a wingspan of 10 meters. In the center, there was an intensely red ball about 70 centimeters in diameter. And this ball had five large wings. The object looked like a large starfish, standing vertically on its lower tips. We could see very well its five points in the shape of wings. The object was perfectly visible. My son even distinguished a kind of rod or antenna between the wings. And in these wings there was a kind of zig-zag. The object did not make any noise. As soon as we moved forward, it rose very slowly to the vertical, hopping, as if it was going up in successive steps. When it arrived at the top of the house, at the level of the tiles, it made a leap over the roof, and then it disappeared at a dizzying pace in the direction of Mont Soleil [a neighborhood of Outreau]. We went out into the street to see it go away. There was nothing left.

Faced with this spectacle, the man admits to being flabbergasted:

- At first, we were unable to think. Then I said to myself, "It must be a flying saucer!" Notice that the craft was nothing like a saucer. Before, when I heard people talking about these flying saucers, I thought they were hallucinating. Those who hear me tell my story today may think the same of me. But I am certain of what I saw, and I was not the only witness, there were many of us. A hallucination of this kind is impossible, so much this machine was big. It was quite a mass!

According to the Hanocqs, the observation lasted a good minute. Two disturbing facts are to be reported. Firstly, the dog of the house did not react although it barks very easily. And, secondly, the next day, the neighboring garden had a peculiar trace. The earth was packed, and some carrots from Mr. Lardeur's small garden were sheared off...

Sources

Nord Matin, September 12, 1973 - *La Croix Dimanche*, September 15, 1973 - *Ouranos* n°9, new series, 4ᵉᵐᵉ quarter 1973, pp. 15 and 16 - *INF2 Dimanche : Objets Volants Non Identifiés,* television program broadcast on December 2, 1973 - *Lumières dans la Nuit* n°133, March 1974, pp. 19-21.

Mr. Hanocq (left). Illustration of the UFO by the author (right).

A very "Peace and Love" ship

Date: July 17, 1971.
Location: Sri Lanka.

10:45 p.m.: Leaving Pattiagama, Parl Abeywickrema, an important tea planter and superintendent of the *Rookwood Estate* in Hewaheta, is returning home. He is accompanied by his two assistants, Oswin de Alwis and Nimal Dunuwille, and Wijesinghe, his driver. These people are driving in a *Morris Station* vehicle. As they drove toward Rookwood, the four men saw a circular object "a little bigger than the full moon" hovering above the mountainous horizon. It was "a breathtaking sight. Mr. Abeywickrema ordered his driver to stop. The four men immediately left the vehicle and observed this amazing spectacle, mute with amazement and then admiration. The sky is limpid. They distinguish perfectly the stationary machine. The object hovers at an altitude of 300 meters. And at a distance of 400 meters. They are formal: the object is circular and provided with two side wings.

After about ten minutes, the UFO gets closer to them at a lightning speed then stops its race at 90 meters of the car. It loses little by little of the altitude and stops only at 30 meters of the ground. Terrified, the driver rushes into the vehicle to hide. In his panic, he released the handbrake and the *Morris Station* began to slide dangerously down the slope. Fortunately, three tea planters jumped on the vehicle and barely managed to prevent it from plunging into a 1,200-meter deep precipice. Soon, the UFO comes to life. Its two side wings retract. The vehicle then becomes completely circular, starts at an angle of 45 degrees, runs towards the southwest at a dizzying speed and disappears.

Back home, the four witnesses were able to provide a very detailed description of the intruder: it was translucent, "a bit like fiberglass", round, 8 meters in diameter and with wings on the sides. Its central part had an amazing fuselage, which was shaped like the famous hippie logo "Peace and Love". This part was illuminated and diffused a fluorescent yellow glow that had nothing to do with the brightness of a star. Its side wings were also illuminated but with less intensity. The craft made no sound, even when it moved. Inside, no movement or living thing was detectable.

Reconstruction of the UFO from Sri Lanka by the author

That day, in the region of Hewaheta, located 190 kilometers from Colombo, several hundred people saw the craft. According to many, it was the first time that a UFO appeared in this part of the Asian sky.

Sources

Weekend, Kandy newspaper, July 30, 1971 - *Flying Saucer Review,* "Case Histories," Supplement No. 7, October 1971, pp. 11-12.

A pie plate with legs

Date: January 1970.
Location: Trondstad, north of Kristiansand, Norway.

Ole Birkeland is a farmer and a shop worker. Those who know him describe him as a solid and sober man.

That January evening, at the stroke of 9:30 p.m., he is at the wheel of his car. Peacefully, he crosses the desert plains beyond the town of Trondstad. After a hard day's work and a bit of overtime, he returns home a little later than usual. He passed the church in Greipstad, where the urban area ends, drove another 1 km through the wilderness and suddenly saw a strange light object in the sky. The intruder, positioned on the side of the road, stops suddenly, changes direction and starts to hover slowly in front of the vehicle of our flabbergasted witness.

- Many details were visible as the object glided slowly, first over and then in front of my car, he explained *afterwards*. I estimate it was 80 to 100 meters away from me... It was an incredibly beautiful sight!

According to the witness, the UFO resembled a "large illuminated pie plate with seven insect legs". Each of these legs ended in a kind of "ball" from which flames escaped "similar to those of a welding flashlight". Totally silent, the object illuminated the surroundings violently, partially blinding Ole Birkeland.

- The headlights on my car were too dim. The area around me was lit up like daylight," he said.

And he will specify:

- I was really close to the UFO. It was hovering almost vertically above me, so I could see it through the windshield of my car. It must have been very large, but it's hard for me to estimate its size accurately. When I got a few hundred meters from the top of Greipstad, where the road goes down to Trondstad, this ship and its light suddenly disappeared, plunging behind a hill in the west direction. All in all, it followed me, at very slow speed, for 3 kilometers. I did not feel any effect of its presence. I didn't hear any sound, but it might have been covered by the engine of my car.

Sources

UFO-NYT, January-February 1971, pp. 17-19 - *Flying Saucer Review,* "Case Histories," Supplement #4, April 1971, pp. 15-16 - Dennis Stacy and Patrick Huyghe, *The Field Guide to UFOs,* Quill, 2000, pp. 64-65.

Left: the UFO seen by Ole Birkeland
Right: reconstruction of the observation (UFO-NYT document)

A flying manta ray

Date: November 6, 1957.
Location: St. Petersburg, Florida, USA.

According to the *St. Petersburg Times* of November 7, 1957, on the night of November 6, at about 5:30 a.m., a dazzling white light passed through the sky, fuelling much debate about the great flying mysteries. Mr. and Mrs. Clark and Mr. and Mrs. C. G. Dillman were witnesses to this phenomenon and agreed to tell their stories. Mr. Tom Clark described a dazzling light with a long orange tail. Mr. Dillman said it was oval, reddish-white, the kind of light that glows at high temperatures. It appeared flashing to the west and disappeared after ten to fifteen seconds. According to Mr. Dillman, it was certainly not a rocket, a *jet*, or a meteor.

The Clarks are definite: it was exactly 5:25 a.m. at the time of the observation. The Dillmans are not as precise but estimate that it was about that time.

- It looked like a manta ray with a curved orange tail," Clark said. It was a very strange sight.

Dillman said that a half hour before witnessing the phenomenon, he discussed stories reported by the *Times* that Wednesday morning about strange lights seen in the sky.

- Until then, I didn't believe in these things at all," he concluded. Now I know they really exist!

When the white light suddenly appeared, Mr. Clark was sitting in the back of the vehicle and Mrs. Clark was driving.

- I could see the light through the windshield of our car, so it must have been close to the ground," said Mr. Clark.

According to him, after 4 to 5 seconds, it plunged and disappeared behind the trees. At that time, the Clark's were driving north on 51ème Street between Emerson and 5ème Avenue South. Mr. Clark said the object made no noise and was moving very quickly.

- The moon was setting in the west, the Clarks said finally, and this object, whatever it was, was emitting so much light that it was blotting out the glow.

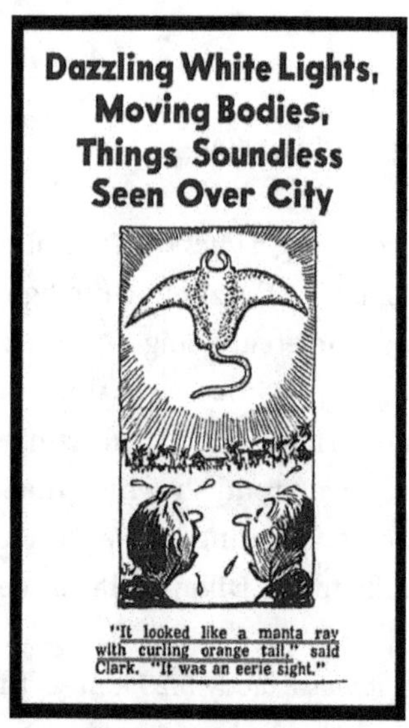

Illustration published in the St Petersburg Times

A bolted square

Date: October 1954.

Location: La Feuillade, a small town in Creuse, France.

On this October morning in 1954, it was about 8:00 a.m. when Julien L., 49 years old, decided to go feed his chickens. The hens were at the bottom of a meadow, quite far from his farm. He went quietly into the meadow and then cut diagonally when an imposing grove blocked his way. He was about fifteen meters from these trees when he saw a flying object appear at their top. Here is what he says:

- That was the year that everyone saw flying saucers landing and Martians coming out. They all said, "I saw that," but I saw something else. It was during the beet season. I had my bag of wheat under my arm and I was in the middle of the meadow, halfway through the coppice. Suddenly, what do I see coming out from above the copse? Balls! Lots of balls following each other! They were between 30 and 40 centimeters in diameter. They were moving forward, turning into each other. Heavily. Yes, it was like something heavy. And they were coming down. I thought: it's not possible, something that heavy, it will land on the other side of the road.

This curious assembly of spheres forms a kind of horizontal capital T which progresses, bar of the T in front. The witness is dumbfounded. The UFO is composed of dull grey balls, of a "wood ash" shade, which all roll in the same direction, a bit like marbles rolling down a slope. It flies low in the trees without a sound and gives the impression of wanting to land.

Julien turns towards the road, looking for a possible witness who could confirm his incredible vision. In vain. The road is deserted. He then brings back his glance on the UFO. This one hovers at about ten meters above him and, even before our man can observe the phenomenon in detail, he is blinded. Hundreds of luminous points dance in his eyes whereas the UFO did not emit any light. The witness states:

- It was not like looking at the sunlight or a car headlight... There, there was nothing. It was in my eyes. No matter how much I turned my head, I couldn't see any better on one side than on the other... I went to feed my chickens five minutes later, because at first I couldn't see anything at all! I could look in any direction, but it was the same everywhere, I could only see big bright stars dancing in front of me. Half an hour later, I still had luminous points in my eyes... I had never seen that. And then, back from the chicken coop [150 yards from the scene of the incident, 30 minutes later], above Bette, I noticed a curious dark, low, diamond-shaped cloud. It looked solid. It had straight, clean edges. It was the only thing in the blue sky. It looked odd to me, but I don't know if it had anything to do with the balls or not. And then it dissipated on the spot... I told my adventure to some neighbors. They laughed and said I had one too many drinks. It would have been at night, I don't say. But in the morning, at 8 a.m...

Sources

Ouranos, new series n°6, 1ᵉʳ quarter 1973, pp. 5-6 - *Lumières dans la Nuit* n°131, January 1974, pp. 13-14 - *UFOmania* n°78, April 2014, pp. 7-9.

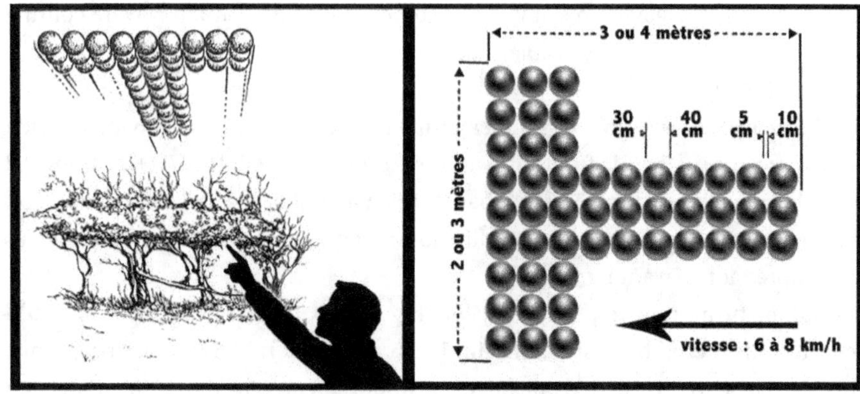

Graphic reconstruction of the UFO of La Feuillade

A rifle bullet from 60 meters

Date: February 19, 1951.
Location: Mount Kilimanjaro, northeast of Tanzania, East Africa.

7 a.m. The *East African Airways* Lodestar, bound for Mombasa, left the runway at Nairobi's terminal smoothly. The twin-engine plane designed by Lockheed carries 9 passengers. At the controls, Captain Jack Bicknell, 30, keeps an eye on the gauge and altimeter. Then he gradually relaxes. Another successful takeoff.

It's a beautiful morning. The visibility is excellent. Not a cloud on the horizon. But at 7:20 a.m., the radio officer, Dennis W. Merrifield, 34 years old, calls Jack Bicknell's attention. Indeed, he had just seen, at about 3000 meters above Kilimanjaro, a luminous and stationary object, "like a white star".

The crew immediately contacted the operators in Nairobi, asking if they knew of any aircraft cruising nearby. The answer was scathing:

- Nothing to report. You should add water to what you are drinking!

Jack Bicknell tells the story:

At first, I didn't dare say anything. We just watched it for a good three minutes, and then we told the passengers. One of the people on board had a pair of very powerful binoculars. With those binoculars, we studied this

UFO. Are we in danger? The black book of ufology

strange thing. Through Eastleigh Airport, we reported our observation in detail. The Eastleigh staff told us that it could be a weather balloon. It was up to us to verify. I took the binoculars and examined the object carefully for several minutes.

When we first saw it, we were about 130 kilometers from Kilimanjaro. Now, thanks to our cruising speed, we were about 80 kilometers from this thing. Through the binoculars, I could see a metallic device, shaped like a rifle bullet, which must have been more than 60 meters long! It had a square, vertical fin at one end. It was silver, rather dull. And on its fuselage, at regular intervals, I distinguished darker vertical bands. Its contours were extremely sharp and precise, with no blurred effect.

I looked to see if it was moving. But he was stationary. It was completely still for seventeen minutes. The passengers exchanged binoculars. Two of them were able to take pictures, and then the object came to life, moving eastward. Finally, it went straight up into the sky and finally disappeared at an altitude of 12,000 meters, at a prodigious speed.

There was no cloud there. This machine left no vapor trail behind it. It had no visible means of propulsion. I calculated that it had covered 96 kilometers in three minutes, so it must have been flying at a speed of 1600 km/h. For me, it was almost certainly a flying machine.

Interviewed in turn, Radio Officer Dennis W. Merrifield, states:

- If it is a flying machine, it is a technology that is 500 years ahead of us. I'd like to think it was a mirage, but there are no mirages in a cloudless sky and a mirage doesn't move.

Upon arrival at their destination, the pilot, the radio officer and the nine passengers (seven men and two women) signed an affidavit. One of them, Ray Overstreet, stated:

- I'm not quite sure, but through the binoculars I saw a row of windows on the craft.

A second passenger, Charles J. Vernon, added:

- This object must have been immense, two or three times the size of the largest known transport plane.

Captain H. B. Fussell, also present on board, rejects the advanced theory of a weather balloon seen during the flight:

- A balloon cannot remain stationary for a while and then suddenly fly away at 600 km/h, especially in such calm and stable weather conditions.

After investigation, no explanation was found satisfactory to explain the nature of the Kilimanjaro UFO. The press of the day concluded, "This is, without doubt, the most authentic of all the flying saucer stories ever reported."

Sources

The Sunday Post, 25 February 1951, p. 15 - *London Sunday Dispatch,* 25 February 1951 - *London Sunday Dispatch,* 4 March 1951 - *The APRO Bulletin,* vol. 2, no. 1, July 15, 1953, p. 2 - Waveney Girvan, *Flying Saucers And Common Sense,* The Citadel Press, 1956, pp. 79-80 - *Flying Saucer Review,* vol. 9, no. 3, May-June 1963, pp. 11-12 - *The UFO Evidence,* NICAP, Washington, May 1964, pp. 123-124 - *Awareness,* vol. 13, no. 3, season 1984-5, pp. 2-3 - *MUFON UFO Journal* no. 274, February 1991, p. 16.

THIS IS WHAT THEY SAW: This diagram was prepared from a sketch by Captain Bicknell. Apart from the dark bands on the fuselage there is a lack of detail which makes the phenomenon even more puzzling. The "fin" at the rear of the machine might indicate some form of jet propulsion.

Drawing of the UFO by Captain Jack Bicknell

II. UFOs and burns:
the emblematic case of Stephen Michalak

Among the cases of "burns" inflicted by UFOs and mentioned in the DIA report made public in April 2022, here is a particularly disturbing example. It is a "CE5" type encounter, that is, one that caused permanent physiological injury. The report states that other effects are attributable to the "highly advanced and unconventional propulsion system" of the incriminating objects, as in this case: "heat" (*heat*), "migraines" (*induced headaches*), "nausea and vomiting" (*nausea, vomiting*), "fatigue" (*weakness*), "dizziness" (*dizziness*), "appetite *loss*" (*appetite loss*), "weight loss" (weight *loss*), "significant odors" (*significant odors*) and "ground traces" (*ground traces*).

The ordeal of an amateur geologist confronted with a flamboyant saucer and subsequently suffering unexplained injuries is a classic. As early as the 1960s, the Falcon Lake incident opened the black file of hazardous encounters and embarrassed both Canadian and North American authorities. Hostile or not, the mysterious celestial objects seem to have frightening powers. Approaching them is not always without risk.

This adventure took place in western Canada, in the province of Manitoba - an Amerindian name meaning "passage of the Great Spirit" - near the border with Ontario.

Date: May 20, 1967.
Location: Flacon Lake, about 100 km east of Winnipeg, Canada.

- My name is Stephen Michalak," says the witness, "and I was born in Poland. After the turbulence of the Second World War and the events that followed, I had to leave my home country and seek refuge abroad. I landed in Canada in 1949 and a few years later I settled in Winnipeg, Manitoba. I now live there with my wife, two sons and daughter in a modest house. I earn my living with a steady job as a

---

mechanic for the *Inland Cement* Company... We live the pleasant life of average Canadians, fully appreciating the advantages this country offers us. Besides my job, I am an amateur gold digger. So, for several years, the first days of spring have been a privileged moment for me to go and search the eastern, wooded and rocky lands of Manitoba. I go there in search of minerals. I even had some concessions... That's why, on the evening of May 19, 1967, I took a bus to Falcon Lake. I rented a small room in a motel on the Trans-Canada Highway with the intention of getting up early the next day and trying my luck. Not for a moment could I imagine the kind of luck I was going to encounter.

Two red and grey saucers

At 5:30 a.m., Stephen Michalak leaves his hotel room. His long geological trek begins. Our man is in his prime. He is 51 years old and likes to get lost in nature and go for long walks. For this, he has a map of the region, a small hammer, a compass, a notebook and some food. The sun rises, radiant. It is a beautiful spring day. Not a cloud on the horizon.

Michalak passes through beautiful pine forests and then decides to settle in a corner, near a large swamp, where some rocks seem particularly interesting.

- When I arrived," he explains, "I disturbed a flock of wild geese. But, little by little, they got used to my presence. Soon, they stopped screaming and went back to their daily routine.

11:00 a.m.: Michalak takes a break and has lunch in the heart of this peaceful and luxuriant nature. A cup of coffee, and there he goes again to examine these veins of quartz which interest him so much.

- At a quarter past noon, the sun was high in the sky, he describes. Small clouds were gathering to the west. As I was cutting my quartz vein, my attention was drawn to the strange and sudden cackling of the geese, who had been quite quiet until then. Something, it is certain, had frightened them. Surely not my presence, which they had been perfectly happy with since the morning. It was then that I saw two cigar-shaped objects with a dome on top. They hovered in the middle of the sky, then gradually lost altitude. They shone with a bright scarlet glow. As these objects approached the ground, I discovered that they were oval in shape. They descended at an even speed, keeping a constant distance between them. Although they were quite distinct, it seemed as if they were a synchronized duo. Suddenly, the object that was farther away - relative to my position - stopped in mid-air while the second one continued its descent slowly to land on the flat surface of a rock, 45 meters from me. The one that remained in the sky was positioned 5 meters above my head. It didn't move for three minutes and then rose quickly. As it gained altitude, it changed color: first bright red, then orange, then gray. Before melting in a cloudy mass, it became again bright red... This vessel, if I dare to call it that, appeared and disappeared so quickly that I have difficulty to estimate the time during which it remained visible. It must be said that the astonishment and the fear caused by these appearances confused my senses and made me lose all notion of time. As for its speed, I have never seen anything on this planet that goes so fast while remaining so silent.

A smell of sulfur

Stephen Michalak is amazed. One would be less amazed. Still kneeling on his quartz vein, hammer in hand, he has trouble understanding what he sees. He does not have the reflex to remove the glasses he wears to protect himself from the stone fragments.

By concentrating on the strange saucer posed with a few meters of him, he discovers that this one measures about ten meters in diameter and passes from the red to the gray, "like a metal heated to white which cools". Moreover, it is enveloped by a golden halo.

- I first distinguished an opening near the top of the object. It emanated a purple light. This light was so intense that it hurt the eyes. Divided between fear and excitement, I was frozen on my rock, unable to make the slightest move. I decided to watch and wait. Very soon, emanating in waves from the ship, hints of hot air accompanied by a pungent smell of sulfur reached me. I perceived a slight humming sound, like a small electric motor running at full speed. Then there was a kind of hissing sound, as if the ship were sucking in air. At that moment, I thought, "If only I had brought a camera!" But that's not the kind of thing you take on a geological walk... And then I remembered I had a notebook and a pencil. So I took my time and drew the thing that was in front of me.

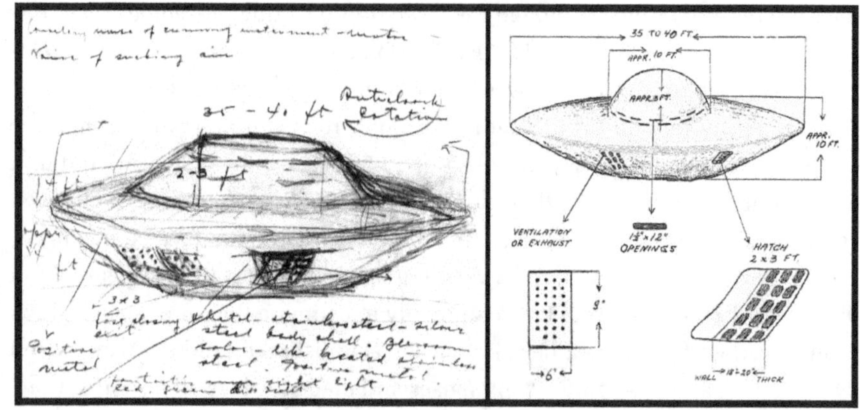

Original sketch made by the witness (left).
Reconstruction of the UFO (right)

Suddenly, a door opens...

- After half an hour, my initial fear subsided somewhat and I gathered my courage to approach this object and observe it. I expected someone to come out and inspect the surrounding area. I had never seen anything like it, so I figured it was definitely a prototype from a secret American space program. I looked for something on the fuselage that said "United States Air Force" or "NASA". I was fascinated by the stream of light emanating from the upper part of the object. This light, mostly purple, was opal in different shades. It was reflected on the ground, more intense than the glaring midday sun. I had to look away often. I could see red spots dancing before my eyes. Suddenly, a door opened on the side of the object. Very slowly, I approached it. I was 20 meters away from this mass of flaming metal when I heard voices. They sounded human but were partially muffled by the noise of the engine and the continuous hissing that escaped from this machine. I could clearly make out two voices. One was higher pitched than the other. This doubled my excitement. Now I was sure that this ship was home.

Emboldened, Stephen Michalak gets closer and throws to the crew that is supposed to be there:

UFO. Are we in danger? The black book of ufology

- Hello, fellow Americans! Got a problem? Come on out! We'll see what we can do about it...

No answer. Inside, nothing moves.

- I stood there not knowing what to do," admits the witness. I had the idea of repeating my request in Russian. I tried again in German, Italian, French and Ukrainian. Still no response. So I decided to go forward again and take a look inside.

A shirt in flames!

And then...

- As the emitted light was hardly bearable, I stepped back to fold down the tinted screen of my glasses. Then I was able to slide my head through the opening of the machine. The interior was a maze of lights. Beams shot horizontally, and diagonally. Lights flashed randomly, without order or sequence. I retreated, still waiting for an answer, and noted the thickness of the body: the walls of the craft must have been 50 centimeters thick.

Suddenly, for the first time, the machine comes to life. Two panels slide open and lock the door. Our witness then sees, on the side of the machine, an exhaust grid, like a ventilation system. This small grid composed of a uniform alignment of round holes will have a great importance for the continuation of our history.

Only listening to his courage, Stephen Michalak reaches out and touches the vessel. It is very hot and seems to be made, at first glance, of a material similar to stainless steel. No joints or welds are visible. The outer surface is polished and looks like tinted glass on which the light plays. While reflecting, the sun creates a diffraction network on this silver background.

Looking down, the witness notices, surprised, that the glove with which he has just touched the vessel is burned. And the rest happens in a flash!

Suddenly, the machine swings to the left. Our witness then faces the small ventilation grid seen earlier. He feels a violent burn on his chest. At this moment, his shirt and his knitwear ignite. A jet of burning air has just shot out of the UFO.

- I quickly ripped off my shirt and knitting. I threw them to the ground. I saw that my chest was severely burned. I felt a shift in the air. The ship rose to the treetops. Like its predecessor, it began to change color and shape; and, in a few seconds, disappeared without a trace.

The compass is going crazy

Between fear and amazement, Stephen Michalak, dumbfounded, remains with his arms hanging down. Unable to move, he sweeps with an empty look the luxuriant decor of this ironically indifferent nature. He has difficulty in understanding what it has just happened. He sees on the ground, close to his clothes, a square of moss which ignites. He hurried to crush the nascent flames. He then thought of an article in *Life Magazine* that he had recently read. It talked about flying saucers, about machines from elsewhere. It made him laugh.

- I thought it was the story of a *reporter with a* fertile imagination," says the amateur gold digger. I was thinking that there was probably some truth in it.

A smell of burnt metal and sulfur still floats in the air. Michalak mechanically picks up his bag, his things. He notices that the needle of his compass is spinning out of control. Is there a magnetic force around that could explain this? A few minutes later, the compass regains its calm and placidly indicates north. It's hard to understand.

- I wanted to get out of there as soon as possible," admits the witness.

Previously, he examines the ground touched by the UFO. He has difficulty to concentrate because he feels nauseous. A headache starts to crush his temples. The place where the machine landed is completely naked, as if swept by a powerful blast. There is no more vegetable debris, nor pebbles. All around, the detritus forms a perfect circle. Suddenly, Stephen Michalak flickers. His headache increases. He is covered in cold sweat. He feels that something is wrong.

- Until then," he says, "I was always a healthy, vigorous man. I weighed all of my 82 kilos. I've gone through the last 25 years without ever getting sick. The only time I had to go to the doctor was for routine visits for my life insurance.

Nothing goes right anymore. He bends over with a groan and vomits. He feels weak and panicky. His strength has left him. He must get back to the motel as soon as possible. Gathering courage, he heads for Falcon Lake.

A way of the cross

- I walked a few feet," he continued, "and had to stop and throw up again. My stomach was heaving and twisting relentlessly. My mouth was dry and burning. My head was threatening to explode from the pain. I was vomiting green bile. The

UFO. Are we in danger? The black book of ufology

red spots that danced before my eyes reappeared. I knelt down by a stream and splashed myself. I had to stay conscious at all costs. Stopping would probably have been fatal. I couldn't use my compass to find my way. I could no longer see the needle. I was looking for familiar natural landmarks. Each step required a considerable effort. I was hoping to be in the right direction to reach civilization where I would be safe. I kept stopping to vomit. My headache was unbearable. My chest was burning. Red marks appeared where the burning air had reached me and burned my shirt. Some of these marks were the size of a dollar coin. I took off my jacket because the fabric was rubbing and irritating these burns. I walked forward, now shirtless.

Stephen Michalak finally reaches the highway. A thousand questions swirl in his head. "Will my wife and kids believe me? And what will my friends and neighbors think? How will I defend myself? Will they all say I'm crazy?

- I knew there was a Mountie detachment nearby," he says. If I could get to them, I might be able to get medical help. Then I thought it was my duty as a citizen to report my observation to the authorities.

A patrol car crosses his path. Saved! He makes big gestures. But the vehicle continues its road without even slowing down. Stunned by such indifference, he progresses more and more painfully.

- As I staggered along the road, I heard someone calling me. I turn around. A police officer! Briefly, I tell him what I have just experienced. I ask him to keep his distance because I am afraid of emitting harmful radiation. I explain to him that I need medical assistance. He retorts that he has something else on his mind. I stare at him, dumbfounded. Obviously, the agent didn't believe a word I said. So he leaves me with my pain and my disappointment. A thought crossed my mind: every human being, powerful or weak, must at some point find within himself the strength and ambition to accomplish what seems impossible. At that moment, I knew that, for me, that time had come.

A foul smell

Finally, at the end of his strength, Stephen Michalak arrives at the hotel. Exhausted, he hesitates. For fear of contaminating the other residents, he prefers to stay in the shelter of a small wood nearby.

- I felt out of this world. I had no strength left. My headache was excruciating, beyond what a human being can endure. I felt as if my eyes were literally popping out of my head. Every time I looked around, the pain was unbearable. Every breath I took brought back a foul smell of sulfur. I held my breath to try to escape it, but to no avail. The smell now seemed to emanate from my whole being, I could do nothing about it.

At 4:00 p.m., Stephen Michalak could barely stand. He decided to enter the hotel. Walking through the restaurant, he asked a hostess for the contact information of a nearby and available doctor. She told him that the local doctor would not be back until July and that the nearest general practitioner lived in Kenova, Ontario, 70 kilometers away.

- I had no choice but to go back to my room and go to bed," says the witness. Still, there must be some way to get medical attention! So I thought about newspapers. My experience might be of interest to the news of the day. So I tried to contact the *Winnipeg Tribune*. But it was Saturday afternoon and the offices were closed. No one was able to help me. I didn't want to worry my wife or the rest of my family, but I finally called the house. I told my wife that I had been in an accident and that my chest was partially burned. My son Mark offered to pick me up that evening at the Winnipeg bus stop. This was a relief. A first feeling of safety came over me.

A real harassment

As evening fell, Stephen Michalak packed his bag and made his way to the bus stop, avoiding the crowd.

- I sat on a stump on the boulevard, he recalls. I suffered a thousand ailments. The stench never left me. Red spots were always dancing in front of my eyes. I thought back to the past years. To the war and its contempt for human life, its sad values, its cowardice. I had known moments when I was close to death. I had survived. This idea comforted me. I wanted to believe that I would emerge victorious from this new trial. When, after an eternity, the bus arrived, I got on and handed my ticket to the driver. I saw in his eyes that he thought I was drunk. If only! I sat in the back of the bus, reassured that I would soon be home... At 8:15 p.m., Mark met me at the Winnipeg bus terminal and immediately drove me to the emergency room of Misericordia Hospital. A Chinese doctor with a poor command of our language took care of me. He prescribed a sedative and asked me how I had done my business. I told him that I had been exposed to airplane exhaust. I was anxious to get home.

Unfortunately, after a night of rest, the witness' condition did not improve. He is unable to eat and regurgitates the sip of tea he tries to ingest. No improvement the following days: diarrhoea, dizziness and persistent nausea are the program. He lost weight. In one day, he lost three kilos. No medication could cure his migraine.

Alerted, a team of journalists from the *Winnipeg Tribune* finally came to interview him.

- I told my story in detail without knowing that this would be the beginning of an endless series of questions and harassment orchestrated by the press, radio, television, the Air Force and various authorities.

The fear of ridicule

Dr. R. D. Oatway, a family doctor, is called in to help. He is surprised by his patient's poor condition. He prescribes a treatment for nausea. For the rest, he hands over to Dr. B. C. Shaw, who recommended antibacterial treatment for the burns. It was then that APRO - a civil association studying UFOs - entered the scene. Barry Thompson suggested to Stephen Michalak that he should do a series of examinations.

- I'm very grateful to Mr. Thompson," says Stephen Michalak. He was the first person to take my story seriously. You could tell he had a handle on it.

Blood tests revealed that his lymphocyte count dropped from 25% to 16%, before returning to normal after four weeks.

At home, it's hell. The phone rings day and night. The news has spread throughout the country and beyond. The press is in a panic.

- Some papers believed my story, others were skeptical," says the new star. They tried to ridicule me. Journalists were digging into my private life. They interviewed my friends and neighbors. They wanted to know if I was a well-adjusted person, a drinker, or even the kind of person who would brag about it.

Blisters and burns in a "checkerboard" pattern

The official investigations then began. The Air Force and the Canadian Mounties came to interview him. Exhausted, Stephen Michalak stopped answering the phone, ran away from the onlookers and was called "pretentious, ungrateful, unsocial".

New doctors examined him, including radiologist T. D. Craddok, and Mr. Berger, a dermatologist. He was sent to the Atomic Energy Research Center in Pinawa, Manitoba, where he underwent several tests. He was found to have no radiation exposure.

On June 10, 1967, six weeks after his encounter, when his general condition had improved, Stephen Michalak felt a violent itch all over his chest. Blisters invaded his chest all the way to his throat. The V-shaped rash even spread to his ears!

On June 23, he set out to find the sighting location with G. A. Hart, an electronics engineer from Winnipeg who was familiar with the geography of Whiteshell Park.

- We located it after six hours. The trail the ship had left on the ground was still perfectly visible. I found the remains of my shirt and a tape measure that I had misplaced that day. We put these items in plastic bags. Then we took soil and stone samples. Finally, we took some pictures. We found that where the machine had come down, some of the tree branches were now dry and dead while the rest of the tree was blooming normally.

On a trip to the site, Master Corporal Davis, Police Officer J. Zacharias, Stewart Hunt (of the National Department of Health and Welfare), Barry Thompson, and Squadron Leader Paul Bissky took new readings. They find traces of radioactivity but not at a level "presenting a real danger". Soil and rock samples were sent to the University of Colorado and to APRO.

In the meantime, a new rash strikes our witness. On September 21, five months after the event, Stephen Michalak was working on the roof of *Inland Cement*, the company he works for, when he felt a burn on his chest and neck.

- At first it felt like a bee sting. But very quickly the pain became intolerable. It spread throughout my body. I went down to the infirmary. The pain got worse, and my throat started to burn. My whole body was swelling. I took off my shirt and found that the checkerboard burn marks on my chest, the ones from the UFO exhaust, were back! The director came running. When he saw me, he sent me to a doctor. Fifteen minutes later, my body was completely purple. I was so swollen that it was impossible this time to take off the shirt I had put back on. A fellow student next to me avoided looking at me, he kept looking away because I must have been so frightening to see. My hands were swollen like balloons. I had no strength left. My vision was blurred and I could barely make out the outline of things. The room spun around me. I lost consciousness, vaguely felt someone laying me on a bed, then nothing.

Once again, Stephen Michalak must be hospitalized.

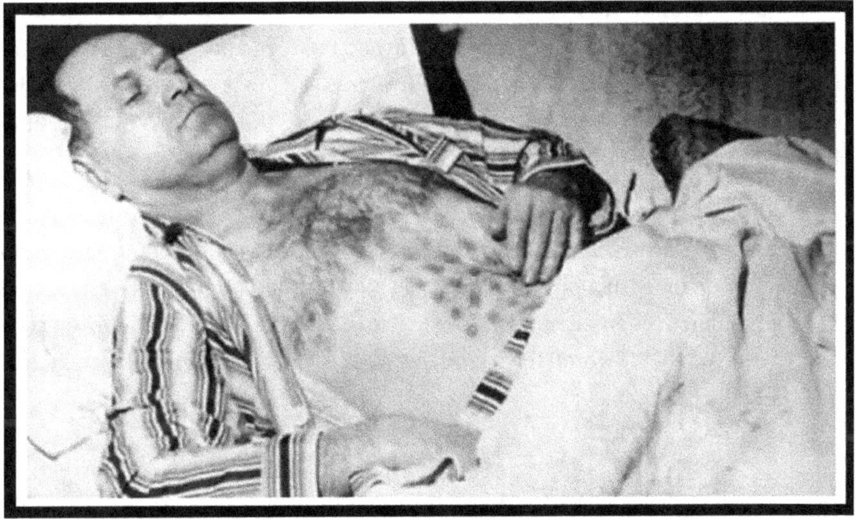

Stephen Michalak and the amazing checkerboard burns on his chest

Strange fragments

The health concerns of the witness leave the various practitioners doubtful.

- The doctors who examined me each gave their theory, recalls the patient. For one of them, I was burned by ultrasonic waves. Another said I was the victim of a thermal reaction caused by a powerful jet of burning air under pressure. One radiologist said my ailments were the result of nuclear fission, like radiation from an atomic reactor. A specialist said my stigma was related to gamma ray exposure.

These rays would have caused my burns and deteriorated the food in my stomach, thus causing this foul odor that never stopped bothering me.

On September 30, Stephen Michalak - momentarily on his feet - returned to the landing site. Everywhere, the leaves withered away as if they had been treated with defoliant. No vegetation grows inside the circle left by the UFO. Everything is now dried up and dead.

- I took new pictures," said the witness. With a Geiger counter, I found a radiation level of 400 milli Röntgen.

On May 19, 1968, accompanied by a friend, Michalak explored again the site of his observation. In the cracks of the rock on which the UFO had landed, he found numerous fragments of metal that turned out to be radioactive. Two larger pieces, in the shape of a "W", are sent for analysis. One is 93% pure silver, the other 96%. They also contain copper and cadmium. The squadron leader Paul Bissky notes in his report:

> The larger fragments seem to have been made to a specific *design*. When one tries to cut them with a knife, they prove to be very resistant. And when they are hit with a metal object or a stone, they do not produce any sound or tinkle. It is interesting to note that they were found at the exact spot where the UFO would have landed. If this is a hoax, it required a great deal of effort.

A balanced man

In August 1968, Stephen Michalak went to the Mayo Clinic in Rochester, Minnesota, to determine the cause of his recurring burns and discomfort. Not covered by standard medical insurance, the cost was paid in full by our patient. The cost was $500, which was quite a bit of money at the time. Staying in a small hotel near the clinic, he underwent a battery of physical and psychological evaluations for two consecutive weeks.

Clinicians' conclusion: the man is healthy. He has neurodermatitis and repeated episodes of syncope, the latter caused by hyperventilation or altered cardiac output. The psychiatric report notes that Michalak is a well-balanced, healthy man, not prone to delusional claims or inventions.

Attempts to explain

The Canadian Mounties, the Canadian Air Force, the U.S. Air Force, and Edward Condon's Colorado Project (a University of Colorado UFO study conducted from 1966 to 1968) investigated this "case.

In the United States, the Condon Commission concluded that:

> If Mr. Michalak's experience were to prove to be physically authentic, it would prove the presence of extraterrestrial vehicles flying in our environment. Nevertheless, attempts to prove the veracity of the facts have raised several inconsistencies and incongruities, developed later in the report.

Commission investigators were unable to prove any alleged fraud and eventually declared the event "unexplained.

In Canada, the incident was discussed several times in the House of Commons as the public wanted to know what the government intended to do about the damage to a Canadian citizen. On November 6, 1967, Leo Cadieux, Minister of Defence, stated that "the Department of National Defence had no intention of making public any reports concerning this alleged sighting. On February 6, 1969, an official announcement confirmed that the files would never be made public because of the danger they might pose to the "public interest. The Department of National Defense eventually classified the incident as "unsolved.

Regarding the checkerboard burns on the witness's torso, some have claimed that they were caused by fly or horsefly bites, thus implying that the appetite and aggressiveness of the Canadian diptera were now perfectly geometric.

Squadron Leader Paul Bissky has developed his own theory. According to him, Stephen Michalak would have consumed five beers in the bar of the Motel the night before his trek. The following morning, still soaked with alcohol, he would have hallucinated in the middle of nature. The investigator kept hammering away at the fact that Stephen Michalak was an inveterate drinker who, once drunk, must have fallen on the burning grill of his barbecue, hence the checkerboard burns. The explanation is funny because, in this hypothesis, the pattern of the witness' burns should be reversed. In the end, the hotel bills denied any consumption of alcohol, and Paul Bissky had to conclude in spite of himself that "certain facts, such as Mr. Michalak's illness and burns, as well as the circular mark observed on the site, still remain unexplained."

Among the attacks on the witness, some malicious tongues postulated that Stephen Michalak had inflicted his own injuries and had invented this zany saucer story in order to have the state pay his medical expenses. Others have claimed that the pseudo-witness, eager for attention, would have put this scenario together to get on the front page of magazines; then, after his hoax, would have published a book about his alleged experience to make money. The reality is quite different. In lieu of a book, Stephen Michalak published a small 40-page booklet at his own expense. He did not benefit financially from it. Very diminished, described as extremely discreet, avoiding the spotlight as much as possible, he ended his days almost reclusive.

Let's ask a final question: why make yourself so sick and accept 25 years of mockery by forging a saucer story in the hope (vain, of course) of making a fortune by selling your story? And how can one inflict such symptoms on oneself that 27 doctors and experts have been unable to explain?

With little resentment towards the visitors he almost saw, Stephen Michalak repeated until his last breath that he alone was responsible for his misadventure.

- As far as I know," he insisted, "I would like to make it clear that the burns and suffering I endured were not caused by aggressive movements of the craft, nor by its occupants. I alone chose to enter into contact with this vessel, and I was burned by its exhaust gases at the moment of takeoff. It is very likely that if I had stayed away, I would never have been burned or suffered as I did. Therefore, I issue a warning to anyone who might encounter such an object: stay far enough away from it to protect yourself and take every precaution against possible maneuvers by it.

As an epilogue...

On October 30, 1999, Chris Rutkowski, lead investigator of the "Michalak case," posted the following message on the web:

> It is with great sadness that I must announce the death of Stephen Michalak last week at the age of 83 (...) I was very young when I knew him. One of my classmates told me that his father had been burned by a UFO. But at the time, bike rides and *baseball* were my main concerns, not so much a friend's sick,

bedridden father. Later, when I went to college and started reading about UFOs and the scientific controversies involved, I suddenly realized that there had been no proper investigation of what I would call "the most significant case in North America.

So I contacted my childhood friend and his family again. I spent hours talking with them about what really happened. I also listened to their common experience. Indeed, I have to say that all family members were affected by this event. They told me with bitterness how they had been treated by the investigators and the media. They wanted nothing more than to be left alone. Yet, Stephen Michalak was stubborn and refused to let up. He never tired of telling his visitors what he had experienced. He never changed a comma in his story. He never claimed that the craft seen that day came from another world. Pragmatically, he said that he did not know what it was.

I remember one event that exemplifies the man that Stephen Michalak was. When *NBC* invited us to participate in the show *Unsolved Mysteries*, I had the chance to spend many hours with his family (...), but the most significant event took place during the taping of the show. Before filming, the director wanted to put Michalak at ease so that he would be relaxed in front of the cameras. They talked about the weather, his job, Canada and really anecdotal things. And then the director suddenly blurted out:

- Stephen, I imagine that being burned by a UFO is the most insane thing that has ever happened to you!

On the set, everyone was stunned when he answered:

- Oh, no, not at all!

And there he recounted what he had experienced in the Nazi death camps, describing both with courage and candor the atrocities he had witnessed firsthand. No one dared to interrupt him. When he fell silent, there was a heavy silence on the set. The entire team was in shock.

Later, a member of the production team tossed me:

- This man is by far the most credible person we have ever interviewed. In the end, what is the burning of a flying saucer compared to the Nazi crematoria? From that moment on, Stephen Michalak was treated with respect and dignity, which he richly deserved. Regarding his encounter with a UFO, we stopped bothering him with :

- Is all this true?

Instead, he was asked:

- Tell us what happened!

Since then, "The Michalak Case" has become an absolute classic. It is receiving national recognition. In April 2018, the Royal Canadian Mint released a 4,000-piece silver coin depicting Stephen Michalak's encounter in Whiteshell National Park. The coin, priced at $129.95, was fluorescent. Through the use of a special ink coating, the UFO depicted glowed in the dark and directed its beam at our witness lying on the ground.

- This is a real honor!" said Stan Michalak. If my father were still alive, he would be deeply moved as he was looking for money that day.

On April 29, 2018, composer Stephen Haiko-Pena composed a choral musical piece entitled *Two Cigar-Shaped Objects*, based on Stephen Michalak's story. The actor playing the witness addressed the UFO in five languages, punctuated by responses performed by a female choir. The Seine Singers, the Celtic group Plain Salt, flutist Kim Gordon, violinist Sylvie Reimer, and pianist David Strang were among the performers.

In May 2019, Stan Michalak and Chris Rutkowski edited a book entitled *When They Appeared*, detailing the Falcon Lake incident and the ordeal experienced by the witness.

Today, it is possible to visit the exact site of the landing, although the location is difficult to access and can only be reached by horseback. The Falcon Beach Ranch offers a two-hour tour called the *UFO Ride* through a beautiful landscape of forests and wetlands.

Sources

Stephen Michalak, *My Encounter With The UFO*, Osnova Publications 1967 : the reference ! - *Winnipeg Tribune*, May 22, 1967 - *The APRO Bulletin*, May-June 1967, pp. 1 and 3 - Royal Canadian Mounted Police reports of May 26, 1967, June 18, 1967, June 26, 1967 and August 10, 1967 - *The Canadian UFO Report*, vol. 1, n°2, March-April 1969, pp. 10-12 - *The Canadian UFO Report*, vol. 1, n°3, May-June 1969, pp. 11-12 - *The Canadian UFO Report*, vol. 1, n°4, July-August 1969, pp. 24-26 - *Lumières dans la Nuit*, Contact Lecteurs n°4, November 1972,

p. 19 - *Inforespace* n°21, June 1975, pp. 11-15 - *Historia Hors Série* n°46, " Les Soucoupes Volantes ", pp. 50-52 - *Flying Saucer Review*, vol. 27, n°1, June 1981, pp. 14-16 - *Flying Saucer Review*, vol. 27, n°2, August 1981, pp. 15-18 - *Flying Saucer Review*, vol. 27, no. 3, November 1981, pp. 21-25 - Timothy Good, *Above Top Secret*, The Lord Hill-Norton, 1988, pp. 195-200 - *NOW*, Toronto, week of July 7-13, 1994 - *MUFON Arizona Newsletter*, vol. 10, No. 2, February 2001, pp. 11-12 - *JUFOF* No. 194, February 2011, pp. 41-47 - case illustrates cover - *JUFOF* No. 195, March 2011, pp. 83-90 - *JUFOF* No. 196, April 2011, pp. 118-123 - Stan Michalak and Chris Rutkowski, *When They Appeared, Falcon Lake 1967: The Inside Story Of A Close Encounter*, August Night Books, 2019.

III. Other cases of UFO sightings inducing burns

As we have seen, the 1,574 pages of the DIA's report list an anthology of alarming injuries suffered by unlucky witnesses. For any ufology enthusiast, the revelations of this espionage branch of the Department of Defense are not surprising. Indeed, for decades, the profuse literature known as "saucerist" reports numerous cases where, following a close observation of unknown devices, traumatized witnesses have suffered painful effects in their flesh.

From the end of the 1940s, the friendly saucer gradually became a potential danger. This phenomenon, as elusive as it may be, has its own miscellanea. Here is a quick chronology.

1947: birth of the expression "flying saucers".

1948: the American Air Force considers, behind the scenes and in a low voice, that these saucers could be *spaceships*.

1950: Studies conducted by the Air Force intelligence services estimate that, during their displacement, these saucers carry out controlled maneuvers.

1954: the JANAP 146 C regulation (promulgated on March 10, 1954) asks civilian and military pilots to transmit to the intelligence services any sighting of aircraft, missiles, submarines or surface vehicles considered suspicious... not to mention UFOs. This information must not, under any circumstances, be communicated to the public under penalty of ten years of imprisonment. For the researcher François Parmentier, "this sword of Damocles has pushed pilots to practice self-censorship. The "saucer" loses its folkloric veneer and becomes a sensitive subject, even a possible threat to national security.

February 1961: the magazine *Flying Saucers* publishes a long article proposing an inventory of events where UFOs seem to have had a harmful effect on witnesses. The journalist George D. Fawcett concludes his paper as follows:

> I hope that the attached information concerning the hostility of UFOs will
> be food for thought for the thousands or even millions of people who are

looking for answers to the enigma of "flying saucers. May the 90 incidents cited, concerning these dangerous and hostile UFOs, help to prepare a defense against their attacks!

1967: Brad Steiger and Joan Whritenour published a book entitled *Flying Saucers Are Hostile: UFO Atrocities From Strange Disappearances To Bizarre Deaths*, 160 pages of shuddering concert.

But what is it really? For that, let us consult the archives we have. If we believe the testimonies, these "objects" would sometimes leave traces on the ground or on the surrounding natural environment: holes, various collapses, burnt grass, broken branches... They would also induce physical disturbances - we have often spoken of electromagnetic effects - on radio and television sets, engines, car headlights or aircraft instruments. More worrying, these UFOs would have a direct, sometimes harmful and lasting influence on humans. The symptoms they cause can be described as follows: asthenia, headaches, tingling, nosebleeds, vision problems. And, as in some of the cases discussed below, there is talk of astonishing and severe body burns.

A UFO with the buzz of a bee

Date: April 24, 1950.

Location: Abbiatte Guazzone, in the province of Varese, a few kilometers from Milan, Italy.

This case is the foundation of the UFO phenomenon and is without doubt one of the most famous episodes in the history of UFOs in Italy. It is almost the first time that such a complete and rigorous investigation has been carried out following the observation of an unknown craft and its occupants.

That evening, around 10:00 p.m., Bruno Facchini, a 42-year-old metal worker, left his house to go to the toilet located at the bottom of his garden. He saw flashing lights coming from the nearby forest. These lights are close to a high voltage pole. Since a violent storm has just passed through the area, our witness fears that an electric cable has fallen to the ground. This could hurt his children. So he put on a pair of boots and, with great caution, walked towards the pylon in question. Stunned, he falls nose to nose with a vessel on the ground, measuring 10 meters wide and 7 meters high. This metallic-looking machine looks like "a gigantic balloon whose top has been flattened".

Even more surprising, a figure wearing a helmet, a heavy grey suit and a mask from which a pipe escapes, is working on this vessel. This silhouette measures approximately 1,70 meter. Behind the translucent visor of its mask, one distingui-shes vaguely a face with the clear skin.

- In the middle of the machine, Bruno will tell us, I saw a ladder illuminated by a green light. I quickly realized that this light came from a kind of lamp that a man was manipulating. This individual was at the top of a kind of pneumatic elevator, like an extendable platform, and seemed to be engaged in welding work.

Bruno Facchini is a pragmatic man. Knowing that Malpensa International Airport and the military airfields of Vergiate and Venegono are close by, he thinks that a pilot should try to repair a military aircraft in trouble. He stepped forward and offered his help. But as he gets closer, he realizes that other figures are busy around the machine. More worrying, as an answer to his proposal, he only gets a series of strange grunts and borborygms. Our man has some notions of French and German, but the sounds emitted by these beings do not resemble an articulated language. They are guttural, monosyllabic sounds.

Bruno Facchini gradually becomes aware that he is facing something unusual. He explains:

- I saw two other people, identically dressed, moving slowly around the craft. I guessed that their suits were heavy and slowed their movements. The machine, illuminated by the welding tool, threw metallic reflections.

For a short moment, he can distinguish the interior of the vessel. There are cylinders, dials. In the surroundings of the machine, the air is exceptionally hot, almost unbreathable.

- I wondered what their intentions were," the witness admits. I had the feeling that they were inviting me on board. Then suddenly I heard a strange sound, like the amplified buzzing of a bee. I realized that I was not in the presence of an airplane and that these creatures were not human beings. I panicked and ran away, but as I ran I looked back and saw that one of these people was pointing something at me.

That something? A small box similar to a "camera" that the humanoid wears around its neck. It points it at the runaway. At that moment, the worker feels an excruciating pain. He feels "as if cut in two" and collapses. His head violently hits a stone.

- I felt like I was hit by a very powerful jet of compressed air that threw me to the ground. I did not lose consciousness, but it was extremely painful. I had time to see these three creatures getting back into this strange ship. They didn't seem to care about me anymore. I am convinced that they only wanted to frighten me and did not intend to harm me. They were busy removing the scaffolding and the ladder. Then the door closed. All the lights went out. Then the noise got louder. The machine took off, gained speed and disappeared into the darkness of the sky. After that, a dead silence fell, and I found myself alone in that field. Only the stars coming out of the clouds were shining in the cool evening air.

This confrontation will not be without incidence. Indeed, a few days after this confrontation, Bruno Facchini felt ill and had to see a doctor. The practitioner noticed that he had a blackened mark on his back, where he said the ray had hit him. It is a kind of burn which will soon spread and gain the whole surface of the back. For more than a month, it will be accompanied by violent pains.

Ten years after this strange encounter, Bruno Facchini will entrust to the investigator Pino Carminati Ghidelli :

- To this day, I have never really recovered from the shock I suffered. I regularly have violent hot flashes even though I don't have a fever.

The day after his observation, Facchini returned to the scene in order to find his cigarette case that he had lost during his escape. He discovers, on the still soft ground, 4 circular marks of 1 meter in diameter. Inside the marks, the grass is burned. While bending down, he collects, here and there, strange fragments of metal, "probably the residues left by the welding".

The Varese police and then the Italian authorities came to investigate. The pieces of metal were sent to the Experimental Institute of Light Metals to be analyzed in its laboratories in Novara. On September 30, 1953, the Institute published its results in report number 530954/4157, stating that the fragments were made of bronze and lead, with a high tin content. The samples do not show any abnormal elements.

In the wake of this, the Italian press echoed the "Facchini case". The famous and very popular *Domenica del Corriere* devoted several issues to it. As well as some very serious magazines of which the *Rivista Aeronautica*, official organ of the Italian Air Force.

Questioned in 1981 by the ufologist Ezio Bernardini, Bruno Facchini persists and signs. Until the end of his life, he will deliver the same version. He specified that, when he saw the Apollo moon landing on television, he was amazed to see that the suits worn by the American astronauts resembled the outfits of his visitors. In 1950, he had described the accoutrements of the humanoids as "similar to suits" and it is by discovering the images of Apollo that he understood that they were space suits.

Like many UFO witnesses, the metal worker suffered from his media exposure. Harassed, mocked by a part of the population, he ended up, with time, by bitterly refusing to evoke his incredible meeting.

A big shot in the Italian Navy once said to him:

- You are damn lucky, Mr. Facchini! I would have given a lot to be able to admire what you have seen, this marvel of technology!

The person concerned hesitated and then said:

- Lucky me? If I had known how much trouble this experience would bring me, I would never have mentioned it. I would have kept my mouth shut, I guarantee it!

Sources

Domenica del Corriere, April 1952 - *Rivista Aeronautica*, May 1953 - *UFO NYT*, November 1963, p. 226 - *Lumières dans la Nuit* n°100 bis, July 1969, p. 4 - *Notiziario UFO* n°37, January-February 1971, pp. 19-22 - *Flying Saucer Review*, vol. 20, n°6, April 1975, pp. 30-32 - *Notiziario UFO* n°104, March 1985-January 1986, pp. 4-7 - which quotes *Corriere dello Spazio* n°2, April 1959, pp. 16-17 - Jenny Randles, *Alien Contact - The First Fifty Years*, Barnes & Noble, 1997, pp. 14 and 15 - Timothy Good, *Contacts extraterrestres*, Presses du Chatelet 1999, pp. 83-86 Roberto Pinotti, *Contacts OVNIS en Italie, volume One (1907-1978)*, Flying Disk France 2022, pp. 22-33.

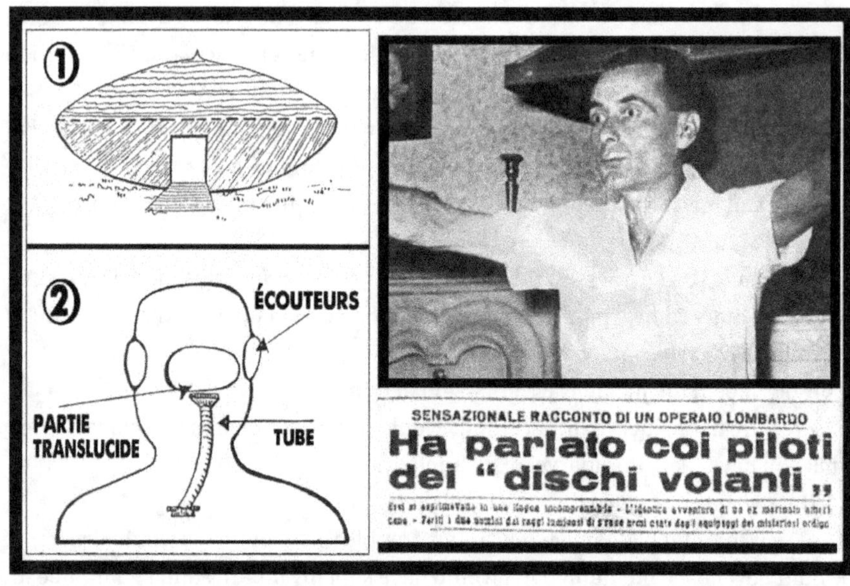

On the left: sketch of the UFO (1) and of the ufonaut (2). On the right: Bruno Facchini

Smooth as a snake

Date: April 8, 1950.
Location: Amarillo, in the state of Texas, USA.

The first witness, age 12, is David Lightfoot and lives with his parents on Blue-bonnet Drive. The second witness, age 9, is Charles Lightfoot and lives with his parents on River Drive. Both witnesses are cousins and attend school on River Road.

At 11:00 a.m., David and Charles are fishing in a river near the nursing home in the northeast part of town. It was a fairly quiet day. Suddenly, the two boys saw an object coming from the south, "like a balloon", which lost altitude and flew over them. Upon closer inspection, the young fishermen realized that it was in fact a disc-shaped object. David exclaims:

- I bet it's a flying saucer. I'm going to look for it!

He immediately runs away, while his cousin Charles, more cautious, stays behind.

The disk spins slowly and disappears behind the nearby hill. Without hesitation, David climbed it. At the top, he notices that the object has landed.

- It was round and looked like a car tire. In fact, it was the size of one. It must have been 45 centimeters long. I could see it very well. It was bulging at the bottom, with no opening. The bottom was stationary, but the top was turning very fast. At the top, there was a small spike sticking out. This peak was fixed and must have been connected to the bottom. When I got to the hill, the contraption was only a few steps away from me. I rushed at it. My fingers barely touched it. It was smooth as a snake, blue-gray and warm.

David doesn't have time to grab it. The top of the craft starts to turn faster. It emitted a kind of whistling sound, took off and flew "in a straight line towards the north-east" before disappearing in a few seconds. As the object took off, it released some kind of gas, a spray that burned David in the face and arm. His father testifies:

- When David left the house this morning, his arms were white, and there was no sun all day. When the boys came running back, telling a story about a flying saucer, I saw that my son's face and arms were red and blistered.

During the following days, David had to be treated with a cream that made the blisters on his skin disappear. Despite this treatment, we are told, his skin remained red "for quite some time".

When questioned by reporters, the boys told their story with calmness but conviction.

- The object stayed on the ground for less than a minute," said Charles, who was standing 90 meters away from the UFO. Then, by golly, it took off as if it were being pulled along by a rope. At no time did it wobble or swing...

- And the middle part of the object, between the base and the top, was very red, like on fire, David added.

The boys don't think that these flying saucers that are being talked about everywhere are from another planet. For them, "it is surely something made by the United States".

On February 28, 1970, 20 years after the events, in a telephone conversation with investigator James McDonald, David Lightfoot admitted that he had stretched his story a bit. The press, fond of *scoops,* distorted the truth quite a bit. According to David Lightfoot, the object never landed but remained stationary

---

at 30 or 60 centimeters above the ground. James McDonald's conclusion: the boy did see an object, but it was quite conventional. David Lightfoot is not convinced.

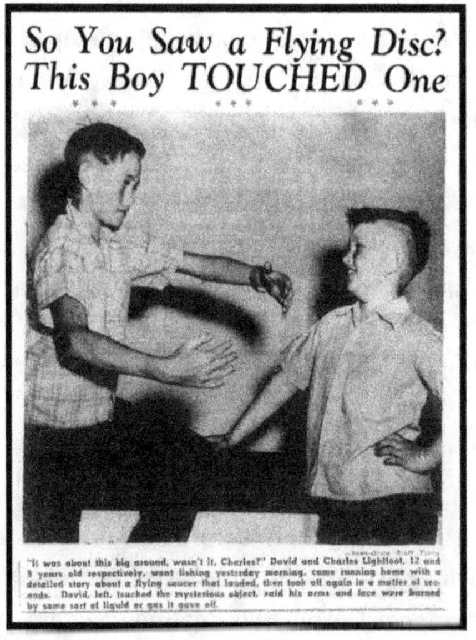

David and Charles Lightfoot, period press

Sources

Sunday News Globe, Amarillo, April 9, 1950 - *Herald Express,* Los Angeles, April 10, 1950 - *The APRO Bulletin,* January 1963, p. 5 - 5 page letter from James McDonald to Ted R. Bloecher, dated March 5, 1970.

A controversial but troubling case

Date: August 19, 1952.
Location: West Palm Beach, Florida, USA.

The following case was much talked about at the time.
21 h 45. Thick night. Suffocating. Moonless. Dunham Sanborn Desvergers, known as Sonny, a 30-year-old Scoutmaster, is driving home. He's driving home

UFO. Are we in danger? The black book of ufology

three young Scout apprentices in his charge (Bob Ruffing, 12, Charles Stevens, 11, and David Rowan, 11). As he approaches Boynton, Sonny sees strange lights in the sky. He counts them: there are six of them, lined up like the windows of an airliner. Without taking his eyes off them, he sees them rapidly losing altitude and descending so low that they brush against the treetops. Sonny thought that a plane was in trouble and about to crash.

He slammed on the brakes and turned back, thinking that he had to help the victims of this crash landing. Since the accident appeared to have occurred a few hundred yards from Military Trail, Desvergers parked his vehicle on the side of the road. He took two flashlights and a machete with him as he had to make his way through the thick vegetation along the road. He orders the kids not to follow him, adding:

- If I'm not back in 10 minutes, go to that house nearby and ask them to call the police!

Then, without wasting a second, Sonny heads for the presumed scene of the disaster.

To clear a way in this jungle is not easy. After about fifty meters, Sonny comes up against a thicket of dwarf palms. For lack of better passage, he engages in the undergrowth which arrives at his belt. He perceives then a strange smell, hardly perceptible, but "acrid and penetrating". Around him, the air is strangely warm. To progress, Sonny locates himself by fixing the polar star. Having traversed about thirty meters, he finally arrives in a clearing. The smell and the heat are now more intense, at the limit of the bearable.

- It was humid and oppressive, he confided. Breathing became difficult.

Our scoutmaster has the unpleasant sensation of being spied on. He stops, raises his head, looks for the North Star with his eyes but does not see it anymore. The other stars have also disappeared. He realizes that the celestial vault, 10 meters above him, is occulted by an immense dark shape. He raises his flashlight and sees a strange object.

- I looked up," he says. Everything was black above me. The sky had disappeared. I shone my flashlight on it and I saw, 1 meter above my head, a strange grey metal contraption, quite dirty. On its surface, I did not detect any rivet or welding. It was so close that I could have touched it with my machete. I was overcome with fear. I said to myself, "I have to get out of here, and fast!" I could make out the shape of this object. It was circular, rather flat, with a dome on top. It didn't emit any light. Suddenly the dome opened, like a hatch, with a sound like a well-oiled safe door opening. A red ball of fire shot out of it and toward me. It was a nebulous fire that projected sparks. This fire enveloped me. An unbearable stench suffocated me, penetrating deep into my nostrils and throat. I dropped my torch and machete. I shielded my face by raising my arms. I fell and lost consciousness.

Meanwhile, as more than ten minutes passed, the boys went to notify the police. Sheriff Mott N. Partin quickly arrived. He is joined by Officer Louis Carroll of Lake Worth. Gradually, in the middle of the brush, Sonny Desvergers regained consciousness.

- I thought I was dead," he explains. I got up but I could hardly walk. My body felt numb. I suddenly thought of the boys waiting for me in the car. To reach them, I started to run in the night, through the bushes. I don't know what I said to them when I found them. Everything was a blur in my head.

Mott N. Partin sees Sonny appear in a sorry state. He will tell the press:

- I have been asked several times if Sonny staged this hoax and acted. If so, believe me, I have never seen such an acting act in my life! In my nineteen year career, I have never seen anyone as terrified as I was that night! When he emerged from the brush, he looked like a wild man. His left arm was burned. On his forearm, all the hair had scorched and the skin was red, irritated. Fortunately, his cap had protected his face. She too was burned in three places. She was sent to Washington for analysis. Sonny later took me to the site of the sighting. I could see that the surrounding grass also had burn marks and was flattened as if someone had laid on it.

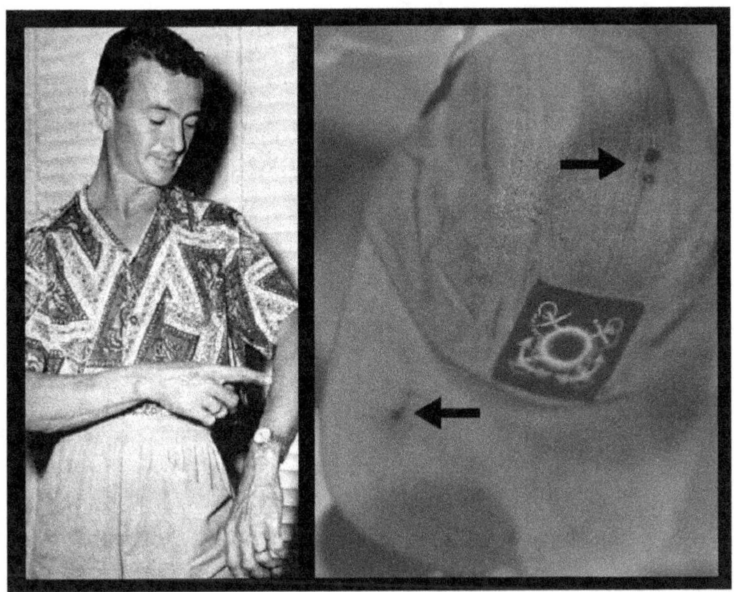

*Sonny Desvergers shows the burns
on his arm (left) and cap (right).*

Captain Edward Ruppelt and six other military personnel (four captains, a lieutenant and a sergeant) came to interview Sonny. On the evening of August 21, an Air Force doctor examined him and found that he had small burns on his arms and the back of his hands. The inside of his nostrils also appeared to be slightly burned. This did not convince the medical officer, although Edward Ruppelt seemed to think the whole story was credible. Sonny Desvergers then asked for permission to tell his story to the press. Edward Ruppelt gave him the green light.

The very next day, the newspapers reported on this terrifying encounter. The story arouses great emotion. Sonny is mediatized, but his words are surprising. He declares:

- It is better, for the public good, if I don't say too much. It could cause panic. The army's theory and mine coincide. I'd like to get it off my chest, but I told them I'd wait until they released me from my duty of silence.

Edward Ruppelt is frankly surprised. He notices that Sonny, proud of his newfound fame, is bragging and trying to take advantage of the event.

The witness's machete and cap are submitted for scientific examination. Grass samples from the field are sent for analysis to the agronomy laboratory at *Battelle Memorial Institute* in Columbus, Ohio. Sonny hires a press agent (a man named Art Kiel) to "sell his story". He told reporters that he had received several threatening phone calls and noticed "a large black car driving around and near his house.

One questions the three apprentice boy scouts. These, rather uneasy, declare to have seen the flashlight of their leader flashing between the trees then the light disappearing of a blow. Then, they would have seen a series of red lights, a little like flares. Six or eight red lights going in all directions. That's why they rushed to the nearby farmers for help. Their speech is hesitant. Edward Ruppelt concludes that the story is a sad hoax.

The Columbus Agronomy Laboratory, however, is changing this. It explains that, once removed from the soil, the roots of the plants received are charred while the aerial parts are unharmed, except for the lowest leaves, which are slightly damaged. The only specimens showing burns are those collected at the location designated by Sonny as having been flown over by the UFO. Those collected from 50 and 75 meters away are completely normal. This is a real coup.

A second twist, however, calls into question the credibility of the UFO hypothesis. Indeed, we discover that the past of the young man is not completely clear. Sonny was expelled from the Marines for illegal absence and car theft. He was also imprisoned in Chillicothe, Ohio. His testimony falls apart...

... but other witnesses, considered in good faith, come forward and outline a third twist in this case. On August 29, at about 7:30 p.m., Mr. and Mrs. Wendell Wells, June Tent (their 15-year-old niece) and two small children, were driving to an outdoor movie theater when they noticed "a bright glow" in the sky. According to the niece, it was "a big yellow and white light" that went through the woods on the left side of the road and fell straight down. June Tent added that the object was the size of a large transport plane but did not resemble any known aircraft. Mr. Wells then turned down Military Trail and the family could see the woods lit up with a strange glow. Because he had a young girl and two children on board, the driver thought it safer not to stop.

A Nellie M. Hahn also reported that on the night of August 19, 1952, she had observed in the east "some kind of orange, bright, round, gigantic balloon above the treetops in a stationary position." Finally, when interviewed by William Nash, Fred J. Brown, an employee of the Everglades Experimental Station west of West Palm

Beach, reported seeing a flying saucer-like object progressing at low altitude. The craft, surrounded by red and yellow lights on its lower rim, measured 10 meters in diameter. In the early morning hours of September 14, it passed directly over the resort, giving off a "bad smell" and emitting a loud buzzing sound that terrorized a herd of cattle.

So, was Sonny Desvergers' story a hoax or, as Jerome Clark suggested, "every ufologist's worst nightmare: a real experience by an unreliable individual"? That's for everyone to decide.

Sources

Daily News, Miami, August 27, 1952 - *Chronicle,* San Francisco, August 31, 1952 - *The American Weekly,* April 19, 1953, pp. 4-8 - *Flying Saucer Review,* vol. 2, n°6, November-December 1956, p. 32 - *Fantastic Universe,* vol. 9, n°1, January 1958, pp. 60-62 - Captain Edward J. Ruppelt, *Face aux soucoupes volantes,* France-Empire 1958, pp. 213-230 - Albert Weinberg, *Le Mystère des soucoupes volantes,* 13ème comic book adventure by Dan Cooper, Lombard 1969 - Jacques Lob and Robert Gigi, *Le Dossier des Soucoupes Volantes,* comic book album, Dargaud Éditeur 1972, pp. 48-53 - Karl T. Pflock, *The Best Hoax In Ufo History?,* document dating from 1997

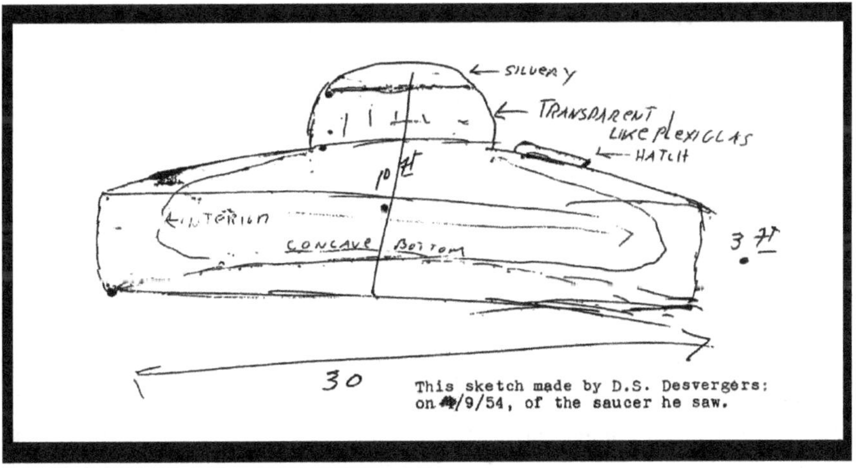

Drawing of the UFO by Sonny Desvergers, 1954

Second degree burns

Date: June 2, 1964.

Location: Hobbs, a small community in New Mexico, in the southern United States.

It is exactly 4:00 p.m. Charles Keith Davis is at his grandmother's house, Mrs. Frank Smith, cutting a cake for a snack. Charles is standing outside on the doorstep watching his grandmother as she works in the boiler room. Suddenly, a strange, elongated metal object descends from the sky and comes to rest above the boy. The old lady, witnessing the scene, is both horrified and powerless. She will say:

- I was so scared I couldn't even scream!

Very quickly, the object takes off again while whistling. As if subjected to a magnetic force, Charles' hair stood up. Before melting in the sky, the UFO releases on the boy a kind of soot mixed with flames. Mrs. Smith runs out and grabs Charles in her arms. She then noticed that her grandson was severely burned in the face. One of his ears was raw, "it looked like a piece of raw meat," the grandmother said. The boy's face is so swollen that his nose is almost indistinguishable, and his eyes are so swollen that he can't open them.

Charles had to be transported to the nearby Lee County Hospital. He remained there for five days. When contacted by APRO investigators, the attending physician confirmed that the boy was admitted with second-degree burns on his face, ears and neck. The doctor said that Charles obviously felt no pain at the time of the burns, which is quite inexplicable. However, he had to be treated with sulphatiazol applied directly to his raw wounds. A few days later, he had to be sedated because his wounds were horribly itchy when they healed. When the press asked the doctor what he thought was the cause of young Charles' burns, he said he had no idea but believed the story of the boy and his grandmother.

When alerted, the FBI responded to the scene. The agents took samples of the boy's skin. They also took away his soot-stained, burned T-shirt and the grandmother's apron, which was also stained when she pressed her grandson against her. Afterwards, no official has ever claimed to have identified the source of Charles' burns.

Source
The APRO Bulletin, November 1964, pp. 1 and 3.

APRO newsletter
headline: "Child Burned in New Mexico".

Blind in one eye

Date: March 13, 1965.
Location: Everglades Park, USA.

Covering an area of 611,000 hectares, the Everglades National Park is located in Florida. It is the largest subtropical natural environment in the United States. It is there that one of the most emblematic ufological cases of the 1960s took place.

James Flynn is a 45-year-old former police officer. He decided to go camping in the park, taking with him his four dogs that he trains to hunt. That Sunday, at nightfall, he prepares his meal around a campfire. Suddenly, around midnight, his dogs run off into the night, barking. Flynn thought they were on the trail of a deer and didn't think anything of it. It's not the first time this has happened. He hears their barks drifting away into the shadowy swamp. Suddenly, a bang sounds. The man is worried. He thinks someone is shooting his dogs. He decided to go and see what was going on.

1:00 a.m.: He drives into the park in his buggy and soon sees, at a distance of 1.5 kilometers according to his estimations, a rather bright yellow light hovering above the trees. This light behaves in a strange way. It moves to return invariably to the same place and then, slowly losing altitude, hovers at 1 meter from the ground.

James Flynn grabs his binoculars and discovers a strange object that is about 9 meters high and 23 meters in diameter. Not far from the top, four rows of

---

portholes emit a yellow light. The object is shaped like an inverted cone. It seems to be made of metal panels assembled by rivets. The ground under the machine is bathed in a yellow-orange light. The observer scrutinizes this astonishing spectacle for thirty to forty minutes, thinking that it is a secret craft from Cape Canaveral. Fearing that this NASA device or capsule was in trouble, the witness decided to help the crew.

He progresses with difficulty through the extremely dense vegetation. Nearby, the noise emitted by the object becomes deafening. James Flynn approaches it cautiously. He waves his arm, waiting for an answer. No response. Anyway, he advances again and enters the orange halo that the object projects on the ground. He waves his arm again, hoping to establish a communication. Suddenly, out of the base of the portholes, a ray of light "like a welder's flashlight" strikes our witness in the forehead, above his right eye, "like a blow from a sledgehammer". The pain is excruciating. The man collapses and loses consciousness.

When our witness comes to, he is blind! Unconscious for many hours, he is lying behind his buggy. Progressively, he recovers partially the sight of his left eye and notices that the ground which was under the machine presents a circular burn trace. Around this circle, the cypress trees are partially damaged. He leaves the camp. Back home, accompanied by his wife, he consulted Paul Brown, an ophthal-mologist. The doctor noticed that the patient's right eye looked like a "bloody marble". He describes the visit as follows:

- Mr. Flynn was very agitated. He kept saying, "I know you won't believe me, but this is what happened to me! And he kept telling the same story. My examination revealed a bruise on the right side of his forehead and above his right eyelid. I could no longer see the retina of his right eye. His left eye, on the other hand, looked normal.

James Flynn was transferred to *Lee Memorial Hospital* in Fort Myers. He stayed there for five days under the care of Dr. Harvie J. Stipe, a doctor he had known for 25 years. The practitioner testifies:

- I was asked to observe Mr. Flynn forty-eight hours after his hospitalization. His eye had an anterior chamber hemorrhage, apparently due to traumatic shock.

The patient also has neurological disturbances. No paralysis but a total absence of tendon reflexes in the biceps, triceps, patellas and Achilles tendon as well as an absence of plantar and abdominal reflexes.

On March 17, Robert Daubenspeck, Deputy Chief of the Lee County Police Department, interviewed Flynn. Daubenspeck told the *Fort Myers News-Press that* he believed that Flynn had been injured while driving his buggy when he hit a low branch. This explanation was immediately challenged by Sheriff Flanders Thomson and William R. Spear, editor of the *News-Press*. Spear notes in his journal:

> James Flynn is a serious citizen. He is pragmatic, down to earth and has never suffered from hallucinations. When he says that a "sledgehammer blow" between the eyes injured his forehead and caused vision loss for which he needs hospital follow-up, and that this "sledgehammer blow" was delivered by a large conical object, he is certain that he believes what he is saying and that he did not knowingly invent this story.

On March 26, accompanied by three people, James Flynn returned to the site of the observation. The group discovers an enormous circular mark on the ground. This circle of burnt grass measures 21 meters in diameter. Inside, everything seems to have been blown away or swept away: there are no leaves, twigs, or material of any kind. Around this mark, eight cypress trees are partially damaged, their high branches charred. No other traces are visible on the surface of this dried-up marsh: no animal, human or vehicle tracks. James Flynn and his friends collected soil samples and sent them to Homestead Air Force Base for analysis. They will not get any return.

For its part, the Air Force tried to discredit James Flynn and stifle his testimony. Officially, for the military, the story was a hoax. However, behind the scenes, they were very interested in it.

The "James Flynn case" was then seriously examined by ufologists, including Navy Captain Charles H. Foresman for NICAP (the largest private UFO investigation organization), and Coral Lorenzen for APRO. To the skeptics, Donald Keyhoe, former Marine Corps major, responded:

- To complete the deception, Flynn would have had to climb the trees, roast the tops and ravage the bark. But there were no footprints at the base of the trees. The mystifier would still have had to hit his forehead hard enough to affect his own eyesight. As for the impaired reflexes, the doctor categorically ruled out the hypothesis of a simulation.

According to Dr. James McDonald who interviewed the witness on October 31, 1966:

James Flynn hypothesized that the craft seen was a secret prototype of the US Army.

- If I were to find out that this thing belongs to the government," he told me, "then I would demand that they pay me compensation for that healthy eye that I had and lost.

It would seem that this UFO had a damaging effect on local living organisms, and the witness paid a high price. In July 1996, during a rare public appearance in Port Charlotte, Florida, he stated:

- I am waiting for the day when someone will reveal the truth about this. I hope I live long enough for that.

Sources

UFO Investigator, vol. III, n°1, March-April 1965, p. 6 - *The APRO Bulletin,* May-June 1965, pp. 1, 3 and 4 - *UFO Investigator,* vol. III, n°3, June-July 1965, p. 3 - *Flying Saucer Review,* vol. 2, n°4, July-August 1965, p. 14 - *UFO NYT* n°6, November-December 1965, pp. 244-247 - which quotes *Fate,* September 1965 - *Phénomènes spatiaux* n°25, September 1970, pp. 11 and 12 - *Lumières dans la nuit* n°123, March 1973, pp. 22 - Donald E. Keyhoe, *Les Étrangers de l'espace,* France-Empire, 1975, pp. 46-48 - Leonard Springfield, *General UFO Alert,* France-Empire, 1978, pp. 258-259 - Jerome Clark, *The UFO Book, Encyclopedia of the Extraterrestrial,* Visible Ink, 1998, pp. 179-182 - *CONTACT* television series, season 2, episode 3 entitled "Encounter in the Swamp," 2015.

A UFO shaped like a loaf of milk

Date: March 29, 1966.
Location: Mountain, Ontario, Canada.

It was 9:15 p.m. While out walking, 13-year-old Charles Cozens spotted two strange objects landing in a field behind the Mountain Police Station on Upper Wellington Street. He climbed the fence to get a closer look at the strange objects. Indeed, one of the objects landed on the ground. It measures "2.5 meters long by 1.20 meters wide and 90 centimeters high". On its periphery, lights "red, blue and green flash like that of a computer". The luminous object "lights up the grass around it" and emits a buzzing sound. It has the shape of "a loaf of milk".

The boy approaches, reaches out and touches the object. It is solid, smooth, "neither hot nor cold, at our body temperature". Charles then distinguishes a kind of antenna on one of the sides of the device. The antenna is "thick at the base" and "thin at the end". The boy reaches out again, touches the antenna... and receives an electric shock, while a flash of lightning shoots out from the strange appendage.

- I ran out of there. I wanted to warn the officers at the police station. But when I turned around, before I left the field, the objects were gone. I thought the police wouldn't believe me. So I went home to tell my parents.

James Cozens, Charles' father, is an industrial designer. His son, very excited, rushes to tell him about his misadventure. James questioned Charles repeatedly, reminding him that the police should only be contacted for serious reasons. Charles remains "adamant and determined". He understands and says he is not lying. Police Officer Arnold Pead was alerted and went to the Cozens' home. He found that the boy had been burned on his hand, the wound forming "a yellowish mark about 7 centimetres long".

Her mother is convinced:

- Charles is a serious boy. He wouldn't have allowed us to call the police if he wasn't telling the truth. We didn't tell anyone about this. We were afraid Charles would be ridiculed. But it's amazing how well he remembered every detail. He was always hardworking, really serious. Not the type to show off.

The story gets out. On the advice of Charles' teacher (then a student at *Our Lady of Lourdes* School), James Cozens consulted a doctor. The doctor found a beautiful burn on the boy's hand that needed attention. At St. Joseph's Hospital, Charles was tested for radioactivity and found to be negative. A blood test did not detect any particular biological anomaly.

Regarding this case, a first press article appeared on April 2, with the headline: "Boy burned by a 'flying ship'!" Mrs. Cozens relates:

- People came from all over, even from Vancouver, to meet and talk with Charles. We made sure that he kept his feet on the ground and was not disturbed by all the attention. He is such a serious boy! He never changed a word of his story. We would have found out quickly if it was a lie. We trust him completely. He was aware of the seriousness of his testimony and of the consequences it could have.

Sources

Hamilton Spectator, April 2, 1966 - *The Montreal Star,* April 4, 1966 - *Hamilton Spectator,* August 9, 1966 - *Phénomènes spatiaux* n°25, September 1970, p. 12 - *Science and The UFO Phenomenon: Statement on Unidentified Flying Objects,* symposium of July 29, 1968 by James E. McDonald.

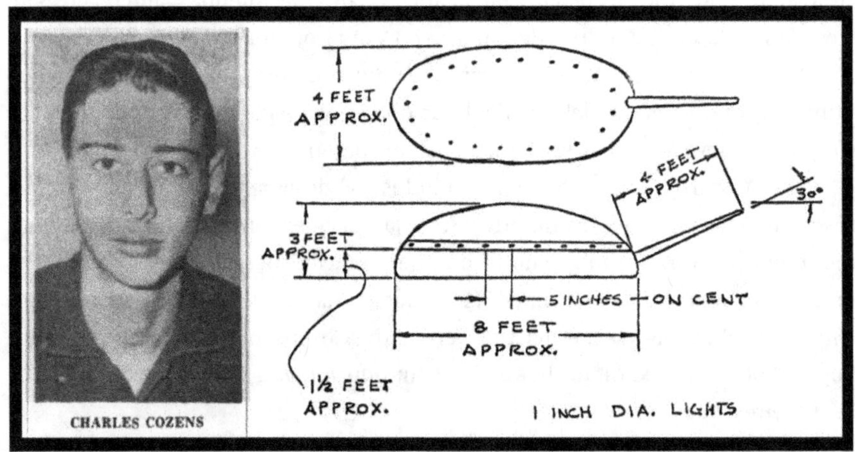

Charles Cozens (left). Drawing of the UFO by James Cozens, his father (right.)

A jacket in flames

Date: March 19, 1968.
Location: Beallsville, Ohio, USA.

It's 8:30 p.m. Twelve-year-old Gregory Wells leaves his grandmother's house, located 4 kilometers from Beallsville, to go to his parents' nearby *mobile home.* The boy carries a jug of water in his hand. The pipes in the *mobile home* had frozen that winter, and he had to get water from his grandparents.

Gregory is almost there when he sees, above the trees, a large, circular, red contraption with four lights. This object emits a strange noise, like that of an "electric generator". It is shaped like a rugby ball.

Gregory sees a small tube at the base of the machine, which pops up and points in his direction. Panic-stricken, he takes his legs and runs towards the *mobile home.*

UFO. Are we in danger? The black book of ufology

A red ray bursts out of the tube and hits Gregory in the right arm. The boy drops the water jug. He falls and screams in pain. His mother, alerted by his screams, runs over immediately. Distraught, she sees that Gregory's jacket has caught fire! Reacting quickly, she grabs the water jug and puts out the flames.

Fortunately, Gregory was wearing a thick sweatshirt under his jacket that day that partially protected him. However, he had to be transported to Barnesville Hospital. Dr. Phillips officially found second-degree burns and applied a Vaseline treatment to the boy's wounds.

Sheriff Sulsberger came to investigate. Gregory's jacket was sent to London for analysis. Gregory's mother and grandmother both testified that they had indeed seen this strange object in the sky. The incendiary device could never be identified.

James E. McDonald, professor of meteorology and dean of physics at the University of Arizona's Institute of Atmospheric Physics, investigated the case. His conclusion:

> To investigate the case, I interviewed a number of people in the Beallsville area. Among them were some who had seen a long, cylindrical object at very low altitude in the vicinity of the Wells' house that night. I cannot report here the many details that were given to me. My conversations with people who know the boy, and especially his teacher, mean that I see no reason to disregard this adventure, despite its unusual content.

Sources

The APRO Bulletin, March-April 1968, pp. 1 and 3 - *Space Phenomena* n°25, September 1970, p. 12.

Blisters and headaches

Date: March 19, 1975.

Location: Allerød, northeast of the Danish island of Sjaelland.

It is 9 pm. A 12-year-old boy is playing in front of his house when he is surprised to see a strange phenomenon. Sitting on the sidewalk, he looked up and saw a "dome-shaped" object in the sky. The upper part of the object is dark, dimly lit. The boy notices that there is a "hole" on the left top of the object. Underneath this strange contraption, he distinguishes two protruding half-spheres.

From its base, the object emits a fan-shaped beam of white light that comple-tely illuminates the road. The UFO then positions itself above the boy. It tilts and directs its beam directly on him. The road on which the boy is is also illuminated. We can see as if it were daylight. The beam emitted by the object is "as strong as the sun". Dazzled, our witness's eyes hurt so much that he had to look away several times.

After two minutes, the object starts to move. It repositioned itself horizontally and then slowly moved away to the south. When it reaches the nearby forest, it makes a sharp right turn and heads west, where it disappears at high speed.

In the days following this observation, the witness suffers from itching caused by red blisters that appeared mainly on his head, arms and hands. He also suffers from migraines. The headaches fade away in a few days. The blisters and itching after a week.

Source

UFO NYT n°3, May-June 1975, pp. 100-101.

Reconstruction of the observation of March 19, 1975 by the author

UFO. Are we in danger? The black book of ufology

A UFO like an umbrella

Date: last week of September 1977.

Location: Poole, in the county of Dorset, England.

Ethel May Field, 62, lives on Sea View Road in Poole. That evening, at the stroke of 11:00 p.m., she went to her backyard to retrieve her laundry that was drying outdoors. Maurice, her 68-year-old husband, and Teresa, her 24-year-old daughter, were inside watching television. Suddenly, Ethel Field hears a strange noise that makes her look up. She saw a circular object in the sky with a dome on top. The object shines with a ghostly gray glow. On its periphery, a string of "blue-yellowish" lights can be seen illuminating the ground.

- This strange thing, the witness said, looked like an umbrella. It was about the size of my garden, that is, it was about 7 meters long.

The UFO then comes to rest above the garden, at a very low altitude, allowing Ethel May Field to see two humanoid silhouettes in the dome at its top. These two characters wear a kind of silver uniform. Their features are "elegant" and the witness believes that they are rather masculine creatures. The being on the right appears to be manipulating joysticks (which the witness does not distinguish); the one on the left stares at Ethel May Field and then waves as if it wants to land.

The object, motionless in the air, is so luminous, so blinding, that Miss Field wants to protect her eyes with her two hands, palms turned towards the sky. When she makes this gesture, a sudden sensation of heat radiates from her palms. For a second, the sixty-year-old feels as if the ground is shaking under her feet. Giving in to panic, she runs into the house and tells her husband and daughter about her adventure. No matter. Miss Field assures that she is going to contact the press and tell them what she has seen. For fear of ridicule, her daughter dissuades her.

Over the next few days, Miss Field's hands develop a sort of infectious rash. A small spot that appeared early on her left palm grew steadily. Soon, both her hands were practically raw and very painful. His doctor diagnosed dermatitis: an inflammation of the skin due to local irritation or external burns caused by the sun or X-rays. In any case, Ethel May Field remained disabled for many days, obliged to wear bandages, giving up her usual activities for a while. The case remains unexplained, and it is not known whether her daughter Teresa appreciated having to pick up the laundry and put it away.

Sources

Daily Express, London, April 21, 1978 - *Flying Saucer Review,* vol. 24, n°2, August 1978, pp. 6-8 - *Daily Echo*, Bournemouth, November 4, 2000.

Ethel May Field shows her bandaged hand (left). Drawing of the UFO (right) (FSR Documents)

Redder than a lobster

Date: May 13, 1978.
Location: Kerman, California, USA.

Manuel Amparano is a police officer. He is 33 years old. That night, at 3:30 a.m., he is on patrol. The night is cool and clear. As the officer drives down Del Norte Avenue, he sees a strong glow in the treetops. At first he thinks it is a fire. Indeed, recently, some young people have taken the annoying habit of setting fire to palm trees. Before alerting the fire department, Manuel Amparano gets closer to the light. He reached the intersection of Del Norte and California avenues. And, above a cotton field, he discovered a "circular object, stationary, similar to a round fireball or a sunset of an intense red". Immobile to 30 or 45 meters above the ground, this object measures between 10 and 15 meters in diameter.

The policeman parks his patrol car - a white Chevrolet Nova - on the side of the road and lowers his window. The phenomenon is very close: only 30 meters away. It is bright but not blinding. The observation lasts about four minutes. The policeman decides to turn his headlights on this strange thing. But, before he does so, the object emits a bluish light beam on the car, like "a camera *flash*". Then it drove away, made a right turn and sped off in a southeasterly direction over the San Joaquin Valley.

After the object disappeared, the witness, shaken, went to the parking lot of highways 145 and 180 where he parked to think. Should he report his sighting or keep quiet? That's when a freelance paperboy named Phil Mahler approaches him and confides:

- While delivering a newspaper on Whitesbridge Road and Grantland Avenue, I saw a red ball in the sky!

Comforted, Manuel Amparano decided to tell his superiors what he had just experienced. At the end of his shift, he contacted the Air National Guard, then the meteorological office, and finally the radar station at Fresno airport. The National Guard told him that no aircraft were in the area at the time of the sighting. The weather bureau says that no weather balloons were launched. The radar telescopes did not detect anything suspicious in the area.

The policeman also contacted a civilian association that investigates UFO phenomena based in Seattle. Later, he received a letter from them stating that an astronomer in Fresno had seen a reddish ball descending near the ground west of Fresno at almost the same time Amparano had observed it. When two other police officers - A.J. Buinyton and Bob Muller - arrived at the station, they were stunned to see the condition of their colleague: he was "redder than a lobster!" His face and neck appear to be burned, although he is unaware of it. The two agents drag him to the bathroom to examine himself in the mirror. The unfortunate man then discovered that his chest had also been burned through his shirt. The two newcomers immediately went to the cotton field where the officer said he had observed the object. They spent about two hours searching the area. Without success.

At 8:00 a.m., back at home, Manuel Amparano tells Barbara, his wife, what he has just experienced. Then explaining that he feels bad because of his burns, he goes to bed quickly. As the hours go by, he is more and more uncomfortable. The weight of the sheets and blankets made him suffer terribly. And when he finally falls asleep, his wife, worried, sees him shaking.

At 5:00 p.m., the witness is not well. The burn is too severe. He goes to the emergency room at Fresno Community Hospital. He is recorded as having "burns from an unknown source". He has never had high blood pressure, but has very high blood pressure. The patient then consulted a private physician. The doctor told him that he appeared to be suffering from exposure to a high-intensity fluorescent lamp or gamma rays. The effects of the burn lasted for five days.

Following a "leak" from the hospital, the news of his condition reaches the media. Manuel Amparano refuses to talk about the incident to journalists, thinking that the excitement that has just arisen will calm down quickly. He is wrong. The phone calls from newspapers, magazines and television stations around the world are increasing. James Van Cleaf, the chief of police, asks his employee not to divulge any details, but the subordinate decides to talk in the hope that the media will stop bothering him. He repeats:

- There was something there, but I don't know if it was actually a UFO.

On the police side, the investigation is well conducted. A report on his observation is recorded on May 13, 1978 at 3:32 am. His testimony is taken seriously because the man is not a crank. His professional career is exemplary. For four years, this graduate of the Modesto City College Police Academy served in the Marine Corps.

If you look at the official Fresno hospital registry, here's what it says:

- The officer was burned through his long-sleeved uniform.
The burns (first degree) subsided after four hours but lasted for two days. Soon, blisters appeared on her face and forearms.
- For a week, he felt a strange burning sensation under his skin. His whole body was painful. He also had severe pain in his groin. He had to be prescribed codeine.

In spite of the investigation (which located fourteen witnesses), the object seen by the policeman in this night of May could never be identified.

Since then, our witness scans the sky with binoculars.

- I know people think I'm crazy," he says resignedly. And I know that, because of this, I have not been promoted. Yet, as an officer, if I witness a murder, I can write a report on it and send the criminals to jail. But when something like that happens, you're considered to be just plain crazy.

Manuel Amparano has filled several boxes with articles about strange celestial manifestations. He bought himself a camera to track down possible UFOs.

- One day, we will finally have the proof that they exist, he assures. Then I will rest, light a cigar and smile!

Sources

Herald Examiner, Los Angeles, June 5, 1978 - *The APRO Bulletin,* vol. 27, no. 2, August 1978, pp. 4-5 - *International UFO Reporter,* September 1978 - *BEE, Fresno,* February 23, 1979 - *UFO Update!* no. 2, Winter 1979, p. 60 - *BEE,* Fresno, May 18, 1997.

Drawing published in the press of that time to illustrate the observation of Manuel Amparano

A lime green laser

Date: September 10, 1981.

Location: Plymouth, a port city in Devon, southwest England.

At the time of the incident, Denise Bishop was 23 years old. Employed in a local car company, she is described by her relatives as "intelligent and down to earth". Until now, she has never been interested in UFO stories and has not read any book on the subject.

At 11:15 p.m., she returned to her parents' home in Weston Mill Hill, a district of the city of Plymouth. As she approached the family home, she saw several lights in the sky. At first, she didn't pay much attention. But as she was about to enter the back door of the house, she froze. The celestial lights form a singular vessel "having the aspect of a crab", hovering above the residences of the nearby hill. Denise estimates that this craft must measure 40 meters wide. She tells:

- The object itself was not bright. It was a dark metallic gray. On its underside I could make out six or seven broad beams of light illuminating the rooftops below. Some of these beams were a pretty pastel tone, pink and purple. Others were white. I was terrified, I rushed to the door. The instant I put my hand on the latch, a thin brush of lime green light shot out from the unlit part of the object and onto the back of my hand. It lasted at least thirty seconds. I was paralyzed. I could only look at the UFO. I was frozen with fear, although the sight of this huge, silent object was fantastic.

Around the house, everything seems quiet. As soon as the green ray, which is not illuminating, is extinguished, Denise, released, hurries to open the door.

- It was, she said, as if the images of a film had been stopped and now the projection was resumed. This ray had interrupted, frozen my gesture. Now that it had been extinguished, I found my motricity again. As I rushed into the house, I had time to see the UFO take off and leave my field of vision.

While rubbing her hand, Denise rushes to her sister to whom she confides her misadventure. The two girls immediately go out on the stoop to scan the surroundings. But the sky is empty again.

- Show your hand, orders the sister.

Nothing to report. The skin seems intact. More fear than harm! Denise sits down to recover from her emotions.

UFO. Are we in danger? The black book of ufology

That's when the dog from the house appears. The animal goes straight to Denise's hand and sniffs it. At that moment, the witness felt a tingling sensation.

- On my hand, there were like little blood spots," she says. In fact, after I washed it thoroughly, I realized it was a burn.

At 2:30 a.m., John Greenwell, the sister's fiancé, arrives. He has just finished his job as a *disc jockey* in a local *nightclub*. When he hears Denise's story, he advises her to call the police... then he changes his mind. He prefers to call the police station himself and finds an agent who gives him the address of a ufology research group based in Plymouth.

A few days later, the civilian investigator Robert Boyd goes to the Bishops' house. When Denise meets him, the situation is reversed: it is the witness who bombards the investigator with questions:

- Do you think they will come back? What if that ray had hit my face or my eyes? And why ME? Did they want a skin sample?

Boyd takes two photographs of Denise's hand, which has a strange mark on it. His notes are unequivocal:

> It appears that some of the outer skin, the epidermis, has been removed, exposing the brighter lower layer of dermis. I tried to convince Denise to go to the emergency room of the local hospital, but she refused. When she complained that the wound really hurt, I told her to dip her hand in cold water, but when she did, it made it worse. We finally opted for an antiseptic cream which gave her some relief.

When Westward TV, the local television station, heard about the affair, they asked Denise to appear on the show. After many requests, she finally, almost a month later, granted an interview to Robert Malone, a reporter for the *Western Evening Herald.*

Derek Mansell, of the ufological organization CIUFOR (*Contact International UFO Research*), interested in this case, then transmits a photo of Denise's hand to a consultant orthopedic surgeon of a large London hospital. For this surgeon, it was a laser burn. He explained that this type of injury heals fairly quickly, but the healing process does not begin for 48 hours. His prognosis held true for Denise. The burn eventually healed and left a scar, similar to a very pale birthmark.

Investigation in the neighborhood revealed that at the time of the sighting, several dogs in the surrounding homes were acting strangely. And a neighbor, Elsie G., reported seeing a strange object hovering in the Plymouth sky that night.

Sources

Western Evening Herald, October 28, 1981 - *The APRO Bulletin,* vol. 30, n°3, 1982, p. 7 - *Flying Saucer Review,* vol. 28, no. 3, January 1983, pp. 15-19 - *Journal Für UFO-Forschung* no. 27, May-June 1983, pp. 70-75 - *Inforespace* no. 64, October 1983, pp. 17-18 - *SHE,* London, July 1986 - Timothy Good, *Above Top Secret: The World-wide UFO Cover-Up,* Quill William Morrow, 1988, pp. 98-101 - Janet and Colin Bord, *Modern Mysteries of Britain,* Diamond Books, 1991, pp. 54 and 55 - John Spencer, *The UFO Encyclopedia,* Avon Books, 1991, p. 44 - *Sunday Independent,* Plymouth, February 2, 1997.

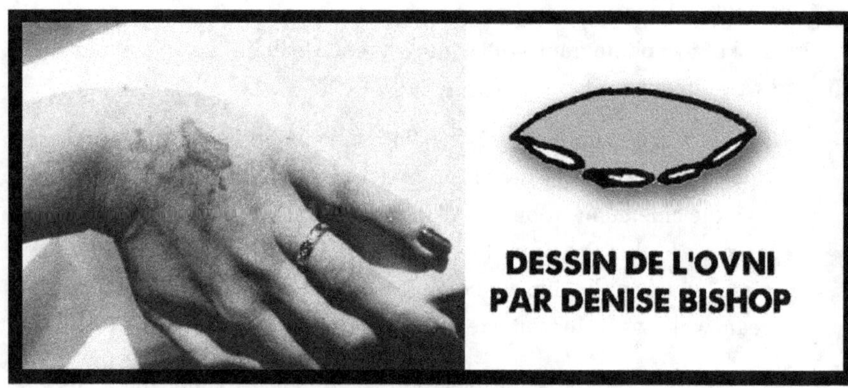

Denise Bishop's hand 36 hours after her burn (left).
Her sketch of the UFO (right)

IV. Valensole: an emblematic case of paralysis with the appearance of entities

Among the effects evoked by the DIA report, it is notably a question of "paralysis". Here is a case of type "CE3" (with the presence of entities seen inside or near the UFO) where a witness found himself unable to make the slightest gesture.

The so-called "Valensole affair" remains one of the most famous episodes of paralysis following a confrontation with an unconventional object. It took place in France and has been reported around the world thanks to an abundant media coverage. Considered as "solid", it opens chapter 4 of the *Cometa Report* (a document written by an association of military and experts, then submitted in April 1999 to Prime Minister Lionel Jospin and President Jacques Chirac). However, to learn more, one must go to the heart of this Provence of which Giono said: "One cannot imagine the discoveries one can make there. This country is of an unheard of malice.

For me, it is indeed in this land of fire and wind, with its ochre and bluish flats, that everything began. As a child, I discovered a phenomenon which, triumphing over a too legible reality, gave rise to confusion, complexity and enchantment. Those who live there know it well: from morning to vespers, every event magnified by light and shadow takes on the appearance of an ancient tragedy.

A huge spider

Date: 1ᵉʳ July 1965.

Location : Valensole, a small town in the Alpes-de-Haute-Provence, located in the heart of a magnificent plateau of lavender and almond trees, France.

That morning, Maurice Masse, 41 years old, got up at 5 am. The day was just beginning to dawn on the promise of a harsh summer day. Without delay, our man left his home, Place du Marché, and went to his field, near the village, at a place called Olivol, near the road to Oraison. Like every morning, work awaits him. However, the man is worried. For a few days, he has noticed that some indelicate hands are taking samples of his precious lavender. Who could dare to steal it like that?

Maurice Masse and his wife (Photo: René Guillois)

Once there, before starting his tractor, Maurice takes a cigarette from his pocket and lights it. Sheltered behind a "hutch" (a stone mound 2 meters high), he consults his watch. It is 5:45 a.m. Suddenly, he hears a whistling sound that evokes "the grinding of a hacksaw. This noise fills the countryside. Maurice freezes. He tries to locate where it could be coming from... No doubt about it: from the lavender field above the vineyard, just a hundred meters away. He goes there with a determined step and sees an ovoid device, placed in the middle of his lavender plants. The device looks like "a rugby ball", he will say later:

- The bottom of the device was 50-60 centimeters from the ground. Above the device, there was a transparent dome, like Plexiglas. Its total height could be 2,50 meters. It had the size of a Dauphine and a matt color.

Maurice Masse estimates that the strange machine measures between 3 and 3.50 meters wide. It rests on six feet mounted on a central pivot sinking into the ground. It looks like, he thinks, a huge spider!

UFO. Are we in danger? The black book of ufology

Funny dwarfs

Intrigued, Maurice Masse steps forward. Astonishment! Besides the machine, he sees two small beings. They are on the ground, squatting, leaning on the lavender plants.

- These two beings did not reach 1 meter in height, he reported. They had a head in the shape of pumpkin, of a volume three times equal to the head of a normal man. They had rather large ears, no chin, a round hole in the place of our mouth, eyes which seemed to me to resemble ours but without eyebrows. They had a large skull without hair. Their build was barely wider than their head. They had arms and legs. They had small hands, and I did not distinguish any fingers other than the thumb.

The first thought of our witness: "As they are small and barely reach my belt, I will catch them and stun them". These two beings, as tall as 8 year olds, are dressed in dark uniforms. They hold instruments that they store in saddlebags attached to their waists. Maurice Masse, more and more disturbed by their appearance, moves forward with the intention of making contact with them. When he reaches 7 meters, they see him and suddenly stand up. One of them points a kind of tube or "gun" at the farmer. Maurice was instantly paralyzed. It is a strange sensation. Our man is conscious. He can breathe, move his eyes, observe and command his muscles to maintain the vertical position, but he is unable to make any movement.

He then takes the opportunity to observe the intruders. These humanoids have no neck. They have "their heads tucked into their shoulders". They communicate with each other with "a sort of gurgling sound" and seem to be enjoying the situation.

- They seemed to be laughing at me," he explains. But I wasn't afraid of their attitude because I didn't feel like they were trying to hurt me

Maurice Masse sees their eyes "which are not mean, on the contrary". After four to five minutes, the small beings return, with an amazing agility, to their aircraft.

- A sliding door rising from the bottom to the top, like a filing cabinet door, closed in a way that seemed automatic to me, he will describe. I could see them behind their dome.

After a thud, the device lifts 50 centimeters off the ground. The tube underneath the device comes out of the ground and the six legs start to turn clockwise. There is

---

no smoke, no dust raised. Finally the machine rises obliquely and disappears in the direction of Manosque.

- It was going faster than a jet plane on takeoff," said the farmer. I was immobilized for quite a long time after the machine left, I estimate 15 minutes.

Little by little, our witness recovered the use of his limbs. He returned to his tractor, lit a cigarette, then mechanically worked the soil of his vineyard until 8:00 a.m. But, at 9 am, he is back home. He is upset. First he tells his father about his adventure. Then at 10 am, he confided in his good friend, Dédé Moisson, owner of the Café des Sports, so that soon the news spread and the police were informed.

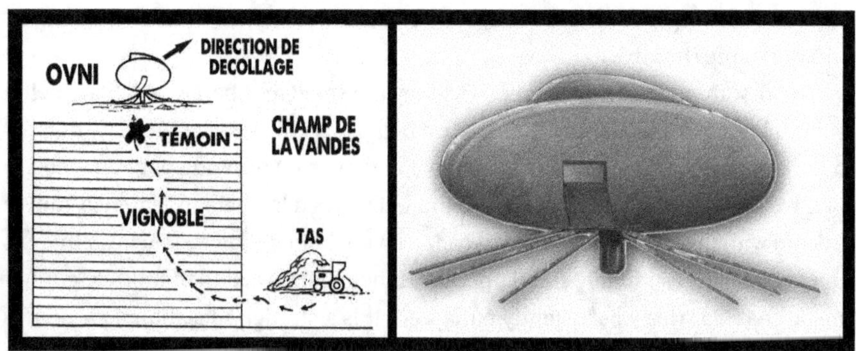

Map of the terrain (left). Reconstruction of the UFO (right)

The surveys

The brigade of Valensole carries out a first investigation. A report specifies:

> On July 2, 1965, around 7:30 p.m., we learned from public rumor that Mr. Masse Maurice, farmer, living in Valensole, would have declared to have seen in his field, on July 1[er] 1965 around 5:45 a.m., an aircraft of unknown conception. Let us summon the interested party to the office of the brigade and let us receive his declaration at 20 h.

Questioned by the marshal Oliva, Maurice Masse delivers a first testimony. He briefly evokes the two small beings. He only spoke about it in detail to his father and made him swear not to repeat anything. He feared to be interned in a psychiatric hospital!

UFO. Are we in danger? The black book of ufology

Two hours later, the Brigade des recherches of Digne joined the agents of Valensole. The men and Marshal Oliva went with the declarant to the lavender field in question. The visit is very short because of the darkness. At 11:15 p.m., the witness gave a second testimony:

- After the aircraft took off, I was initially moved (*sic*) and I did not approach it. Then, fifteen or twenty minutes later, I went near the site. I noticed that there was a hole. Around the hole, the earth was soggy in the basin. When I came back in the evening at about 8:30 p.m., with my daughter, I noticed that the earth had become hard as cement.

The next morning, the gendarmes return alone to the scene to take some pictures. After investigation, they found traces on the ground. The *Cometa Report* states:

> The investigations of the gendarmerie established the existence, at the place indicated by Maurice Masse, of a basin printed in the ground, which was soaked at this place.

According to the minutes of the gendarmerie of Digne :

> In the center of this basin was a cylindrical hole 18 centimeters in diameter and about 40 centimeters deep. There were also four shallow furrows, 8 centimeters wide and about 2 meters long each, which formed a kind of cross, with the cylindrical hole as its center. The earth at this point was compact.

On August 18, 1965, Maurice Masse voluntarily went to the police station. Believing that he had not told them everything when he was questioned on July 2, he made a third sworn statement. This time, he was questioned for eight hours by the gendarmerie captain Valnet who had come from Digne for this purpose. The conclusions of the captain are as follows:

- The witness told the truth. He is a man of good sense, serious and who does not let himself be fooled.

A last investigation - on a private basis this time - is led by Mr. Chautard, adviser to the Court of Appeal of Lyon. It began on September 6, 1965 and was communicated to GEPA, the Groupement d'Étude des Phénomènes Aériens. Mr. Chautard first spoke with Azias and Santoni, the two gendarmes who had carried out the first investigation, then with Captain Valnet, as well as with Mr. Richaud, mayor of Valensole, Mr. Ciapello, secretary of the town hall, Mrs. Tardieu, assistant secretary, and Father Gourjon, priest of Valensole. Mr. Chautard concluded:

- All of them unanimously attested to Maurice Masse's perfect honorability. He is considered to be a sober, calm, well-balanced man. He is 41 years old, married and has two children. He runs a lavender distillery. His business is doing well. The conversations I had with him, with his wife, with his father and with his mother confirmed my conviction that he had not invented this story.

In the end, it is regrettable that a soil sample was only briefly studied. No trace of radioactivity was found. Only a high level of calcium was noted: 18.3%. No thorough analysis was carried out whereas, disturbing fact, at the place of the landing, the lavender will stop growing during 10 years!

A bitter man

From July 3, the press seized on the affair. Some journalists speculated that the saucer was in fact an Alouette II or III helicopter of the French army. Indeed, that summer, military exercises were underway under the name Provence 65. To this, Maurice Masse answers:

- I had first thought of an army "Alouette", but I am used to seeing these helicopters landing often on my field or next to it. And I do not fail to talk with the pilots who are hunters like me.

On July 4, he makes the point in *Le Provençal*:

- I am not delusional, I did not dream, what I saw in my field, I saw it well!

Like most witnesses of UFOs, Maurice Masse will pay dearly for his singular encounter. His field was ransacked by the gendarmes, journalists and onlookers who flocked to his field. Everyone wants to see the place where the "saucer" was seen. Everyone wants to photograph and film the witness, who has acknowledged in *Le Provençal*:

- My first reaction was to run the plow through the field and remove all traces of the plow. I should have obeyed my first impulse. My field is now in an indescribable state, and I am literally being chased by a pack of *reporters* and onlookers, not to mention official interrogations. I have given so many accounts of what has happened to me that I am tired of it.

Victor Nathan, the journalist, concludes:

> This is probably why Mr. Masse decided to disappear. Just like the mysterious device he had seen, he vanished and yesterday, in Valensole, a crowd of people was looking for him, but in vain.

In reality, to escape the pack of reporters, Maurice Masse left Valensole on July 3 to take refuge at a relative's house in Giens, but he was located by a journalist from Europe 1 who interviewed him. On his return from Giens, our witness broke down. In the evening, he burst into tears in front of his wife and children who did not know the details of his adventure.

Just yesterday, the press presented it as follows:

> With his sunburned features and broad neck and shoulders, he has the classic appearance of a peasant. A good hunter, a good fisherman, he has also inherited this southern faconde which sings of the joy of living and the sun.

Since his mysterious encounter, Maurice Masse is not the same. He hides, refuses to speak. *Le Méridional* of July 6, 1965 notes the change:

> As for the author of the story, Mr. Maurice Masse, some inhabitants of Valensole have firmly dissuaded us from meeting him. This man would be, since yesterday morning, in the grip of a nervous breakdown. This distressing news was confirmed to us by several reliable witnesses.

Unexplainable physiological effects

From now on, rumors are rife. Some people think that it is a hoax, "a sea serpent from the Bas-Alpes". This hurts Maurice, even if the local press tries to defend him:

> To tell the truth, there are few who question the veracity of his statements. Maurice Masse is well known in Valensole. He is not a crank or a prankster. It is believed that if he claims to have seen a mysterious device in his lavender field, it is because he has really witnessed this unusual sight.

Strangely enough, three days after his observation, Maurice Masse fell into a heavy sleep that lasted sixteen hours. During the following months, he suffered from hypersomnia, sleeping between twelve and fifteen hours per night. In addition to this persistent sleepiness, his hands began to tremble. And, on his wrist, the watches stop mysteriously.

As the days went by, Valensole gradually regained its calm, but for any "saucers" worthy of the name, the Olivol district had become an obligatory place of pilgrimage. Despite requests, Maurice Masse refuses to talk about that morning of July 1er 1965.

The case of "the saucer of Valensole" is quickly exported. The British ufology magazine *Flying Saucer Review*, a reference, devoted no less than seven issues to it. In 1976, the American comic magazine *UFO Flying Saucers* immortalized it on its cover and in an episode entitled "Frozen *In* His Tracks".

"They're not mean!"

On August 8, 1965, the ufologist Aimé Michel went to Valensole to conduct his own investigation. He manages to interview Maurice Masse who, tracked down, is described at the same time as "nervous and evasive". Concerning the small beings, he ends up however letting go:

- They are not evil. Their intentions towards us are good. That I am sure of... If these beings wanted to harm us, they could, with their machine, blow up the whole plateau of Valensole and even further.

Aimé Michel then showed Maurice Masse a reproduction of the UFO seen in Socorro, New Mexico, on April 24, 1964, by the policeman Lonnie Zamora. This strange device seems almost identical to the one in Valensole. The reaction of the farmer was immediate. Aimé Michel tells:

> The effect it had on him was fantastic. I had the impression that when Mr. Masse saw this image, he literally gasped as if he was contemplating his own death. At first he thought someone had photographed HIS own ship. When I revealed to him that this craft had been seen in the United States by a police officer, he was relieved and said:
>
> - You see that I did not dream and that I am not crazy!

That same day, Aimé Michel met two other washermen: Aimé Magnan and André Neuvières. They were at Olivol on the morning of July 1er , a few hundred meters from Maurice Masse's farm. They distinctly heard the strident whistle, "a little like that of a circular saw" but saw nothing in the sky. They assure us that "no helicopter was the cause". However, according to them, "there was cinema, that morning, at Olivol!"

On August 12, 1967, Aimé Michel returned to Valensole. Accompanied by the ufologist Charles Bowen, he questioned a much calmer Maurice Masse. The witness's answers are terse and straightforward.

- It's true that I haven't said everything," he admits. I've already told too much. I should have kept it all to myself. What I refuse to confide in you, I have not revealed to anyone, not even to my wife. And nobody will make me talk. I will die without revealing anything. It is therefore useless to insist.

Aimé Michel then tells him the singular adventure of the Hill couple, on September 19, 1961, in New Hampshire. Barney and Betty Hill, confronted with strange entities, were forced to enter a vessel to be subjected to humiliating medical examinations. Masse immediately retorts:

- If these people say that they have been forced by these beings, they are lying. For THEY do not force anyone. If this couple had said "No" or "We don't want", then THEY would have left them alone.

A heavy secret

For those who approach him, it is obvious that Maurice Masse is hiding a secret. It is true that he accepted to meet with a few investigators, such as Guy Tarade, Aimé Michel and Jacques Vallée in May 1979. But his comments are always measured. Pierre Guérin assures us:

- Masse would later reveal to Aimé Michel that there were things that happened during the meeting that he would never tell anyone, even his father, because they would think he was crazy.

Similarly, the journalist René Pacaut met Maurice Masse in 1972. The farmer would have declared to him:

- I can't say everything I saw. No one would believe me.

Hervé Laronde will write of him:

- There is something indefinable about this humble man, something that suggests that he knows more than he is willing to admit! Yes, he certainly knows more about UFOs and their origins than any of us.

As proof, on January 9, 1992, Maurice Masse confided to the journalist Christiane Maréchal of Le *Méridional*:

- I was not afraid of these beings. I hunted wild boar for 37 years. I was in the war. One day, I fell into the Verdon river without knowing how to swim... Nothing worse could happen to me !

He then pauses before adding:

- In the night, you can't distinguish the shape of their machines, it's full of lights of different colors, it's beautiful! You know, they are not mean, say it well, that!

Maurice Masse passed away on May 14, 2004, carrying his unmentionable secret with him forever in a cloud of stars.

Sources

PV n°445 of July 2, 1965 of the Valensole brigade - PV n°105 of July 2, 1965 of the Digne research brigade - PV n°145 of Captain Valnet of August 18, 1965, Digne research brigade - *Flying Saucer Review,* vol. II, n°5, September-October 1965, pp. 9-11 - *Flying Saucer Review*, vol. II, n°6, November-December 1965, pp. 5-9 - *Flying Saucer Review,* vol. 12, n°2, March-April 1966, pp. 32-33 - *Flying Saucer Review,* vol. 12, n°3, May-June 1966, pp. 22-25 - *Flying Saucer Review,* vol. 14, n°1, January-February 1968, pp. 6-12 (this issue of the British magazine features Maurice Masse on its cover and devotes a 7-page article to him) - *Flying Saucer Review,* vol. 15, n°1, January-February 1969, p. 7 - *Flying Saucer Review,* vol. 15, n°4, July-August 1969, pp. 8-12 - Jean-Claude Bourret, *La nouvelle vague des soucoupes volantes,* France Empire, 1974, pp. 113-123 - Jacques Lob et Robert Gigi, *OVNI : Dimension autre,* album de BD, Dargaud 1975, pp. 10-11 - *UFO Flying Saucers,* U.S.A., BD n°12, November 1976 (the case illustrates the cover) - *Inforespace* n°53, September 1980, pp. 2-16 - *Sunday Mirror,* July 6, 1986 - Jacques Vallée, *Confrontations*, Robert Laffont, 1990, pp. 137-142 - *Télé Poche,* 1992, BD on the Valensole case entitled *Un parfum de lavande - Sciences & Vie : 1947-1997, 50 ans d'OVNIS,* article by Pierre Lagrange entitled *Mystère à Valensole,* pp. 54-59 - *Le Rapport Cometa,* J'ai Lu n°7883, 1999, p. 56 - Pierre Guérin, *OVNI, les mécanismes d'une désinformation,* Albin Michel, 2000, p. 130 - Lynn Picknett, *The Mammoth Book of UFOs*, Carroll and Graf Publishers, 2001, pp. 83-84 - Bernard Thouanel, *Objets Volants Non Identifiés,* Michel Lafon, 2003, pp. 88-89

  UFO. Are we in danger? The black book of ufology

Fréderic Mistral square in Valensole (photo by the author)

V. Other cases of paralysis

As advised by the main manager and producer of military intelligence in the Defence service, in order to try to understand this phenomenon, let us look at the events of the past. They are generous with so-called "stun cases." The DIA report states that these sudden losses of mobility can be accompanied or followed by "eye *injuries*", "electrical *shock*", "*pain*" or "emotional *shock* and intense fear". Here are some amazing examples.

Let's go back into these stories where, as Einstein said, "we have to kill ourselves" before we can grasp their puzzling mystery.

The case of Moises Campelo

Date: May 1991.
Location: Campo Redondo, Rio Grande do Norte State, northern Brazil.

Moises Campelo, a young farmer in his thirties, leaves his brother's house to go to his home located 1.5 kilometers behind the hills. The evening has just fallen on this rainy Sunday. Moises has been walking for five minutes when he sees a light on the crest of a distant mountain. "It must be a car", he thinks distractedly, rather focused on the road ahead. And then, surprise, in a split second, the strange light is above him.

Moises raises the eyes. It is difficult to look at this monstrosity suspended in the air because of its intense light. Very quickly, he realizes that it is a machine "of the size of a house" which turns slowly on itself. He tells:

- Almost instantly, I found myself paralyzed, and I told myself that this UFO was going to take me away. It lit up everything around me, and it gave off a lot of heat.

Moises feels as if he is being "sucked up". Astonishment gave way to panic. Our witness, still standing, feels that he is rising into the air. Nothing physical

---

- neither cable, nor grapple - however seized him. He is the plaything of an invisible force.

- I was lifted 1.5 meters off the ground," he said. I couldn't speak or scream for help, and I couldn't move either. The light was very hot. I was terrified.

Moises' body has become so rigid that a packet of cookies he is carrying under his arm is literally crushed. This strange ordeal lasts almost five minutes. Then, against all odds, the "invisible force" diminishes and Moises is "gently deposited" on the ground. Not being able to stand on his feet anymore, he collapses. Throwing a panicked glance around him, he notices that the UFO remains close, stationary, at tree height, emitting the same unbearable light.

Moises, whose eyes burned terribly, was unable to walk. To reach his house, he crawls along the path "like a lizard". He reaches a small tree under which he rests for a while. But, when he decides to resume his walk, the UFO moves and positions itself again above him. Drawn by the same invisible force, the peasant rises again in the air. This time, he is in a crouched and immobile position, 1 meter from the ground.

- I hit my head on the branches as I was climbing," he says. I was paralyzed again and this time I was very cold. I couldn't move. I was unable to scream for help, and the light started hurting again.

The mysterious machine turns tirelessly on itself while Moises, conscious in spite of his state of terror, starts to pray. This second episode of levitation lasts about fifteen minutes, then the UFO, until then silent, moves away by emitting a dull hum like that of "a turbine at low speed", then disappears. Moises then falls back heavily on the ground. Terrified at the idea that the intruder could reappear, our witness runs to his house. He recounts:

- My left eye started to swell and pop out of my head. I couldn't see anything with it the whole time it took me to get home.

Interviewed in 1992 and 1993 by ufologist Bob Pratt, Moises confided that following this terrifying confrontation, he suffered chronic physiological effects.

- My left side went numb for three or four months," he said, "in my waist and hip. It felt like I was paralyzed. My left eye swelled up so much that I couldn't sleep at night for quite a while after that because I couldn't close it. He was blind for a few days, and I still have problems with him.

Sources

MUFON UFO Journal n°453, January 2006, p. 18 - Bob Pratt, *Ovnis danger - Appel à la vigilance*, Éditions Trajectoire, 2010, pp. 19-29 - Thiago Luiz Ticchetti, *Contacts ovnis au Brésil*, Flying Disk France, 2021.

The case of Natasha Barinova

Date: October 11, 1989.
Location: Maelski commune, near Nalchik, in the Caucasus, Russia.

Natasha Barinova, 16 years old, studies in a technical college where she is very appreciated by her teachers. On this October day, it is about 6 p.m. when Natasha is walking home. As she reached the courtyard in front of her house, she saw a kind of net falling from the sky, in the center of which shone a very bright white point. Immediately, she feels caught. The strange net lifts her up! Terrified, she tried to push it away but felt an electric shock. She screams but her voice, suddenly shrill and high-pitched, is distorted as if the space around her altered the acoustic waves.

Hearing her screams, her family members rush into the yard. What they see is beyond comprehension. Natasha is suspended in mid-air. A disc-shaped object hovers, stationary, less than 50 feet above her. Then the disc moves away and disappears. Natasha falls back heavily on the ground. Unable to move, she remains paralyzed during a long moment.

Questioned by Jacques Vallée, Professor Vladimir Azhazha, who heard about the affair, said:

- It was as if something had tried to tear the skin off her fingers. The tips of his phalanges have actually grown larger.

Natasha had to be hospitalized for severe burns on her hands and post-traumatic stress.

Sources

Jacques Vallée, *UFO Chronicles of The Soviet Union: A Cosmic Samizdat*, Ballantine Books, 1992, pp. 36-37 - *MUFON UFO Journal* n°453, January 2006, p. 18.

The case of Marius Dewilde

Date: September 10, 1954.

Location: Quarouble, in the Nord-Pas-de-Calais region, about 10 km from Valenciennes, France.

Marius Adolphe Dewilde (known as Mario), a 33-year-old metal worker, lives in an isolated gatehouse on the edge of the Bois de la Fontaine. We are exactly 1.5 kilometers from the national road. A dirt road, barely passable, leads to the house. The place is not very frequented. There are two railroads there. On the first one, used by the mines, passes a train per day. The second one is used by a freight train morning and evening. So there is not much traffic. It is on this second track that the unthinkable will happen.

On September 10, the night is calm. Sitting in his kitchen, Marius Dewilde is reading the newspaper. An article published in *La Voix du Nord* about the sinking of the trawler *L'Abeille IV* caught his attention. Suddenly, something makes him prick up his ears:

- My wife and son had just gone to bed and I was reading by the fire," he says. The clock hanging over the stove marked 10:30 p.m., when my attention was drawn to the barking of my dog Kiki. The animal was howling to death. Believing there was a prowler in the yard, I grabbed my flashlight and went outside.

Arriving in the garden, Marius Dewilde sees on the railroad track, less than 6 meters from his door, on the left, a kind of dark mass. This one, of oval shape, measures approximately 6 meters long and 3 meters high. He said to himself: "A farmer must have unhitched his cart. I'll have to notify the station agents first thing in the morning to remove it, otherwise there will be an accident."

But the dog redoubled its cries. Marius Dewilde says:

- I heard on my right a noise of hurried steps. There is a path called "the smugglers' path", because they sometimes use it at night to cross the French-Belgian border.

As the dog starts barking again in this direction, Marius Dewilde turns on his electric lamp and shines it on the path.

- I saw two beings like I had never seen before, 3 or 4 meters from me, just behind the fence that separated me from them. They were walking one behind the other towards the dark mass on the rails. One of them, the one walking in front, turned towards me. The beam of my lamp caught a glint of glass or metal on his face. I had clearly the impression that he had the head enclosed in a helmet of diving suit. The two beings were moreover dressed in suits similar to those of the divers. They were of very small size, probably less than 1 meter, but extremely broad of shoulders...

Marius Dewilde tried to block their way, determined to "capture at least one of them". But an extremely powerful ray bursts out of the dark mass on the rails and reaches him. Marius Dewilde wants to shout. It was impossible. He tried to move, but his legs would no longer obey him. He is paralyzed! He hears the two little creatures running on the concrete slab in front of his door and then disappearing into their machine which rises, swinging "like a helicopter". A thick vapor gushes under the object with a hissing sound. This one goes up vertically to about thirty meters. Its aluminum color is adorned with a red-orange shade. Then it flies towards the west in the direction of Anzin.

- A minute later, the witness said, everything was gone.

Interdict, our man scans the sky and the surroundings. What to think of all this? He is however sure not to have dreamed.

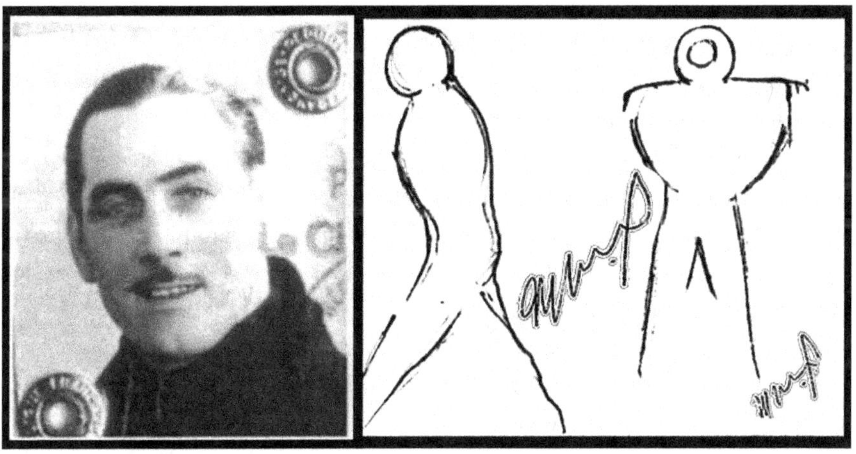

Marius Dewilde in 1958 (left). Drawings of the entities by the witness (right)

Livid, out of breath, and "taken of violent colics", he jumps on his moped to warn the nearest police station. It was closed. He pushes to the police station of Onnaing where he can finally tell his misadventure.

Following this, several investigations are carried out. The Lille Air and Border Police, then the Paris Police, arrived on the scene equipped with Geiger counters. The agents discovered symmetrical notches on the sleepers and noticed that the ballast was blackened. At this point, the gravel was crumbling between the fingers as if it had been subjected to a very high temperature. SNCF engineers estimate that "the pressure revealed by these marks corresponds to a machine weighing 30 tons".

The prefecture and the sub-prefecture are also interested in the case. The gendarmerie, the police under the direction of the commissioner Gouchet, the DST, the customs as well as other more or less official services question Marius Dewilde. The story fascinated the press. Most of the newspapers (*Libération, Radar, Le Parisien, Combat, Le Figaro, Nord-France, Points de vue et images du monde, L'Aurore, Nord-Éclair, La Semaine du Nord...*) reported on this incredible encounter. The case of Quarouble crosses our borders and goes around the world. The American edition of *Time* tells about it in its issue of October 25, 1954, by evoking "paralyzing pygmies". And *Life* magazine publishes a photo of Dewilde proudly carrying a crossbeam on his shoulder...

However, the witness's cheeky and controversial personality quickly leads his detractors to claim that it is all a big joke designed to make him interesting. The commissioner who leads the investigation does not agree:

- Marius can tell what he wants to anyone; but to me he will not tell stories. So, everything he said is true.

A testimony seems to corroborate the sincerity of the witness. On September 10, at the same time, Fleurix Crétu, 42 years old, in charge of the machine room of the pumping station of the company *Eau & Force* of Vicq, near Quarouble, lived a strange experience. In the middle of his work, he suddenly saw a powerful illumination outside, very white, which invaded the whole station. This caused a sharp drop in the voltage of the electrical circuits, and then everything broke down. It took a good hour to restart everything. Meanwhile, Fleurix Crétu's wife arrived at the station. She came on foot and explained that she had just witnessed a strange spectacle:

- A bright, oblique beam of light came down from the sky, widening, searching the surrounding area and then the pumping station. The beam was so wide at its base that it covered the entire station.

Fleurix Crétu also noticed that his wristwatch had stopped. It could never be repaired. This happened less than 2 kilometers as the crow flies from Marius Dewilde's little house, near the 79th level crossing.

Sources

Point de Vue, Images du Monde n°329, September 1954, pp. 3-5 - *Daily Express,* September 13, 1954 - *The Daily Telegraph,* September 14, 1954 - *Nord-Éclair,* September 16, 1954 - *Lowell Sunday Sun,* September 19, 1954 - *Le Soir Illustré,* September 22, 1954 - *Radar,* September 26, 1954, pp. 1 and 3 - *Life,* 1er November 1954, pp. 28-29 - *States Times,* Baton Rouge, December 3, 1954 - Jimmy Guieu, *Black-out sur les soucoupes volantes,* Fleuve Noir, 1956, pp. 113-116 - *Ouranos* n°24, 1959, pp. 11-13 - *Ouranos* n°25, 1960, pp. 20-25 - Aimé Michel, *Mystérieux objets célestes,* Robert Laffont, " Les autres mondes et leurs origines ", 1977, pp. 62-69 - Henry Durrant, *Premières enquêtes sur les humanoïdes extraterrestres,* Robert Laffont 1977, pp. 33-37 - Marius Dewilde and Roger Luc Mary, *Ne résistez pas aux extra-terrestres,* Éditions du Rocher, 1980 - *Lumières dans la Nuit* n°419, September 2014, pp. 8-24 - *Top Secret* n°17, pp. 21-25 - Jean-Marie Bigorne, *Chasseur d'ovnis (UFO hunter),* Le Temps Présent, 2014, pp. 159-174.

Marius Dewilde examines the tracks on the railroad (left).
State Times article, December 3, 1954 (right).

The case of Luigi Rapuzzi

Date: August 14, 1947.

Location: Raveo, near Villa Santina, in the region of Friuli Venezia Giulia, northeast Italy.

This is the very first European testimony describing an unconventional craft landed on the ground and accompanied by two humanoids. This astonishing event took place almost two months after the observation of the pilot Kenneth Arnold over Mount Rainier. Luigi Rapuzzi, who witnessed this amazing adventure, is a painter and novelist. He was then known under the name of L. R. Johannis.

During the first two weeks of August 1947," he says, "I was visiting a small village called Raveo. As a child, I spent a large part of my summers there. I was always interested in geology and anthropology. I devoted all my free time to studying these disciplines, which are my favorites, and to practicing one of the activities that is essential to them: the systematic search for fossils.

For this purpose, on August 14, Luigi Rapuzzi goes up the hilly bed of a mountain stream called the Chiarso. This short valley ends on the slopes of the Gentile Pass. The adventurer brought a small backpack and his geologist's ice axe. Along the left bank of the almost dry stream, he follows a path that winds through fir tree clumps and alluvial rubble deposits. On leaving a fir forest, he noticed a large lenticular object of bright red color about fifty meters away, on the rocky bank. As he suffers from myopia, he puts on his glasses. Getting closer to the thing, he realizes that it is a disc, apparently in varnished metal, "like the metal of an ordinary toy".

At the top of it," he says, "I could see a sort of shiny metal antenna, telescopic in shape, sticking out of it. It looked like the ones we see today on our cars. At that time, I must say that I knew nothing about flying saucers. I think that the Italian newspapers had not yet mentioned the subject.

This object, about ten meters wide, is embedded on the side of the mountain, in a large transverse crack of the friable rock. It is located about 6 meters above the bed of the stream. Luigi Rapuzzi decides to go and examine it more closely. Before doing so, he looked around, looking for someone to help him if the need arose. Then he saw two young boys about 50 meters away, at the edge of a grove.

At least, that's what I thought," he says. I yelled to get their attention, showed them the disk, and walked toward them. When I was halfway across the room, I stopped, petrified. These two boys were like no other dwarves I had ever seen or even imagined. They walked slowly in my direction, with small steps, arms hanging down and heads still. They stopped very close to me. I had no strength left. I was as if paralyzed, as if in a kind of dream, but I was able to observe them and note the smallest details. These details are forever engraved in me. I could, even today, make a portrait or even a cast of these extraordinary beings. At the time, I was torn between amazement and fear.

These dwarfs are no more than 90 centimeters tall. They wear a dark blue jumpsuit made of a material that is difficult to describe - "translucent", Luigi Rapuzzi will suggest. Their collars and thick belts are bright red. So are their wrists and leggings.

Their heads," the witness continued, "from the impression I got, were bigger than a normal man's head. It made them look a little cartoonish. However, I don't think anyone would have laughed at the look on their faces. At this point, I have to say that the terms I use to describe them are only indications. I don't know, today, if these characteristics that I define as a nose, a mouth, eyes and hands correspond to their reality, nor if it would not be more correct to name them in another way.

Luigi Rapuzzi notices that these beings have no hair. Instead, they wear a kind of large brown cap, like a mountaineer's hat. The skin on their faces is an earthy green. The only color that comes close, the witness thinks, is that of the modeling clay commonly used by sculptors or that of clay soaked in water. Their nose is straight, geometrically cut and very long. Underneath, one can see a simple slit, in the shape of a circumflex accent, which opens and closes at intervals, a bit like the mouth of a fish.

Their eyes were enormous, prominent and round," says Luigi Rapuzzi. They looked and felt like two very ripe yellow-green plums. In the center of the eyes, without eyebrows or eyelashes, I noticed a kind of vertical pupil. What I would call their eyelids consisted of a ring, of a shade between green and yellow, which surrounded their hemispherical eyes like the frame of a pair of glasses. For a moment which seemed infinite to me, I remained to contemplate these extraordinary beings. It is only much later that I could estimate the time that this face-to-face lasted. I think that this silent confrontation did not exceed two or three minutes.

Then I raised my arm, the one holding the ice axe. I waved it first in their direction and then in the direction of the disk. In an overexcited voice, I started to shout. I asked them who they were, where they were from and if I could help them. They turned around. I don't remember what I said next, because it all happened so fast. Today, I think the two beings interpreted my eager gestures as a threat. I'm not sure, but today I would avoid reacting like that.

At that moment, one of the creatures puts his right hand on his belt, from which a thin stream of smoke or some kind of ray shoots out.

I collapsed," says the witness, "and an invisible force ripped my ice axe from my hand. Only once in my life have I had the opportunity to experience a violent electric shock. It was in 1924, when I was a student at the Technical Institute of Udine, in a physics class. Well, I can tell you that the moment that ray or smoke reached me, I felt a similar sensation. Moreover, the slightest effort to get up required an energy that I did not have.

The two dwarfs get closer to the witness on the ground at 2 meters. And they lean on the ice axe that has fallen nearby. Luigi manages to roll to the side. He then sees one of the dwarves pick up the tool which is longer than him. The hand of this creature is green. It has eight fingers, four of which are opposable. In reality, it is not really a hand. It's more like a claw, as the fingers have no joints.

I also noticed that the chest of both beings was quivering, a bit like the chest of a dog panting after a long run. I made an inordinate effort to get up, and finally managed to sit down, but I had to keep my elbows on the ground so I wouldn't fall back.

Meanwhile, the two entities join their circular vessel. Luigi sees them climbing, with a slow but determined step, until the crack of the rock. Then they penetrate in the disk embedded almost vertically on the slope of the mountain. After a few moments, the vessel springs out of the rock then rises in the air. A cascade of stones and earth rolls down into the river bed. It is the only noise that breaks the silence of this *no man's land.* Further down, almost dry, the stream flows, silent, over the rocks.

> The disk remained stationary in the air for a while, hanging like a huge gong. I could clearly see its sharp edge 4 or 5 meters away from me. I was seized with terror because I thought it was going to come down and cut me in half like a worm. I'm not really sure anymore, but I think I screamed. Anyway, I remember that I did everything I could to get up and run away, without success. I kept falling on my back, torn with pain.

Suddenly, the disc tilts slightly, moves away and ends up disappearing on the horizon. A huge blast sweeps the witness who rolls on the ground, his eyes full of dust. He then finds himself on the stones of the river bed.

> I don't know how long I stood there. Finally, I managed to sit down again. That's when I looked at my watch. It was 9:14.
> I had to sleep for an hour. I felt like all my bones were broken. I was shaking like after a night of drinking. I searched my bag for my coffee thermos. It was in pieces. What surprised me was that there was no trace of its metal case. My fork and aluminum lunchbox were also gone. In my bag, everything was soaked in coffee, including a packet of sketches of the area that I always carry with me.
> So I had to settle for coffee-soaked bread. I threw away my salami and the rest of my food. Then I went in search of my ice axe. In vain. Yet it would have been useful, especially as a walking stick. Gathering my strength, it was only around noon that I was able to return to my room. I arrived at Raveo at 2 pm and went to bed. I told the owner of the hostel where I was staying that I had fallen from a rock. She told me that this should be a lesson to me from now on, that it was high time I stopped picking up those damn rocks (she knew me for more than 35 years, since I was a kid).

The next morning, armed with a new ice axe and, I confess, a *revolver*, I returned to the site. Naturally, there was no one there. I climbed up to the crack in the rock. I thought that the two creatures might have thrown my old ice axe, which I was so fond of, into it. I found nothing.

I think my beloved ice axe is now somewhere in a museum, on another planet. I hope someone up there is trying to decipher what is engraved on its shaft: notches, my name, two stylized alpine flowers, an eagle and a mountaineer's motto.

Sources

Flying Saucer Review, special issue 1*: The Humanoids,* October-November 1966, p. 2 - which quotes *Clypeus,* n°2-5, May 1964 - *Lights in the Night,* Contact readers n°100 bis, July 1969, p. 3 - *Notiziario UFO,* year III, n°3, March 1980, p. 33 - *Notiziario UFO,* year 34, n°1, May 1999, pp. 17-22 - *Cuadernos de Ufología,* Anuario n°31, 2005, p. 150 - *Outer Limits Magazine* n°13, April 2018, pp. 64-69 - *Phenomena Magazine* n°123, July 2019, pp. 6-11 - Roberto Pinotti, *UFO Contacts in Italy, volume 1 (1907-1978),* Flying Disk France, 2022, pp. 10-22.

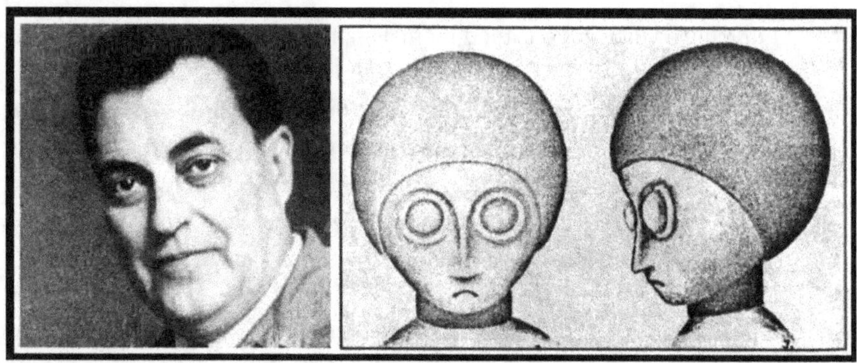

Luigi Rapuzzi, alias L. R. Johannis (left).
His drawing of the humanoids (right).

VI. In Venezuela, hairy and paralyzing dwarfs

Other latitude: other paralysis caused by "singular beings".

They arrive, we don't know from where. And we don't know how. Witnesses say that their ships, looking like storms, throw through the night flashes that cut like blades. But who are these ufonauts, with multicolored skins, strapped with *Star Trek-like* uniforms or sometimes naked as a hand?

In the stories that follow, these celestial balladeers have the appearance of hairy dwarfs. In living memory, they were seen in September 1954 in France before being found, two months later, in Venezuela.

These archaic, warlike creatures bear a striking resemblance to the Japanese *Kappas* or the Tzeltal *Ikals* of Mexico. Some will say that they are just that: a cultural resonance, the archetypal echo of a dream from our legends. Others will bet that they haunt the top of the sky and descend from our stars, in Pullman saucers, as if from a simple staircase. But what is the part of the dream and the part of reality?

The dwarves of Petare

Date: November 28, 1954.

Location: Petare, in the suburbs of Caracas, Venezuela, South America.

It is between 2 and 2:30 am. The night is quiet and deep. In the streets of Petare, Gustavo Gonzáles De León, a 25-year-old Cuban merchant from Havana, is driving his van. Accompanied by José Ponce, his 19-year-old assistant, he is going to pick up cold cuts from a wholesaler to sell them at daybreak in the local market. As the two men walked up Bella Vista Street, which leads to the warehouse area, they noticed that it was lit up as if in broad daylight. As they proceed, they come across a bright "object" that blocks their path. This stationary object, above the road, has the shape of a metallic sphere measuring between 3 and 4 meters in diameter.

On the sides of the machine, one distinguishes two kinds of portholes measuring 50 centimeters each. The upper part of the object is overhung by a kind of dome. What surprises our two men the most is that the machine floats at 50 centimeters of the road, and that it seems suspended as by magic, without any support. Indeed, we can't see any wheels, tripods or landing gear.

- What is this thing?" wonders Gustavo.

He stops his van in order to better observe her. Then very quickly, the curiosity succeeding to the amazement, the two clerks, of a common agreement, leave their vehicle.

A creature with the eyes of a cat

Circumspectly, with small steps, they approach. A dramatic turn of events, 8 meters from the object, Gustavo Gonzáles falls face to face with a creature that measures barely 1 meter high!

This humanoid being is hairy. Its body is entirely covered with a stiff and dark hair. His head is round. Does he actually wear a helmet? It is difficult to know. In any case, we can't distinguish his nose, his ears, or his mouth. We only see two big and frightening eyes. Two oval eyes that shine and reflect the light of the headlights like cat's eyes.

The humanoid seems to wear no clothes except for a kind of small loincloth. And he is barefoot.

Faced with this amazing being, Gustavo feels as if paralyzed. With great effort, fighting against himself, he finally manages to put one foot in front of the other, progressing painfully towards the humanoid.

UFO. Are we in danger? The black book of ufology

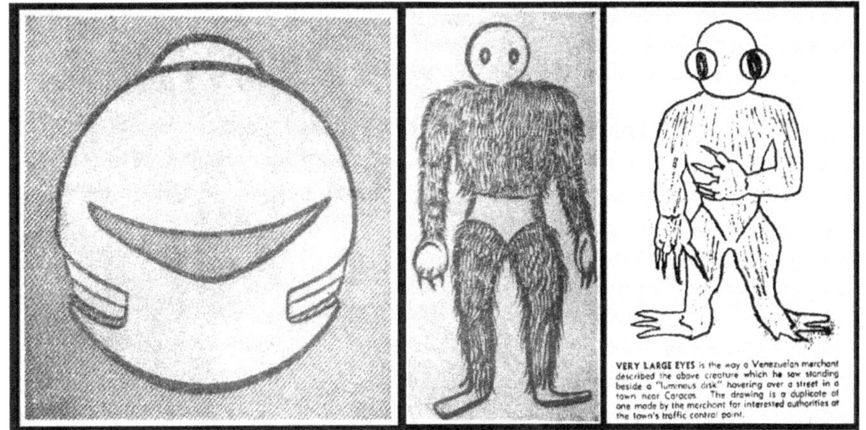

The UFO (left). The hairy dwarf (center)
and from Gustavo's description (right)

A fight without mercy

There, everything gets carried away. The young Cuban, won by a crazy idea, throws himself on this hairy dwarf and grabs him. He seizes him firmly between his arms, "in the way of a judo hold". Having belted him, he drags him, triumphant, towards the van.

The first thing that amazes Gustavo Gonzáles is the low weight of this energetic person: he weighs between 20 and 35 kg, at most. The young man is jubilant. That's quite a catch! He tells himself that he and José will deliver this creature to the nearby police station. And when they tell the officers about their incredible adventure, they will be believed. They will be the heroes of the day, showing off their incredible trophy.

Unfortunately, Gustavo Gonzáles' elation is short-lived. The little guy turned out to be much stronger than his stature and weight would have suggested. Almost effortlessly, he managed to get out of the way with a terrific "cat's leap" of almost 2 meters. And, in the stride, it assaults its attacker with a terrible blow, of an unheard-of violence, which sends him tumbling at 5 meters!

The shopkeeper bites the dust, momentarily stunned. But, refusing to declare himself defeated, he gets up with the firm intention of fighting. Strange,

---

because at this moment, his body is traversed by a strong vibration, as if he entered in trance.

The hairy dwarf proves to be of an astonishing flexibility. He leaps again on Gustavo. This one, terrified, instinctively takes out his knife to defend himself. And he stabs the humanoid in the shoulder. Let us say rather that he tries to stab him. Because, to his great surprise, the blade of the knife bounces and slides on the dwarf as if he had a "rhinoceros skin".

The Cuban also notices that the man has rounded hands, equipped with four razor-like claws. And these sharp claws try to reach him.

As if that wasn't enough, Gustavo Gonzáles sees two other identical creatures out of the corner of his eye. One of the dwarves comes to the rescue of his teammate. He holds in his hand a kind of luminous cylinder that he points at the young man who, totally dazzled, is paralyzed and blind. The belligerent ufonaut takes advantage of this to flee and return to his spherical vessel.

When Gustavo recovers his sight, he notices, disappointed, that the street is deserted. The ship and the humanoids have melted into the night forever.

Reconstruction from a Cuban magazine, 1954

Other humanoids

José Ponce, Gustavo's sidekick, got out of the van. Younger than his comrade, therefore impressionable, he noted, with fear, the unusual vigor of the dwarf with sharp claws. And he saw two other humanoids, similar to the first one, appearing from the embankments on the right of the road. According to him, these beings had joined hands. They were carrying something like stones or clods of earth. When they saw the young man, they jumped with a disconcerting lightness and agility inside the sphere, through a visible opening on its side. Almost in a state of shock, José then turned and fled, heading for the police station, four blocks away.

A few moments later, he was joined by Gustavo Gonzáles. The witnesses are greeted by two guards: Manuel Moreno and E. Dominguez, who first check if the young men are drunk or under the influence of drugs. The agents note that they are extremely nervous and disturbed. In fact, Gustavo breaks down, having a real nervous breakdown. It takes him a long time to calm down. They then notice bruises on his left side.

- That's when I tried to catch the hairy visitor who came out of the machine," he says.

After drinking a glass of water and recovering, Gustavo finally told the guard about his terrible encounter. In the end, the agents note in their statement that at 2:30 a.m., two men showed up at their post, which is under the jurisdiction of the *Inspectoria General del Tránsito* (*General* Transport Inspectorate). That these men were not drunk, that they were sane, that they were coherent. Certainly, their story was surprising. But it was very well argued, rich in details, and seemed credible given the amount of information provided.

Reliable young people

We immediately contacted the two men's bosses: Johan Schafer, owner of the deli of the same name, and Antonio Cherchi, the manager. These managers stated that our witnesses were sober, honest, very serious, always punctual and never caused any problems. If they say that they have been in contact with something disturbing, we can only believe them.

By midday, the press office of the General Command of the Caracas City Police informed the press. Major Jesús Antonio Yanes said that an unprecedented event had just taken place, that it seemed serious but very unusual. The *reporters*, eager for a *scoop*, jumped at the opportunity. One of the country's most influential newspapers, *El Nacional*, immediately published a front-page story about the incident. The journalists believe that the two men are completely reliable. They said that they could not be called drunkards, since the police would not have been shy about reporting it. The story spread like wildfire. Everywhere from Caracas to Maracaibo, people are talking about it.

"El Nacional", November 29, 1954

Left: "He claims he saw a strange, glowing craft and fought with one of its three diminutive occupants"

On the right: "I managed to catch one of these little creatures. It weighed a little over 100 pounds. It had huge eyes, like a toad's.
And it was hairy like a monkey," said Gustavo González de León.
His deputy, José Ponce, attended the fight."

The press gets involved

The same day, the second daily newspaper of the country, *El Universal*, also dedicates its front page to the setbacks of our apprentice butchers. The headline reads in bold letters: "According to eyewitness, a flying saucer landed in Petare."

On November 30, *El Universal* published *interviews with* witnesses, police officers and the owner of the deli. It was reported that hundreds of people, having lost their sleep, gathered in Buena Vista de Petare street and stormed the police station. Terrified, they demand an explanation. For several days, these citizens have been watching anxiously for the sky.

UFO. Are we in danger? The black book of ufology

Also on November 30, *El Nacional* carried this catchy headline on its front page: "A typographer also saw a flying saucer in the Amacuro Delta. Two occupants came down from it". We learn that a psychosis has taken hold of the country. Two thousand people besieged the office of the General Inspectorate of Transport, demanding details about the famous flying saucer. Diadamo Paolo, the Italian baker on Buena Vista Street who usually delivers his goods before daybreak, has just changed his schedule.

- From now on, I'll deliver my bread at 7 a.m.," he says. I don't want to be faced with these weird things. It would give me a heart attack. I believe in the existence of flying saucers and these creatures.

Fernando de Moya, a 39-year-old typographer, confides:

- It was after reading González's story that I decided to tell what I experienced a few days ago in the Amacuro Delta area. Until then, I didn't tell anyone for fear of being called crazy. Last November 3 and 4, I saw the same thing as González and Ponce. While mooring my boat in the territory of the Guaraunos Indians, I saw - dumb with surprise - two creatures that were standing 6 meters away from a round and luminous machine. The two Indians who accompanied me, very nervous, fled immediately and abandoned me. The strange creatures moved by executing small jumps. They were bending down, obviously collecting something which they then transported in their kind of vessel and then returned unceasingly to their task. The machine was equipped with two portholes. Protected by several rocks, I got closer. I then saw that these creatures were hardly 1 meter high. Their heads were round, with two huge eyes. Their vessel was stationary at 2 meters from the ground...

As we can see, *hombrecillos* falling from the sky are now the talk of the town. On November 30, the national daily *La Esfera* confirmed that the population, with its eyes riveted to the sky, "fears an imminent invasion of Martians (*Marcianos*)". In the local press in December, José Ponce stated that the creatures were "hairy like monkeys" and that their round hands looked like "goose feet".

Gustavo Gonzáles de León, who was momentarily transferred to the central emergency station of Salas, where the medical staff on duty took care of him, is now a star. But, for the young Cuban, the situation is unenviable. Pursued by the journalists, he must lend himself to their incessant solicitations. Stalked relentlessly, he was forced to leave his home at 72 Bolivia Street in Catia to take refuge with friends, the Monzón family, who lived at Bloque 20, apartment C8 in Tablitas.

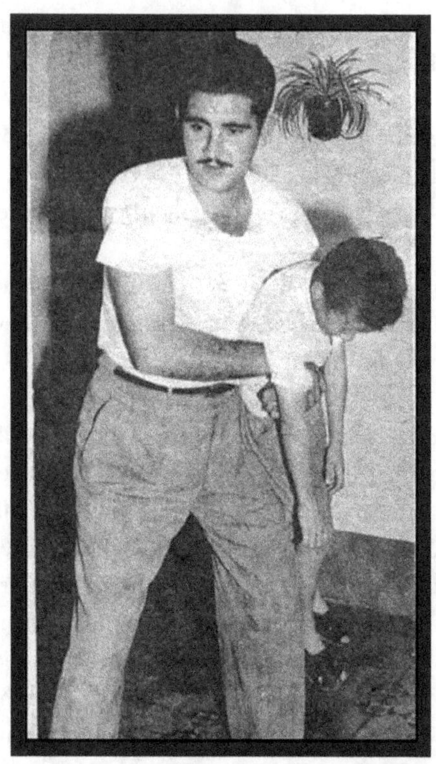

Gustavo shows reporters how he grabbed the humanoid

Witnesses confirm

Following an investigation carried out in the whole neighborhood, several witnesses came forward and affirmed that they had seen and heard, on the morning of November 29, certain details corroborating the observation of Gustavo and José. María Antonieta Avellaneda said she heard a bang and a whistling sound between 1 and 2 a.m. All her life, she will affirm that she saw a dark mark left on the ground by the saucer, "like burnt earth". At that time, the street was not yet paved. Concepción Barrachán saw a strange luminous device that made no noise. Manuel María Soria observed a powerful light illuminating his vehicle, forcing him to stop momentarily. Elsa Duderstad, who lives at 9 Los Palos Grandes Street, saw towards Petare a very intense light in the shape of a disk. Her son Rodolfo confirms. The Caobos, who live along the old railroad, saw a very bright light that illuminated their rooms, "like a very intense star". Dr. Julio Garces of the Hospital Pérez de León (Petare), said he heard like a scream of terror in the street Bella Vista, after 2 am. Later, the doctor will affirm that he witnessed the whole scene. He was then invited to Washington to discuss the case of the "little humanoids" of Petare with the North American authorities.

The mysterious hairy dwarfs also spit on the imagination of the illustrators of the world tour. In France, the excellent tandem Jacques Lob (scriptwriter) and Robert Gigi (illustrator) proposed, superbly illustrated, the case of Petare in the issue of the newspaper *Pilote* n° 640, published in 1972. These plates in colors will be then included in their album of comic strip *Those come from elsewhere* (Dargaud, 1973). The Venezuelan dwarfs will have, for the occasion, the honors of the cover.

Nowadays...

Years have passed, but the case of the *hombrecillos* of Petare is far from being forgotten. Gillman, the most famous *hard rock band* in Venezuela, included in its album *Escalofrío* (1994), a song detailing the observation of Gustavo and José: *El Extraño Caso de Petare* (The Strange Case *of Petare).*

In 2014, the magazine *Año Cero* devoted a 6-page article to the case of the *enanos peludos* (hairy dwarfs). We learn that, 60 years after the case, the team of the program *Fourth Millennium*, broadcast by the Spanish channel *El Mundo*, went to the place. The journalist Pablo Villarrubia, the archaeologist Pablo Novoa Álvarez, the ufologist Fernando Magdalena and the Venezuelan journalist Héctor Escalante led the investigation. They were able to find some witnesses still alive. In particular the lawyer Marileiva Jugo who knew well Gustavo González and who declared:

- He was a highly regarded person in the community. I have lived in Petare for 45 years, and I can tell you that what happened then is true: that morning they really saw a UFO and monstrous beings. Some people thought that González had gone crazy, but he was a perfectly balanced man. The police interviewed the two witnesses, and the agents took pictures of the place where the craft was floating. All his life, González told the same story, without changing a single word of his account

---

and of the experience he had with his companion. Alas, he died two years ago [in 2012]. And he swore, until his last breath, that all this was true.

Since then, Petare has changed a lot. It has become one of the most dangerous places in the country. Robberies, murders and kidnappings are a daily occurrence. In 2020, it is estimated that one million inhabitants (almost twice as many as in 2000) are surviving in misery in this ghetto, which is considered to be "the largest working-class district on the continent".

Sources

The APRO Bulletin, vol. 3, no. 3, November 15, 1954, p. 11 - *The APRO Bulletin,* vol. 3, n°5, April 15, 1955, pp. 1-2 - *Amazing,* vol. 31, no. 10, October 1957, pp. 88-89 - Horacio González Ganteaume, *Los Platillos Voladores Sobre Venezuela,* Ediciones Halbrane 1961 - Jacques Vallée, *Anatomy Of A Phenomenon,* Ace Books, 1965, pp. 199-200 - Coral E. Lorenzen, *Flying Saucers. The Startling Evidence of The Invasion From Outer Space,* Signet Books, 1966, pp. 57-58 - *Inforespace* n°11, 1973, p. 2 - Charles Bowen, *In Search Of Humanoids,* J'ai Lu, 1974, pp. 68 and 113-114 - F. Aniceto Lugo, *Los Visitantes del Espacio,* Orión, 1976 - *Lo Inexplicado,* vol. VI, n°70, 1981, p. 1378, article "Violencia y UFO" - *Año Cero* n°292, 2014, pp. 26-31 - *UFO* n°247, Brazil, June 2017.

The dwarfs of the Curva de Chirico

Date: December 9, 1954.
Location: "Curva de Chirico", 4 km from Carora, in the north of Venezuela.

23 h 45. It has been dark for quite some time. Lorenzo Flores, 18 years old, and Jesús Gómez, 17 years old, from the town of Carora, came to hunt rabbits, at night, along the Transandine road. The evening was quiet, without any history. Having fired all their cartridges, and having for weapons only an old unloaded rifle and an old machete, they decide to return.

Suddenly, in the undergrowth, less than 50 meters away, they see very intense lights. Intrigued, they think that a car has gone off the road and may have been in an accident. But, progressing painfully through the brush, they discover, stunned, that it is something else:

- There was a round device there, which had the shape of two inverted bowls, one on top of the other, says Lorenzo Flores. The device measured 3 meters in diameter or a little more. Fire was coming out of its base. It was stationary, suspended in the air at about 80 centimeters from the ground. Suddenly, we saw four small men, about 1 meter high, emerge from the device. As soon as they saw us, the four of them rushed to Jesús, my comrade. They grabbed him and tried to force him into their machine. What to do? I had my rifle, but it was not loaded. So to save my friend, I used it as a club. I hit them with the butt of my gun. I hit them hard, but it felt like I hit a rock, something very hard. In fact, my gun broke in two without causing any harm to these strange creatures. Thank God, by struggling, we managed to escape.

Bodies covered in hair

Afterwards, the two boys went to the central police station in Carora. Their shirts were torn. And Jesús Gómez had scratches all over his body, obviously caused by the intruders' claws.

Jesús Gómez told the police:

- It was too dark to make out the eyes or claws of these humanoids, but we could see that their bodies were covered with very thick hair. They were four small beings, all the same size but with terrible strength. We thought they were going to drag us into their ship.

- To escape from these dwarves, Lorenzo Flores later explained, our only recourse was to flee and get to the road which was about 20 meters away. When we turned around to see where the strange ship was, it had gone. So we stayed on the road. A truck of the firm *Inlaca* arrived. The driver saw us and made us board. He affirmed to have seen an intense light coming from the place where we were and a strange device flying away, just before midnight. The driver of the truck then took us directly to the police where we presented ourselves to tell what had happened. We arrived there without shoes and with our shirts all torn.

In this document of the time,
we can see the tattered shirts of Lorenzo and Jesus

Funny prints

It is easy to imagine the face of the police authorities when they see two rascals coming in, their clothes in tatters, on the verge of a nervous breakdown. But the police were quick to react and formed an investigation committee composed of officers Ramón González and Ramón Gudiño, as well as agents Víctor Morales, Modesto Suárez, Rafael Ereú and Serafín Hernández. Without delay, these men went to the site in question. In a plaza, 25 meters from the road, they found Lorenzo's rifle broken in two, as well as the machete and bicycles abandoned by the two hunters.

On the ground, they find obvious signs of a struggle. And very interesting: among the boys' shoeprints, they note the presence of smaller prints, comparable "to those that could be left by monkeys". But which in the end do not correspond to this type of animal. Finally, there is still a strong smell in the air, similar to sulfur.

Testifying under the dictatorship

At this stage of our story, it is necessary to specify that between 1953 and 1958, Venezuela underwent the dictatorship of the military putschist Marcos Pérez Jiménez. It was a troubled and violent period, in which all opposition was destroyed and the secret police was omnipresent. In addition, in 1954, the United States - supposedly a great democracy - had just awarded the American Legion of Merit to this fearsome tyrant. In short, this is a time when it is very risky to deal with the police. Our two hunters are therefore in a delicate situation.

Besides, very soon they undergo a second interrogation led by Manuel Azuaje, chief of the police of Carora, who concludes:

- These two boys are well known in Carora as being very honest. It seems very strange that they would make up such a story to attract the attention of the authorities.

During this second interrogation, the two boys revealed that Jesús Gómez, in the hands of the hairy dwarves, tried to defend himself with his machete but, terrorized, he fainted. Lorenzo Flores then took the machete and struck the intruders several times, but to no avail: the creatures were harder than stone. It was then that he decided to hit them with his rifle, which broke under the shock.

The impossible scam

The tone changes when our two witnesses are transferred before Captain Julio Chacón Mejias, head of the National Security, the dreaded police of the dictatorship at the time. The two young people are then subjected to a more severe interrogation. Questioned separately, they test the harsh methods used by these agents.

In the end, Julio Chacón Mejias, faithful to his legendary psychorigidity, affirms that all that is only invention and staging. However, in spite of the repeated intimidations of the agents of the Security, our two young hunters maintain courageously their account. Impossible to take them in default. The two young Venezuelans are then examined by the psychiatrist Sam Castrillo, director of the clinic of Barquisimeto. Result: they are judged sane, reliable and completely responsible. Investigators and authorities are disconcerted. And they end up admitting that Flores and Gomez could indeed have been in the presence of a flying saucer and somewhat belligerent occupants.

The two young people, described as impressionable and very shy, go through a difficult ordeal. A crowd of people wants to meet them at all costs. Journalists pursue them day and night and harass them. The district judge, Daniel Pompeyo Graterón, travels in person to question them. In a non-stop back-and-forth, an overexcited multitude rushes in and demands details.

Faced with a journalist from the daily *El Nacional,* Jesús Gómez, the youngest, finally breaks down and confides:

- The whole thing was a huge nightmare for me. I'm sure I saw this record and these dwarfs at the Curva de Chirico. My regret is that now people will call me crazy or even a thug. And they will say that with my friend Lorenzo Flores, who has just been taken to the clinic of Barquisimeto for psychiatric tests, we would have conceived such a swindle...

EL NACIONAL

Fundador: ✝ HENRIQUE OTERO VIZCARRONDO

CARACAS: SABADO 11 DE DICIEMBRE DE 1954   PRECIO: Bs. 0,37½

ATERRIZO UN DISCO VOLADOR EN CARORA

2 Jóvenes Cazadores Lucharon Contra Varios Extraños Seres

El suceso ocurrió aproximadamente a las once y cuarenta y cinco de la noche. Los enanos trataron de capturar a uno de los cazadores

Daily newspaper El Nacional, December 11, 1954: "A flying saucer landed in Carora. Two young hunters fought against several strange creatures. The events took place between 11:40 pm and about 5 am. The dwarves attempted to kidnap one of the hunters."

A troubling case

For Horacio Gonzales, APRO's Venezuelan correspondent, despite the efforts of National Security to silence the two hunters, this case is genuine. Especially since it is certain, in his words, that a young man from a very poor background would not deliberately break his rifle in order to pull off such a scam. For these people living in great precariousness, a rifle, even an old one, remains a thing of great value, difficult to obtain. Therefore, it should be treated with the utmost care.

The case of the Carora *enanos* quickly spread to the United States. Carol Lorenzen, co-founder of APRO, wrote about it in her book *The Great Flying Saucer Hoax* published in 1962 and republished in October 1966 under the title *Flying Saucers, The Startling Evidence Of The Invasion From Outer Space*. North American cartoonists adapted the two hunters' misadventure in the first issue of the comic book magazine *Flying Saucers* published in 1968.

Sources

Flying Saucer Review, vol. 14, n°3, May-June 1968, p. 14 - Charles Bowen, *En quête des humanoïdes*, J'ai Lu, 1974, pp. 115-116 - Eric Zurcher, *Les apparitions d'humanoïdes*, Éditions Alain Lefeuvre 1979, pp. 245-246

Illustration taken from Flying Saucers: "Lorenzo hits with all his might but... 'I broke my gun, and that monster (or whatever it is) didn't feel a thing!'"

The dwarfs of San Carlos

Date: December 16, 1954.
Location: San Carlos, Venezuela.

Jesús Paz has dinner with three friends in a restaurant in San Carlos. After a good evening, the friends drive home. Near the park of the Ministry of Agriculture (which serves as an exhibition center), Jesús is seized by an urge and asks the driver to stop. He gets out of the car and, to relieve himself, disappears behind a clump of bushes along the road.

His companions, who were waiting for him, suddenly heard a terrible cry that would make your hair stand on end. No doubt about it: it is Jesús calling for help! Rushing to the scene, the young men discover Jesús Paz lying unconscious on the ground. Stunned, they also see a small humanoid, "a hairy dwarf" according to them, which runs away and takes refuge in a shiny disc-shaped device, stationary above the ground. One of the boys, Luis Mejia, a national guard, desperately searches for his weapon and then realizes, in disappointment, that he has left it at headquarters. He then picks up a stone and throws it at the machine, which takes off and moves away with a kind of whistling sound.

Jesús Paz was rushed to the city's hospital. According to the medical examination, he is in a state of shock. He has several cuts, "large, long and deep" on his right side and along his spine. Doctors say he appears to have been lacerated by a wild animal. Questioned by the authorities, the three friends gave the same account.

When he came to his senses, Jesús Paz told the police that he had gone to a flower bed to relieve himself. His footsteps were muffled by the thick grass and he surprised a small hairy humanoid creature examining the flowers. Wanting to avoid it, he tried to turn back, but the belligerent dwarf attacked him, scratching him, tearing his shirt and landing a heavy blow on his neck. Before being knocked out, Jesús just had the strength to scream to alert his comrades.

Sources

The APRO Bulletin, vol. 3, n°4, January 15, 1955, pp. 1-2 - *Coral E. Lorenzen, The Startling Evidence Of The Invasion From Outer Space*, Signet Book, 1966, pp. 56-57 - Frank Edwards, *Les Soucoupes volantes, affaire sérieuse*, Robert Laffont, 1967, pp. 155-156 - Charles Bowen, *En quête des humanoïdes*, J'ai Lu, 1974, p. 70 and p. 117

The dwarfs of Valencia

Date: December 20, 1954.

Location: Valencia, capital of the state of Carabobo, in northern Venezuela.

*The daily newspaper El Nacional of Caracas of December 21, 1954 reported
a rather disconcerting news item.*

It was screaming, shirtless, eyes wild, that Jose Parra, 18 years old, presented himself at 2:00 a.m. at the National Security Station of Valencia, saying that he had just been attacked by six dwarfs emerging from a flying saucer. The encounter took place in front of the cement factory, near the gutter that borders the Circunvalación ring road.

Lopez Ayaro, head of criminology, recorded Parra's statement and ordered that he be remanded in custody until he regained his composure. At the same time, Ayaro sent a team of investigators to the place indicated by Parra, to see if the alleged dwarves had left any traces of their passage. The investigators found footprints, but could not determine whether they were human or animal.

José Parra insisted that his encounter with the dwarves that came out of a flying saucer was true. He explained that he *jogged* on the ring road to lose weight because it is part of his training as an apprentice jockey at the National Racetrack in Caracas.

- I need to lose a kilo," explained José Parra. So I get up very early and jog for an hour along the highway. When I arrived in front of the cement factory, I saw six men, small and rather hairy, who were picking up large stones on the side of the road to transport them to a saucer that was waiting there, motionless, as if suspended in the air, less than 3 meters from the ground. I was amazed by this and even more by the saucer. I wanted to run away to try to get someone's attention, but one of the dwarves came after me and paralyzed me with purple light rays. Then all the creatures returned to the ship, which rose and disappeared. When I recovered, I immediately came here to the National Security Station to tell what had happened to me.

José Parra showed that he was affected by the facts he reported. He stated that, until now, he did not believe in flying saucers or hairy dwarfs. Now he knows that all this is real.

Sources

El Nacional, Caracas, December 21, 1954 - *Amazing Stories,* vol. 31, n°10, October 1957, p. 92 - Coral E. Lorenzen, *Flying Saucers, The Startling Evidence of The Invasion From Outer Space,* Signet Books, 1966, p. 57 - Charles Bowen, *En quête des humanoïdes,* J'ai Lu, 1974, p. 71 and pp. 117-118.

VII. Stunning face-offs

Among the secondary and damaging effects caused by the presence of a UFO, the report of the principal manager of American military intelligence evokes not only cases of "paralysis", but also episodes of "loss of consciousness" (*unconsciousness*) and "force field impact" (*force field impact*). This can be accompanied by "disorientation *and confusion*" and "*skin sores, rash*".

Here are some dramatic examples from around the world...

The case of Roger Mougeolle

Date: April 24, 1954 (year of an international "wave" of UFO sightings).

Location : Rouges Eaux, commune located in the Vosges department, Grand Est region, France.

In February 1976, Roger Mougeolle confided in the investigators of the magazine *Lumières dans la Nuit*. He is an extremely weakened man, who expresses himself with difficulty and speaks in a low voice. And what he tells is truly amazing.

In 1954, he was a lumberjack. And in good health. Afterwards, he changed profession and, for many years, he participated in the construction of Vosges chalets. At that time, it was not known that handling glass wool without protection was dangerous to health. That is why, in February 1976, Roger Mougeolle was almost permanently bedridden in a clinic in Bruyères, with lungs saturated with fine glass particles. In spite of this, he found the strength to tell the story of the adventure he had lived 22 years earlier, in the middle of the forest.

On April 24, 1954, Roger Mougeolle went to a vast hill in the Vosges, south of the place called La Grande Cheminée, not far from the village of Rouges Eaux. This area of the commune of Bois-de-Champ (8 kilometers north-east of the town of Bruyères) is renowned for the quality of its trees. A hard day awaits the vigorous 37-year-old, accompanied by Gilbert Doridant, a 19-year-old "simpleton" in charge of burning the useless branches while Roger prunes the trunks of the felled trees.

The two men are in the middle of their work when they are startled by a strange noise coming from the sky. It sounded like "a train passing over a metal bridge or the bursting of a high-caliber bomb. When the noise stops, three large objects appear above the hill. They have the shape of "a very elongated ellipse or a large cigar. Their slowness and volume give the impression of an enormous mass." Two of these objects silently move away and disappear. The third, against all expectations, lands in the clearing, 50 meters from the two stunned loggers.

According to Roger Mougeolle, the machine is grey in color, uniform. On its surface, one does not distinguish any mark, any welding, any protuberance. But what impresses the witness more than anything else is its gigantic size. Its length seems to exceed 200 meters. While its width and its height are estimated between 80 and 100 meters!

This colossal vessel stops a few centimeters from the ground. Roger is persuaded that it is a dirigible balloon. Not at all afraid, he moves towards this enormous mass. On the other hand, Gilbert is terrified and runs away with all his legs. Very shocked, he will refuse thereafter to put the feet in this clearing.

Very intrigued, Roger comes to put his hand on this strange vessel. Its surface is smooth, cold, "hard as steel". It is then that he realizes that this immense object, completely motionless and silent, is not an airship. He then seizes his axe and strikes the surface of the UFO with the flat of the blade. Not with an aggressive aim, far from there: just to realize, "to see" he will say later. The shock of the blade then produces a dull sound "like the one you hear when you hit a big piece of steel".

What follows is literally stunning. Roger is suddenly projected with violence 5 or 6 meters from the UFO. It is not, he will say, a breath of air that propelled him to the foot of a rock. It is rather a force of unknown nature and "distributed uniformly on all the parts of his body". Paralyzed, Roger has the clear impression that "by its only presence, the object deprives him of his freedom of movement". Finally, very slowly, this colossal mass comes to life, takes off and disappears in the sky. At this moment, our witness finds his mobility.

Struck by the size of the objects described, investigators at the time wondered:

- How is it possible, given the exceptional dimension of these UFOs, that there were no other witnesses, notably in the nearby village of Vanénont?

The explanation is not rocket science: in 1954, this region was hardly populated, and the few roads in the area were rarely used.

We only have the account of Roger Mougeolle. Gilbert Doridant could not testify, having perished in 1957, crushed by a load of tree trunks whose attachments had broken.

Sources

Lumières dans la Nuit n°261-262, March-April 1986, p. 44 - *Lumières dans la Nuit* n°275-276, May-June 1987, pp. 27-30 - Michel Figuet and Jean-Louis Ruchon, *OVNI, le premier dossier complet des rencontres rapprochées en France,* p. 69, which quotes *Nostradamus* - Timothy Good, *Contacts Extraterrestres*, Presses du Chatelet, 1999, pp. 148-149.

Reconstruction of Roger Mougeolle's case by the author

The case of Jeanne Rossignon

Date: mid-October 1954.

Location : Thin-le-Moutier, in the Ardennes department, in the Grand Est region, France.

An autumn morning dawns in the small rural town of Thin-le-Moutier. Going about her tasks, Jeanne Rossignon, a farmer, goes to a field near the village where her cows are grazing. It is time to gather them and bring them back to the barn to be milked. At the top of a small hill, the farmer is stunned. A strange machine is placed there, in front of her, less than 30 meters away. Jeanne lost consciousness and fell heavily to the ground.

When she comes to, the machine has disappeared. Jeanne returns painfully to her home. She was so ill that she had to go to bed. Immediately, "a strange dermatosis appears". And for several days, her skin "looked like a toad's skin". According to Professor Villequez, a specialist in dermatology and attached to the Faculty of Medicine in Dijon, "such reactions are frequent following a violent emotional shock. The young woman therefore did not invent this story."

This case was notably reported by the daily newspaper *L'Est Républicain* which titled then: "Flying saucers give skin diseases!" By specifying that Jeanne enjoys, in the country, the general esteem.

Sources

L'Est Républicain, October 21, 1954 - Jacques Vallée, *Chroniques des apparitions extra-terrestres*, J'ai Lu, 1972, p. 283, who quotes *Challenge* - Charles Garreau and Raymond Lavier, *Face aux extra-terrestres*, Jean-Pierre Delarge, Mame 1975, pp. 27-28 - *Lumières dans la Nuit* n°374, September 2004, p. 25.

The case of Dr. Luis Leónidas Sánchez Vegas

Date: August 7, 1967.
Location: Caracas, Venezuela, South America.

Luis Leónidas Sánchez Vegas is a prominent and popular doctor. His dedication to the country's underprivileged populations has earned him the respect of all. So when he confided his strange adventure to the famous daily newspaper *El Mundo*, his testimony was like a bomb.

That day, the patient who came to his office did not look very human. Bald, small in stature, he wears a kind of silver suit. His head is very large and slightly deformed. He has no lips, just a slit in place of the mouth. And his face is crossed by huge eyebrows. Speaking in perfect Spanish, he tells the doctor not to worry if his body temperature is high.

UFO. Are we in danger? The black book of ufology

- This is quite normal," he explains, "because I am not originally from your planet.

Intrigued, Doctor Sánchez Vegas examines this strange patient. And he goes from surprise to surprise. The character does not have ears. His dentition is reduced to ten teeth: five on his upper jaw and five on his lower jaw. Very voluble and visibly at ease, the visitor then starts to tell his life story. He confides that he has no parents. That the mode of reproduction of his people is very different from that of the Earthmen. And that on his distant planet, foreign languages are learned with the help of a machine.

Then he ends on a serious note. According to him, 9000 years ago, the Earth experienced a terrible cataclysm. If we, humans, continue to abuse and destroy our biotope, we will surely run into a new catastrophe.

This encounter shook the doctor to the point that he collapsed and had to be rushed to hospital. His brother Julio, also a doctor, contacted the daily newspaper *El Mundo*, which reported the shocking encounter in these words:

The doctor is one of the most influential figures in the medical profession in Caracas. After his conversation with a small being from another world, he had a heart attack. He had to be taken to a specialized clinic. His testimony and that of a young man living on Avila Avenue, in the suburbs of San Bernardino, suggest that these two citizens were confronted with the same interplanetary visitor. The doctor and the young witness, named Pedro Riera, agree on the following details: the being was small, with a big head, very agile and dressed in a strange suit that seemed to be made of a metallic-looking material.

The doctor and the young man, 20 years old and employed in an advertising agency, claim to have seen this interplanetary being on August 7, in the same area of the city, at significantly different times. Four other people, including a policeman, affirm to have seen that day the vessel used by the extraterrestrial visitor. These people are Carmen Ortega, a student, Andrés and José Pascual, and a police officer who wishes to remain anonymous. These new witnesses inform us that a strange object remained parked for several hours, on the morning of August 7, in front of the Eduvigis building, on Avila de San Bernardino Avenue.

Pedro Riera is one of the occupants of the Eduvigis building. According to him, the creature broke into his apartment. He then tried to grab it by its clothing, but the being escaped through the window and joined his vessel parked on the left side of Avila Avenue. That same day, the doctor said that he received a strange visitor whose description corresponds point for point to the one provided by Pedro Riera.

The doctor told us that this being claimed to come from another planet. He spoke perfectly in Spanish. He spoke about the scientific and technological advances of his world and said that his people have eradicated the diseases that the earthlings suffer.

He also spoke of wars, of bellicose behavior in general, but revealed that all this no longer existed on his planet. He added that his mission on earth was to meet scientists and then transport them to his planet to teach them about all these advances, in the name of progress and for the benefit of all living beings capable of reasoning.

This strange being nevertheless confided to the doctor that the fact of transporting Earthlings in his world ran up against two major difficulties: the weight and the control of space. He indeed explained that on his distant planet, an Earthman would see his weight and his strength triple (...) But, in spite of these potential difficulties, both physical and mental, and according to some studies, human beings would not suffer too much from this change.

Sources

El Mundo, August 19, 1967 - *El Universal*, August 20, 1967 - *Ultimas Noticias*, Caracas, August 19, 1967 - *El Mundo*, August 22, 1967 - *The APRO Bulletin*, September-October 1967, p. 12 - *Flying Saucer Review* vol. 14, n°3, May-June 1968, pp. 18-19 - Jacques Vallée, case n°866 *of Un siècle d'atterrissage, Lumières dans la Nuit* n°110, February 1971, p. 6.

The case of Esteban D. Cova

Date: August 26, 1967.

Location: Maiquetia airport, located on the Caribbean Sea coast, about 10 km north of Caracas, Venezuela.

It's 2 a.m. Esteban D. Cova, Private 1ère in the Marines, finishes his service. Showered, changed, he leaves the Air Mail hangar and returns to his barracks. Suddenly, a small being accosts him. This creature is barely 1 meter high. Our soldier finds it hideous. According to him, the dwarf has a large head and bulging eyes. Its body is covered with "hairy fabric or metal bristling with wires". Moreover, it emits a kind of whistling which produces a funny effect on our witness. This one then feels like a tingling in all his body.

In perfect Spanish, the creature asks:

- Will you come with me? I need the presence of a new human being!

Seized with fear, the soldier faints. When he came to, he rushed to tell the base commander about his unbelievable face-to-face encounter. Later, the commander will tell investigators:

- I am convinced that something really terrified this Private First Class. And I'll take his word for it.

Sources

The APRO Bulletin, September-October 1967, p. 13 - Jacques Vallée, case n°873 of *Un siècle d'atterrissage, Lumières dans la Nuit,* n°110, February 1971, p. 7.

The case of Clifford Muchena

Date: August 15, 1981.

Location: La Rochelle, a beautiful 108-hectare estate located near the border between Mozambique and Zimbabwe, Africa.

Built and developed in 1951 by Sir Stephen and Lady Virginia Courtauld, the La Rochelle estate was donated to the people of Zimbabwe in 1972. A true haven of peace in the heart of a generous nature, the place has become a must for tourists visiting the region. It includes an observation tower, a futuristic building called *The Fantasy and* a long, narrow building known as "The Tea Room". The estate employs about 30 foresters and employees, including Clifford Muchena. South African investigator Cynthia Hind describes it this way:

> Pleasant-faced, uneducated, 5'6" tall, yet athletic, Clifford reads and speaks
> perfectly good English.

Here is what he says...

It was about 6:30 p.m. when I saw a ball of light near the tea room. This ball, very large, could be seen by everyone. It was first seen spinning inside the observation tower. The first witnesses, totally terrified, thought that the tower was on fire because flames were coming out of the window.

I ran to the side of the house to ring the alarm bell. The ball of light then went along the main building. It passed me and then headed towards *The Fantasy*. I stopped ringing the bell and ran to the building to see what was going on. I saw that it was lit up and filled with flames. Then I saw three men standing there. I was terribly scared and wondered what kind of fire it was.

At first I thought one of these men was Mr. Connolley, one of our directors, who had come because of the disaster. So I called him by name. These men were tall, over six feet tall each. When I called out to Mr. Connolley, these beings turned around very slowly, and I was very scared. They were wearing whitish overalls that glowed. The color looked like this *(he pulls out a 20 cent coin from his pocket)*. I couldn't make out their faces because the light was too strong. I had to shield my eyes with my hand. I couldn't see if they were wearing something on their heads. I was totally blinded. The moment I raised my hand to protect my face, I fell. My God, I was so scared!

When the investigator asks Clifford the cause of his fall, he replies:
- These men could not have pushed me because, at that moment, they were standing 3 meters away from me. No, it was rather a great power that emanated from them...
He hesitates for a moment and then concludes:
- Here, more than 20 people have seen them. Many people think that they were ghosts. I say that maybe they were the spirits of my ancestors.
A second witness then agreed to speak. She is Eunice Kachiti, a Forestry Commission maid who is in charge of the women's craft workshop on the estate. Here is what she said:

That Saturday, I was at home when I saw fire on this tree *(she points to a black box in the middle of the lawn)*. There were two men standing there.

UFO. Are we in danger? The black book of ufology

They were strange. They had torches or flashlights in their hands. They were wearing blue jeans. I couldn't make out the upper half of their bodies because their flashlights were only shining on their legs. I think they were standing and looking at the ball of light in front of them. It seemed to me that their lamps were longer than the torches we use here, with a more elongated end.

The ball of light began to move toward the tea room. The color of the ball changed from yellow to bright red. As it moved, it grew to be about 5 feet wide. It started from the box over there. Then it stayed near the house for about two or three minutes, and then it went back to the tree. During all this time, the two men did not move. At first I thought they were just ordinary visitors watching the fire.

The ball of light then returned to the tea room. Later, it went up the wall of the observation tower and into the upper room. I don't know if the two men had anything to do with this ball of light. I think they were just looking at it because it was jumping in the air and bouncing higher and higher. When it slid inside the tower, it looked like the tower was burning. When I looked back to where the men were, they were gone. Then the fire went out.

As far as we know, and according to the recollections of those involved, there were no visitors in La Rochelle that afternoon. So who were these strange characters?

Finally, one last detail: the African personnel had never heard of UFOs or possible occupants. It is therefore unlikely that they were influenced by local or even international ufology stories. However, in Africa, "night lights" are part of local folklore. In Zimbabwe at the time, the story of Maganga was widely told.

One night, Maganga was walking home when he saw a very bright light in front of him. He became frightened and immediately turned around, running along the path. To his astonishment, the light rematerialized in front of him. No matter how fast he ran, the light was still ahead of him and getting closer. Suddenly it disappeared, but invisible hands grabbed Maganga by the throat. The man was thrown to the ground. Gathering some strength, he managed to crawl to the nearest *kraal* (cattle pen). He took refuge there, partially paralyzed and without speech. Only a ghost-hunting *nganga* (witch doctor) was able to restore his speech. He ordered the witness to ingest medicinal plants that caused him to vomit a green foam.

The narrator of this story is none other than a district commissioner in Rhodesia. He says that when he first saw Maganga, he was convinced that the man was dying. When he returned, he saw Maganga in excellent health.

There are many similar stories recorded in the annals of Rhodesian history. Many involve dogs either being healed by the *nganga* or dying as a result of these encounters.

Sources

MUFON UFO Journal n°183, May 1983, pp. 6-10 - *UFO Afrinews* n°1, July 1988, pp. 9-10 - Jenny Randles, *Alien Abductions, The Mystery Solved,* Inner Light, 1988, pp. 156-157 - *UFO Afrinews* n°2, June 1989, pp. 7-8 - John Spencer, *World Atlas of UFOs,* Smithmark, 1992, pp. 153-156 - *UFO Afrinews* n°15, January 1997, pp. 3-4 - *The World's Greatest Alien Abduction Mysteries,* Chancellor Press, 2001, p. 164 - Lynn Picknett, *The Mammoth Book of UFOs,* Caroll & Graf, 2001, p. 329.

Clifford Muchena (left). View of the La Rochelle estate (right).

The case of Robert Taylor

A land of legends

Scotland, a land of spells and wonders, is most famous for its ghostly mansions and for Loch Ness, where a shy monster with a girl's name frolics away from the cameras of the curious. If we are to believe the great Shakespeare, and his legendary

Macbeth, this country was born in terrible convulsions. In the beginning, says the writer, there was only a deserted, windswept moor. And three witches, crouching around a bubbling cauldron, muttering and cursing.

More recently, for those who love the mysteries of the sky, Scotland has become a destination of choice for observing strange flying objects. The *Observer* newspaper declared in June 2002 that the number of UFO sightings there was "phenomenal". These sightings were concentrated in West Lothian and particularly around the town of Bonnybridge. For investigator and ufologist Ron Halliday, "one of the theories is that the Bonnybridge area is a window to another dimension." The sightings are so numerous that the city councilman has requested a twinning with Roswell... You can't make this up!

The most famous, most credible and most studied UFO sighting in the United Kingdom took place in Scotland. It happened in the center of the country, in a region called the Lowlands. These "lowlands", which run from the Clyde in the west to the Forth and Tay in the east, are home to most of the local population.

Meeting in the forest

Date: November 9, 1979.

Location: Livingston, a small town located between Edinburgh and Glasgow, in the heart of a region called West Lothian, Scotland.

This is where Robert Taylor, our witness, lives. At 61 years old, married with five children, Bob (as he is known to all) is a World War II hero. He served as a tank driver and participated in the evacuation of Dunkirk and then the D-Day landings.

For the past few years, Bob has lived with his wife in a modest house at 4 Broomieknowe Drive in Livingston. He now works for the Forestry Department of the local development corporation. One of his main tasks is to patrol a part of the Dechmont Forest, not far from the M8 freeway which connects Glasgow to Edinburgh.

Bob Taylor soldier (left). And at the time of his observation (right).

On November 9, 1979, Bob had just finished his coffee break. At 10:00 a.m. sharp, he leaves his home at the wheel of his pickup truck, a Bedford. He is accompanied by his faithful dog, an Irish setter, named Lara, who follows him everywhere. He goes to a forestry plantation which borders the M8 freeway. He has to check if everything is in order, if the young trees are growing well and if the fences are in good condition to prevent some runaway sheep from wandering into the nearby woods. As the vegetation is dense, Bob parks his vehicle on the side of a road and continues his journey on foot to the great joy of Lara who, finally free, gambols around, sniffing the delicious autumn scents.

Soon, the wooded area Bob is walking through becomes a clearing. Having walked this path so many times, he knows the area perfectly. However, it is here that he will experience an episode that will change his life forever. Suddenly, as he entered this open space, the forester froze, dumbfounded. What is this strange object lying in the clearing?

A strange machine

The machine has the shape of a dome. It is stationary and seems to hover clearly above the ground. It does not turn on itself. Of a uniform dark gray, it does not emit any sound. And its texture is strangely reminiscent of sandpaper. Stranger: the surface of the object is like moving. Part of its body is periodically altered, first in one place, then in another. Bob has the distinct impression that the object is trying to camouflage itself.

UFO. Are we in danger? The black book of ufology

The changes cause the UFO to lose some of its gray texture. Instead, a surface appears that looks smooth and shiny. Bob has trouble judging whether this object is becoming successively transparent or reflective. Either way, what he sees defies logic.

The object measures approximately 6 meters in diameter for a height of approximately 3 meters. Its upper part, about 2.5 meters high, is a hemispherical dome. The dome appears to be mounted on a flange or a protruding circular rim, like the brim of a hat. The lower part of the object is not visible. It is either darker or in shadow.

On the protruding rim that goes around the machine, there are regularly spaced rods topped by what appear to be "propellers" or "bow ties." These appendages are immobile. Above this rim, on the surface of the dome, Bob distinguishes circular spots of a darker tone. Perhaps they are portholes. No other details are visible.

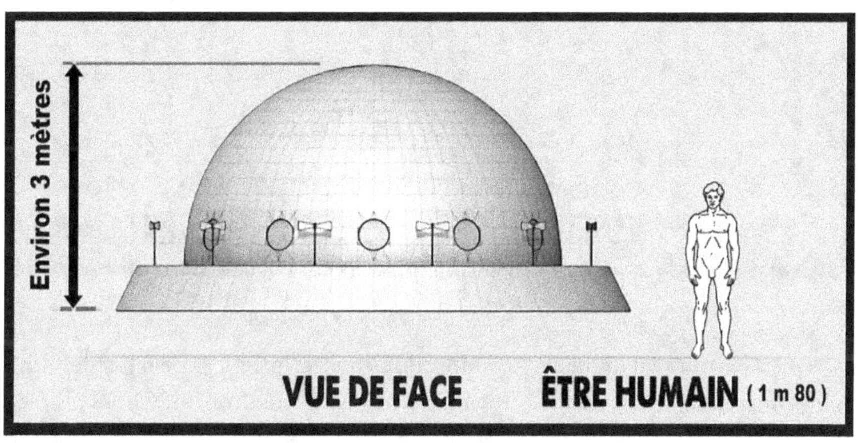

Illustration of the UFO seen by Bob Taylor

Hypnotized, Bob remains a good minute to contemplate this astonishing spectacle. Incredibly, parts of the craft fade away and, all of a sudden, we can see, through him, the background of the forest. The next moment, the UFO becomes solid again. It is to understand nothing there! The only sounds that we perceive in the clearing are the furious barks of Lara. The dog obviously does not appreciate the presence of the intruder.

Belligerent spheres

Suddenly, two gray spheres appear from the base of the machine like robots. They start to roll on the grass of the meadow. These spheres measure about 90 centimeters in diameter. They are bristling with six spikes and resemble the mines of the Second World War. Their color and texture are identical to that of the large machine. As their spikes sink into the wet earth, a sucking sound is heard.

In a few seconds, these two spherical objects melt on Bob. Now our man is terrified. "It's all unreal," he thinks, frozen in fear.

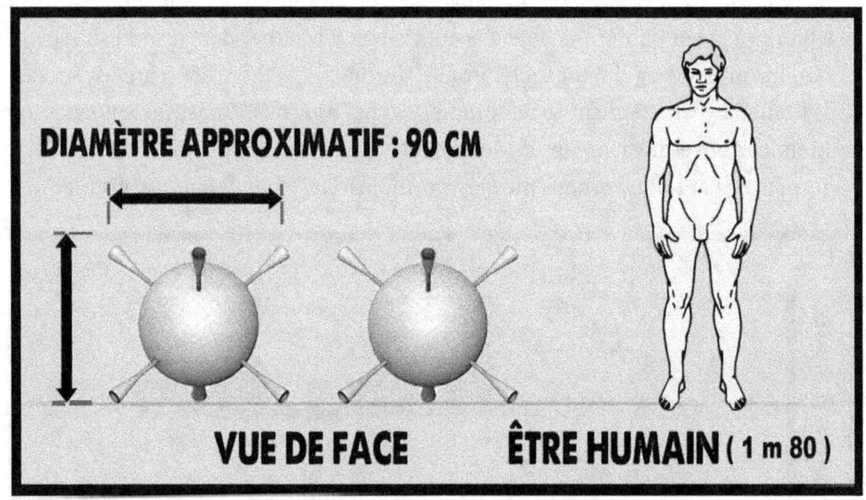

Illustration of the spheres seen by Bob Taylor

Quickly, the two spheres surround Bob then grip him on each side of his pants, just under his pockets. Subjected to a strong traction, our witness is then violently pulled forward, in direction of the UFO. He tries to resist, his boots ploughing the ground. At the same moment, he is assailed by a strong odor which floats in the air and seems to emanate from the two spheres. That makes him think of the pungent and nauseating smell of burned brake linings. Our forester suffocates. At the same time, he perceives a whistling sound, similar to that of a cane being whirled in the air. He loses consciousness and collapses face down.

He remained unconscious for nearly twenty minutes. When he gradually came to, he noticed that he could neither speak nor walk. He has totally lost the use of his legs! Near him, the faithful Lara, very excited, barks furiously. The good dog did not abandon him. Bob notices that the UFO and the two spheres have disappeared. He is then persuaded that it is Lara who made them flee. And, as a result, saved him from this very bad situation.

Our man is very thirsty and has a terrible headache. As if that wasn't enough, he feels feverish and his chin, obviously injured, burns. Unable to get up, he starts to crawl. With difficulty he covers the 90 meters that separate him from the path. Then he crawled the 430 meters to his car through the mud and wet earth. Once he reached his goal, he climbed into the van and tried to reach his supervisor through the on-board radio. Alas, he is mute!

As best he could, he managed to get the van into gear. But, too weak, he made a false maneuver, stuck the vehicle in the ditch and mired it. It was now impossible to get it out. Painfully, always flanked by Lara, he decides to return on foot. Taking a shortcut, he cuts through woods and fields. A long journey awaits him: his home is more than 1.5 kilometers away.

The investigation is launched

Bob arrives home around 11:15. He is covered in mud. When Mary, his wife, sees him, she is stunned. She hears him muttering that he has just been assaulted. She wants to call the police. Bob dissuades her. He explains to her that he was attacked by a *spaceship*. For sure, they will take him for a madman. Mary contacts Malcolm Drummond, 58, Bob's boss and head of the Forestry Department. It is 11:20 a.m. During this call, Bob takes the opportunity to take a bath.

Unable to believe the news, Malcolm Drummond first telephones a local doctor, asking him to go to the Taylors' home immediately. Then, without wasting a second, he arrives at Bob's house and questions the witness who is still in his bath.

Soon after, Dr. Gordon James Adams from the Blackburn Health Center arrived to examine Bob. Other than a scrape on his chin and two on the outside of each thigh, he found no major problems. The forester had no head injuries or neurological problems. Blood pressure, eye fundus and nervous system examinations reveal no abnormalities. However, this UFO story disturbs Malcolm Drummond. He knows Bob very well and is convinced that he is not lying. For him, there is no doubt: our man was indeed attacked by two strange "spheres", emerging from a "spaceship". Therefore, he thinks, we must be able to find evidence of this "landing" in the clearing.

Drummond, Bob and several Forestry Department employees go to the site of the encounter. They discovered numerous marks on the ground. The area was then fenced off and off limits. Drummond notified the police of the incident. At the scene, officers took photos, took measurements and searched the area thoroughly. Seven police officers (including an officer from the *Criminal Investigation Department*, CID) were involved in the investigation. The incident - unprecedented - is then considered an "assault" by one or more unidentified "third parties".

The lab in action

The marks on the ground are of two types. First, there are two long parallel ladder-like "tracks", each measuring 2.5 meters. Surprisingly, although these tracks appear to have been caused by a heavy object, the prints only touch the grass. Indeed, the ground under the vegetation is neither altered nor even crushed.

Around these two "tracks", there are forty holes. They are about 10 x 10 centimeters wide. Inside, there is fresh earth. And all of them are at an angle of about 30 degrees to the ground.

Meanwhile, Dr. Adams examines Bob's clothing and notes, in surprise, the presence of two long snags on the pants. The garment is torn under the pockets, exactly where the witness claims these strange spheres grabbed him. An S-shaped hole is also visible on one of the legs of the long johns.

The pants are transferred to the police of Edinburgh which, in its forensic laboratory, will subject it to several tests. Coming from the stock of clothes of the police force, they are made of a very thick and solid fabric. First conclusion: it took a considerable force, like the pressure of a pair of pliers, to cause these two cuts. And no doubt, the snags in the fabric correspond to an outward pulling force. According to the officers' analysis, the incisions seem to confirm that the unconscious man was dragged violently across the meadow.

The press gets involved

Soon, a large number of people, especially Forestry Department staff, are made aware of the incident. The news went around the country. The press was not to be outdone. The local *Livingston Post* opened the celebrations with the first story of the "assault" by robots from elsewhere. *The Scottsman*, *The Evening News* of Edinburgh and *The Glasgow Herald* followed. The next day, all the newspapers

UFO. Are we in danger? The black book of ufology

published detailed reports. And it is through the *Sunday Express* that Great Britain discovers this incredible face-to-face.

The journalists interview Bob and his relatives. Malcolm Drummond states:

- If anyone else had told me this story, I would have laughed out loud. But Mr. Taylor is a reasonable, sensible man whom I respect. He has been through a real ordeal. His torn pants prove it. The thing that left its mark on the prairie floor must have weighed a ton!

When asked, one of the spokespersons of the national police stated:

- This man did see something!

The work of the investigators did not stop at studying the traces on the ground. During the following weeks, some of them, who live near the witness, notice the persistence of a scratch on his hip (precisely where the tear in the pants was located). In addition, in the days following the assault, Bob lost his appetite. So did Lara, his dog (this is the only notable reaction of the animal). This lack of appetite will persist for about six days after the encounter.

An official UFO case

Bob was in great demand. Everybody wants to meet him, to approach him, to question him. His UFO story fascinated England and then the rest of the world. The ufological press treats the case with, in general, rigor and seriousness. As for the British national press, it is crazy about this case which it considers very solid. It will not cease to evoke it during the following years.

In February 1992, an article announced that the Livingston case was now considered "an official UFO encounter":

It was Scotland's most famous close encounter with a UFO. More than a decade later, the Livingston Development Corporation has decided to erect a small memorial at the site of the sighting. We believe that the recognition of such an incident is a world first. Today, Bob Taylor is 73 years old and now lives in Pertshire. He stated:

- I am still positive that it was an unconventional vessel.

The place of the incident became a very popular place for British people to walk. And the meeting place of many ufologists. On the spot, a sign invites the outdoor enthusiast to do "the Dechmont UFO trail". One can read the following text:

> Did you know that on the morning of November 9, 1979, Dechmont Forest was the site of an unusual encounter, now known as the "Robert Taylor Incident"? Follow the marked trail to discover more details about this strange event and to take full advantage of both the beautiful wooded areas, wildlife, and views of Dechmont Law.

A commemorative plaque was sealed in a rock. But frequently stolen, we will stop replacing it.

"Give me back my pants!"

On January 26, 1995, a tasty paper appeared in *The Press and Journal* of Aberdeen. Its title: "The man of the UFO wants his pants back! We learn that clumsy policemen misplaced Bob's famous pants, however considered as a relic.

> Mr. Taylor's pants, we read, are an object of international fascination. Examined by ufology experts and psychics who have attempted divination experiments on them, they have traveled the world. Now Mr. Taylor is desperate to get it back. He says that it is up to the police to carry out their research since they are the ones who confiscated the garment for analysis. Mr. Taylor admitted last night that this UFO saga has exhausted him.
>
> - I have been telling my story for too long," he said. I'm retired and I'm a tired man. It's time for me to turn the page and put it behind me. But, anyway, I want my pants back! They've been all over the world - the United States, Japan and God knows where. I have no idea where they are now. It's up to the police to find him!

Attempts to explain

Most British citizens gave credence to Bob Taylor's account. However, to explain this unusual face-to-face encounter, some more pragmatic minds have rejected the possibility of an "outer space visit" and proposed a handful of more rational hypotheses. Here is an anthology of them.

UFO. Are we in danger? The black book of ufology

An episode of ball lightning (or globular lightning)

In 1982, the author Stuart Campbell, then an investigator for BUFORA (a British UFO research organization), put forward a first explanation. According to him, our witness would have been confronted with an extremely rare phenomenon of *"black ball* lightning". Not very convincing, the hypothesis is quickly abandoned. Indeed, these luminous spheres appearing only during violent storms. However, the weather conditions that morning (cold and dry, with no threat of rain) were not favorable to their formation. Moreover, their life span is very short: between one and five seconds. And, in the end, this proposal explains neither the marks on the ground nor the tears of Bob Taylor's pants...

The mirage of Venus

In 1986, the same Steuart Campbell put forward a second explanation: this strange incident was due to a "Venus mirage". He suggests that when the witness entered the Dechmont Woods clearing, he was the victim of a mirage caused by the planet Venus and two other astronomical bodies that were above Deer Hill, a nearby hill facing him. This mirage is said to have caused the forester to have an epileptic fit. Campbell then offers an explanation for the various details that are problematic.

The two spiky spheres? Simply Venus and Mercury, seen in broad daylight and distorted by Bob's flickering vision in the middle of a crisis. The tracks on the ground? The Forestry Department would have undertaken, shortly before, work in the woods by laying drainage pipes. The snags in the pants? Bob probably tore his garment while crawling to his van.

Upon investigation, this assumption is undermined. First of all, the Forestry Department formally denied having undertaken any work in the clearing. Secondly, it is rare for Venus and Mercury to be visible in daylight. Moreover, at this particular time, they were obscured behind Dear Hill. For them to be visible, a providential temperature inversion phenomenon would have been necessary. Another disturbing detail is that Bob Taylor's medical file states that he has never, until now, suffered from epileptic seizures. Could this be a first? Finally, how to explain, in this hypothesis, the defensive and irritated attitude of the dog? How on earth could planets have left traces on the ground, perforated a pair of pants, all this while making a dog howl?

A military innovation

There has also been talk of a rare and experimental army device to combat armored vehicles. The fact that it never left any other trace makes this hypothesis very unlikely. And does this device really exist?

Poisoning

According to David Slater, editor of *UFO Matrix* magazine, Bob may have been poisoned by an herb with psychotropic properties: belladonna, commonly known as "devil's grass. The foliage and berries of this herbaceous plant of the Solanaceae family contain alkaloids that can cause hallucinations. Bob, during his walk, could have mechanically ingested some berries... But, on the one hand, the witness denied having eaten anything during his walk and, on the other hand, no belladonna plant was found in this sector of the Dechmont woods.

A hoax

This accusation does not hold water. Those who knew Bob described him as a pragmatic, discreet man of great honesty and "incapable of conceiving of such a sham". The Livingston police confirmed that he was not interested in fame and that he systematically avoided any excessive attention.

Conclusion

The Dechmont Woods incident remains a complex case, still unexplained. Considered as a classic, it still benefits today - and this is not common! - of an official recognition. Thus, the September 1994 edition of the *Daily Star Of Scotland* recalls the main lines of the encounter experienced by Bob, adding:

> The official report issued by the CDI, the Criminal Investigation Department, ultimately concluded that "Mr. Taylor is a highly respected member of the community. He is described as a conscientious and reliable man who is incapable of fabricating such a story. In fact, several people claimed to have seen, at that time, a round, white, dull object in the sky above the forest."

Conclusion: no satisfactory explanation can be retained. And the hypothesis of an extraterrestrial vessel is not to be excluded.

Robert Taylor died in March 2007. He never varied in his statements. However, concerned about his credibility, he maintained until his last day that he had seen a spaceship in the woods of Dechmont. Concerning the various hypotheses put forward to explain his misadventure, he declared to the researcher Malcolm Robinson:

- I can remember everything that happened that morning like it was yesterday. So there's no way that silly stories about ball lightning or Venus over Deer Hill can change my mind... Anyway, I would never want to go through that again.

Before concluding, laconically:

- Ah, if only my dog could talk!

Sources

Daily Record, November 1979 - *Flying Saucer Review,* vol. 25, no. 6, November-December 1979, pp. 2-7 (the case illustrates the cover) - *ALPHA no. 8, May-June 1980, pp. 5-6 - Flying Saucer Review,* vol. 26, n°1, Spring 1980, pp. 25-28 - *The APRO Bulletin,* vol. 29, n°1, July 1980, pp. 1-3 - *Flying Saucer Review,* vol. 26, no. 3, September 1980, pp. 2-4 - Steuart Campbell, *Close Encounter At Livingston*, 64-page dossier published in July 1982 by the British UFO Research Association (BUFORA Ltd.) - *West Lothian Courier,* August 20, 1990 - *Lothian Courier,* November 2, 1990 - *Fortean Times* no. 56, Winter 1990, pp. 48-49 - *UFO Magazine,* vol. 11, n°1, March-April 1992, p. 2 - Steuart Campbell, *The UFO Mystery Solved*, Explicit Books, 1994, pp. 143-158 - *Strange Times* n°1, 2001, pp. 33-34 - Lynn Picknett, *The Mammoth Book of UFOs,* Carroll and Graf, 2001, pp. 127-128 - *UFO Data Magazine,* Jan-Feb 2007, pp. 5-11 (the case illustrates the cover) - *JUFOF* n°203, May 2012, pp. 142-144 (the case illustrates the cover) - TV series *CONTACT*, season 2, episode 7 entitled "Intrusion in the Forest", 2014 - Malcolm Robinson, *The Dechmont Woods Incident,* Flying Disk France, 2021 (the reference book!)

VIII. UFOs and fatal encounters

This chapter is without question the darkest of the UFO dossier. Fortunately, the fatal cases that it lists remain marginal. The death of the victims, sometimes attributed to a UFO, is not always demonstrated (some saw "only a ray of light" falling from the sky, others "a light" and "an enormous silhouette" appearing from nowhere). However, at the time, the press and many of the actors of these dramas chose to accuse these mysterious objects.

It is obvious that the first Brazilian case (in which a young lumberjack tragically perished on Crab Island) was the preamble of a wave of offensive UFOs unique in ufological history. And hardly contestable.

Because of their violence, it is to be feared that the following events will disconcert or even put off some readers insofar as they upset the "angelic" theories of the phenomenon and undermine any attempt at a rational interpretation. Nevertheless, it would be unreasonable to conclude that this phenomenon is necessarily lethal. According to the ufologist Joël Mesnard, in 1997, a study was conducted on these so-called "hostile" sightings. There were 200 of them throughout the world, of which nearly a third were in Brazil. Why there? No one knows. Joël Mesnard's conclusion:

> The problem, even if it does not manifest itself on a devastating scale, is too serious to consider anything. Should we be afraid of UFOs? It seems desirable to remain cautious, if necessary, but we must remain aware of the very limited extent of these phenomena... Risk is inherent to life, and what we know about UFOs and their physical effects does not justify giving in to fear. It is wiser to give in to curiosity.

A death on Crab Island

Date: April 15, 1977.

Location: Crab Island, located in the estuary of the Mearin River, about 20 km south of São Marcos Bay, in northeastern Brazil.

The island of the Crabs (or *ilha dos Caranguejos* in Portuguese) is 40 kilometers long and 11 kilometers wide. It is an inhospitable land, swampy, infested with mosquitoes.

On that day, three brothers and a close relative living in Alcântara, in the state of Maranhão, went to the island to cut down trees to make poles that they would then sell on the continent. There are Apolinário Mendes Sousa (31), Firmino (38) and José Corrêa (22), and their brother-in-law Aureliano Bispo Alves (36). After dropping anchor in a small river in the interior of the island, they set to work without delay.

6 p.m.: the lumberjacks have worked hard, without a break. The day, still very hot, is coming to an end. The time for a well-deserved rest has come. The four guys are eager to go home. But the tide is low. They had to wait until midnight for it to rise and free their boat (the *Maria Rosa*), which had been trapped in the mud until then. To kill time, the workers had a bite to eat and discussed everything. At 8 pm, exhausted, they decided to give themselves a few hours of sleep. Used to the place, they are used to wake up around midnight to hoist the logs on board and go back to São Luís taking advantage of the tide.

José, Firmino and Aureliano take up residence in the ship's hold, whose door is covered with a piece of cloth to keep out mosquitoes. Apolinário prefers to rest on the deck.

5 a.m.: Apolinário is awakened from his sleep by a haunting cry. He leaps up, rushes into the hold and discovers a terrible sight. Aureliano lies on the floor, bathed in several centimeters of water and whimpering. He is unable to get up. And Firmino is covered with burns.

- He was burned and swollen, he will describe. His skin was in tatters. I tried to talk to him but he didn't respond. His eyes were closed, I couldn't open them. I was terrified.

Apolinário runs to the hammock where José is sleeping to ask for help, but he understands that his younger brother is dead. His body is cold and in rigor mortis. One of his legs is hanging out of the hammock. Apolinário painstakingly tries to put it back in. Then, looking around, something strikes him: there is no sign of damage in the ship's hold. Nor any trace of fire.

What to do, then, with a brother and brother-in-law in poor condition, and a third brother dead? Devastated by grief, Apolinário struggles against tears. The only able-bodied man on board now, he cannot hope for any help. To make matters worse, the tide was low again and he was forced to wait several hours before leaving the island. For more than eight hours, our woodcutter gnawed at his brakes. Around 2 pm, he managed to raise the anchor and returned to the mainland as best he could. It was a long and exhausting journey that he had to manage alone, whereas usually three men maneuvered the sails and held the rudder of this 12-meter long boat.

Our boatman finally reaches the port of Itaqui, in São Luís, in the late afternoon.
- God helped me," he said. Without his help, we would all be dead!

However, his ordeal is not over. Now, he has to walk 10 kilometers to inform the local police about the drama. And ask Pedrinho, his elder brother, to assist him.

First, Apolinário and Pedrinho took Firmino, who was the most burned, to the hospital in São Luís (he was in a coma for a week and stayed there for a month). Apolinário then went to the police station and reported the tragedy to the chief officer, José Argôlo, and to Commissioner Venceslau Vasconcelos. The policemen, accompanied by the soldier Orlando, go to *Maria Rosa* to assess the extent of the damage. They discover the corpse of Jose and the terrible wounds of Aureliano. The commissioner Venceslau Vasconcelos declared in an interview to the daily newspaper *O Estado do Maranhão* :

- As for the burns, they seemed to have been caused by a red-hot iron. However, this was not the case. It was really weird. I didn't see any signs of fire or fire starting on the ship.

Aureliano Alves, who was only injured, could hardly speak. And his look, we are told, was strange. Terrified.

Terrible wounds

According to the reports of the Forensic Institute of the Secretariat of Public Security of the State of Maranhão, the following was discovered

Firmino has second-degree burns, infected, with blackened edges, associated with edema. These wounds measure approximately 10 centimeters long and 6 centimeters wide. They are located on the thorax and the left arm covered with blisters on all its front face. The report of April 29, 1977 states that:

The young man was admitted to the hospital in a coma state. When he woke up, he had visual disturbances. Currently, the patient is drowsy, semiconscious, with decreased muscle tone and miosis - a decrease in pupil diameter - bilaterally.

Aureliano presented with severe pain in his right shoulder and left side. The report of May 2, 1977, mentions a second-degree infected burn, with blackened edges, 14 centimeters long by 2 centimeters wide, extending from the right scapulo-humeral joint to the posterior part of the deltoid region on the same side. A second infected burn, with blackened edges, 17 centimeters long by 2 centimeters wide, extends down from her left shoulder to the left side of her back. A second degree burn, also infected, was found on her right buttock.

As far as these two men are concerned, the *coroners* have decided that their burns were caused by "cosmic electricity". The diagnosis quickly became extremely controversial.

If the survivors suffered serious burns and long-lasting psychological consequences, **José Corrêa** died. The report of May 2, 1977, signed by doctors Raimundo Sergio de Brito Pereira and José Ribamar Miranda Filho, forensic doctors, states that

> Jose's body, dressed in black pants and red boxers, showed a rigor mortis. After removing his clothes, we found the absence of any type of external body injury (fracture, burns, etc.), except for a deviation of the right labial commissure. We conclude that Mr. José Corrêa died of a stroke caused by arterial hypertension, as a consequence of emotional shock.

No explanation is given for the hypothetical cause of the shock in question. And no autopsy can be performed on José's body. After being exposed to the sun for more than twenty-four hours, his body was in a state of advanced decomposition. He was quickly buried in the cemetery of São Raimundo in Anjo da Guarda.

A thick mystery and unanswered questions

Doctors and experts consult each other. They came to the following conclusion: it was lightning that caused the death and burns of these men. Following this declaration, a strong controversy broke out among the citizens. Newspapers, radio and television stations in São Luís were also indignant. For them, the cause is quite different. In fact, for some time now, strange flying "objects" have been seen in the skies of the Brazilian Northeast, many of which seem hostile. These "aggressive" UFOs, qualified as "vampires", are beginning to worry the population.

Dr. Carneiro Belfort, director of the forensic institute, is doubtful.

- I wanted to see Firmino," he explains, "because the papers said his injuries were caused by UFOs. I needed to verify this personally. I have never seen a UFO and I don't believe in their existence. The burns were characteristic of those inflicted by lightning, but I can't say that categorically. If not, I don't know what it could have been. This man told me that he saw "a fire" before he lost consciousness.

In Brazil, the term *fogo* (fire) is commonly used to describe a UFO. What did Firmino see and then confide in his delirium? Doctor José Oliveira, attached to the forensic institute, wonders in turn:

- Firmino had numerous second degree burns and could have died. In my opinion, lightning was responsible for this. However, if it had been lightning, the boat should have been damaged or burned. But it didn't. And the man who died should also have been burned.

Evoking the burn on Aureliano's buttock, Oliveira is surprised:

- If he had been struck by lightning, his clothes would have suffered the same fate!

However, his shorts were intact. This remains inexplicable.

The hypothesis of lightning is then challenged by sergeant Atenor Costa, meteorologist of the Brazilian Air Force at São Luís airport. And by Clésio Muniz, chief of criminal investigation of the Maranhão police. Indeed, the records of the weather station are formal: there were no thunderstorms or lightning between 5 pm on April 25, 1977 and 6 am on April 26, 1977. The night was therefore "clear and calm". Sergeant Costa goes further:

- There is no way that a lightning bolt could have fallen to the ground, hit the sand and then bounced off and gone sideways to hit the boat. This does not happen. If it had, then the lightning would have burned the canvas protecting the door. It would not have struck two or three men at the same time when they were far apart in the boat... Furthermore, it is simply impossible for lightning to burn two men and kill a third without leaving a mark on his body.

This is corroborated by Natalino Filho, director of the weather station:

- The lightning could have struck the water and then travelled the distance to the boat, as water is a good conductor of electricity. But, in this case, Apolinário should have been killed since he was lying on the ground closest to the water, and there were no burns on the boat. I inspected him personally. It is a hellish mystery.

This raises other questions, still unanswered. How do we explain the injuries to Firmino, whose arm muscles were so badly damaged that the fingers of his left hand remained chronically contracted? How to explain that the men woke up so late and in places where they had not been lying down? Firmino was found under Aureliano's hammock when he had settled at the front of the boat. And Aureliano was found in the place where Firmino had been lying down. However, the two men do not remember having changed places.

Moreover, adding mystery to mystery, Benedito Gonçalo Amarante, Apolinário's uncle, the first member of the family to learn of José's death, is said to have received a surprising confidence from his nephew. Apolinário told him that, at a certain time in the morning, our Brazilians had seen a strange light that had rushed under the rough curtain of the boat door. Then appeared an "enormous silhouette" that "extinguished" their consciousness. When the men woke up, they were injured. And the youngest of them was dead.

The police investigation

Subsequently, the 5ème Police District conducted a thorough investigation. Its men went to the island, inspected the boat, interviewed the survivors and then the actors of the tragedy - relatives, forensic doctors and carers. The following hypotheses were then excluded:
- consumption of alcohol or drugs,
- food poisoning,
- exposure to toxic gases,
- a dispute between men that resulted in a physical fight.

As a result, the police are unable to determine the causes of the tragic incident on Crab Island. This strongly annoys citizens and journalists.

A local newspaper launches the offensive by stating: "Our clear impression is that the modest police of Maranhão are not able to solve the mystery of the Crab Island. The daily *O Estado do Maranhão* drives the point home:

The thing seems so fantastic that some newspapers suggest that we do not have a police force in São Luís capable of dealing with beings from other planets. So, we have to qualify as "modest" a police structure that has serious difficulties to face some marginal facts from our own planet. So, when it comes to facts from other worlds...

It is more or less proven that strange devices that shoot light rays and are considered as "flying saucers" travel the sky of Brazil. The hypothesis is then emitted that the Island of the Crabs was attacked by one of these disks. And our police, who are only used to the heavy task of forbidding those played at full volume by our suburban transistors, late at night, on our own island, can only feel completely disarmed when faced with discs flying over another island long considered mysterious.

Why would these flying saucers, possibly piloted by superior and highly evolved beings, come here in order to torment the lives of poor fishermen? As if, here below, these men did not have their share of sufferings! Would these inhabitants of other worlds be more ignorant than the humble people of our planet?

To this day, the case remains controversial and the subject of much debate. It has never been known what injured two men and killed a third.

An amazing mental block

The famous ufologist Bob Pratt often visited Brazil, where he seriously investigated this case. He contacted Dr. Silviu Lago, a physician, professor of medicine and hypnotherapist, who had been practicing for 45 years. He asked him to subject our survivors to a regressive hypnosis session. The three men agreed to the experiment because they had all been suffering from depression since the tragedy. They hoped that such an experience could help them.

From December 14 to 17, 1978, Dr. Lago spent sixteen hours with the survivors. He concluded that the three men were telling the truth. But he was unable to get any clues about what happened that night.

- They can't remember any details of what happened to them after they went to bed," he observed. I'm not used to dealing with this kind of mental block. This is a very strange and complicated case.

A strange place

Among the islands of the Maranhão coast, the Crab Island is known for its many legends and fantastic stories. It is not recommended to walk there alone for fear of disappearing forever in the heart of its vegetation. It is said that one hears, at night, strange religious songs, evoking the lamentations of souls in pain. Occultists believe that the island shelters powerful spirits likely to offer protection to those who wish it. In short, for many residents, the island is an enchanted place, conducive to supernatural phenomena.

When, in 1977, Alvaro Martins, a journalist for the daily newspaper *O Liberal*, planned to go there to cover the strange incidents that were taking place there, the officials urged him not to. The day before his departure, he received a formal cancellation order: the São Luís air base did not want journalists in the region because, according to them, the island was home to a UFO outbreak... You can't make this up.

Sources

Jornal O Imparcial, April 29, 1977, April 30, 1977, 1ᵉʳ May 1977, May 14, 1977 - *O Estado do Maranhão*, São Luís, May 3, 1977, p. 3; May 4, 1977, p. 2; May 7, 1977, p. 4; May 13, 1977, p. 2; May 31, 1977, p. 2; June 7, 1977, p. 2 17-18 - Daniel Rebisso Giese, *Vampiros Extraterrestres na Amazônia*, Belém, 1991, pp. 129-137 - Bob Pratt, *UFO Danger*, Éditions Trajectoire, 2010, pp. 201-214 - *Top Secret* n°6, 2003, p. 25 - *UFO* n°98, Brazil, April 2004, p. 32 - Thiago Luiz Ticchetti, *UFO Contacts in Brazil*, Flying Disk France, 2021.

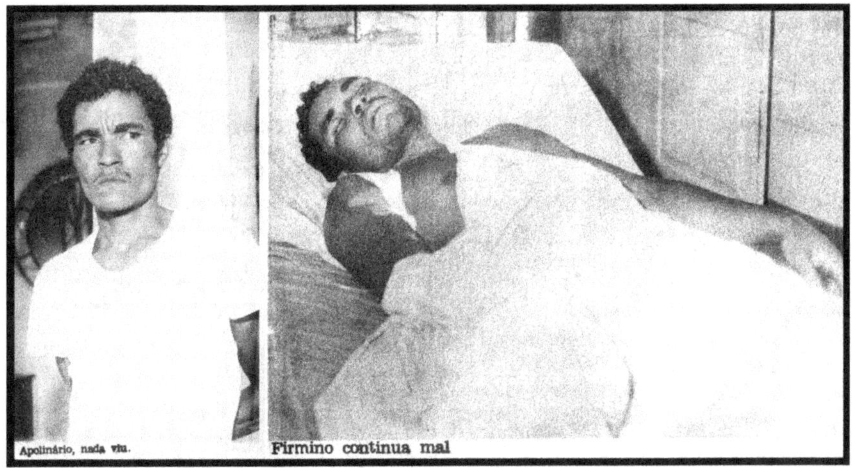

Apolinário Mendes Sousa, who saw nothing (left). Firmino in a coma (right).
(Jornal O Imparcial, May 1977)

An epidemic of offensive UFOs

Date: summer 1977.

Location: Northeast Brazil and a large part of the Amazon. In particular the village of Colares.

After the tragedy of the Island of the Crabs, an uninterrupted wave of UFOs perceived as offensive began all over the Brazilian Northeast and the Amazon. These *chupa-chupa*, as the natives call them, attack the villagers with green and red rays. And seem to draw their blood. They are, reports the local press, real airborne "vampires". The people affected by these rays then suffer from asthenia, burns, loss of reflexes and appetite, and some die. A secret report of the Air Force, published by the Brazilian magazine *UFO*, is precise on this point:

> The affected people suffer from what we can call a severe nervous crisis, for lack of a better name, crisis that in the great majority of cases results in partial or complete paralysis, voice extinction, chills, dizziness, intense heat, hoarseness, tachycardia, tremors, headaches with progressive swelling of the affected parts.

The UFOs appear mainly over small rural communities, located on the banks of the Amazonian rivers. The wave is so big that the mayor of Colares, an island belonging to the municipality of Vigia, sends an official letter to the headquarters of the 1er Regional Air Command (1er COMAR) in Belém to report that these strange devices are terrorizing the residents and fishermen, compromising their activities. The mayor urgently requests the help of the Brazilian Air Force. And while waiting for a military intervention, provides weapons to the villagers so they can defend themselves!

The local population, traumatized, spends its sleepless nights watching the sky. The men gather in the squares, bang on cans, shoot fireworks to try to keep the invaders away. Women and children run away, seeking refuge with their families in the interior of the continent. Soon, Colares is almost deserted.

What seemed to be only a collective hysteria will become so worrying that the Brazilian armed force ends up intervening. It lands on the scene in October 1977. Its confidential mission was led by Captain Hollanda, whose real name was Uyrangê Bolívar Soares Nogueira de Hollanda Lima. It was named *Operação PRATO* (Operation Plate). During the few months of their presence on the spot, the soldiers will be many times confronted with these hostile intruders. They will realize more than five hundred photographs of unidentified flying objects and more than sixteen hours of video images. They returned to their hierarchy a consequent report of two thousand pages, authenticating the most impressive wave of UFOs that Brazil has known.

In Colares, in July 1977, the 24-year-old doctor Wellaide Cecim Carvalho de Oliveira was confronted with astonishing symptoms. In charge of the Health Unit, she saw patients who said they had been "attacked" by flying, blood-sucking objects. They present burns on their face, throat and chest. As well as small atypical perforations within these burns. The patients are devoid of strength. And their blood tests show a very low hemoglobin level. The doctor will take care of eighty victims corresponding to this clinical picture. All of them suffer from severe anemia. And three of them will die.

A first woman - 72 years old - goes to the unit one morning. She was very agitated and said she had been attacked and burned by a *chupa-chupa*. She opened her blouse and showed a large red spot on her left breast with small punctures. The doctor tried to calm her down and prescribed 5 milligrams of diazepam, an anxiolytic of the benzodiazepine family. Her condition is worrying: the Brazilian can hardly raise her glass of water to drink. She has difficulty breathing, suffers from dizziness and feels weak. Three hours later, her condition deteriorated. She went into a deep coma, her body completely rigid, losing her breath. She had to be rushed to Belem to be hospitalized. Due to her rigidity, she was transported with her legs out of the vehicle. A few hours later, a death certificate issued by the Renato Chaves Forensic Institute announced that the unfortunate woman had died of cardiac arrest due to her injuries.

Wellaide Cecim Carvalho de Oliveira is then confronted with a second victim, a younger patient this time, aged 44. This Brazilian woman also suffers from hypertension. She has just been attacked at home by a ray of light that passed through her window. She died shortly after.

- However, the attacks affected more men than women, says the doctor, and more young adults than elderly people. Very few cases of children were recorded. None of them were under 10 years old. I didn't treat any very young or very old victims, as if there was a respect for these age groups. All the victims were thin and none were overweight or obese. All were brown or of Native American descent. No whites or blondes fell prey to these objects. In fact, there were only half a dozen on the island.

On the aggressions, Wellaide Cecim Carvalho de Oliveira has collected some information:

- The artifacts, often cylindrical in shape, reached an extreme degree of boldness when they began to emit their rays of light through the cracks of the island's wooden and adobe houses. The walls of these houses usually had no covering. The rays emitted by the UFOs penetrated through the smallest crevices with skill and purpose. To protect themselves, people filled these cracks with various papers, newspapers or magazines. They even filled the keyholes, that's to say the situation which reigned then ...[1]

Finally, concerning the phenomenon of *chupa-chupa*, the doctor puts forward a hypothesis:

- I have come to believe - regardless of who is flying these machines - that "they" were really desperate, to the point of doing everything they could to reach the victims. I don't know why, but I don't think their intent was purely and simply malicious. They obviously needed something that these people had... I think at that time

---

1. See the chapter that the author devotes to this affair in *Ovnis, les 12 dossiers que le Pentagone ne s'explique pas* (Max Milo, 2021).

there was a squadron of ships that were lost in the Amazon that were desperate for fuel or something to get back to their place of origin. Who are we, mere mortals, to know what fuel they used? Ours comes from alcohol or oil. But what about theirs? Does it not come from human beings? I think they took the life energy of people and turned it into something useful for them.

Sources

O Estado do Maranhão, São Luís, July 16 and 17, 1977, p. 1 - *UFO* n°101, Brazil, July 2004, pp. 8-26 - *UFO* n°116 and n°117, Brazil, November and December 2005 - *Nexus* n°83, November-December 2012, pp. 84-95 - Thiago Luiz Ticchetti, *UFO contacts in Brazil*, Flying Disk France, 2021.

Drawings of chupa-chupa made by the witnesses in the press of the time

UFO. Are we in danger? The black book of ufology

Second death on Crab Island

Date: April 30, 1986
Location: Crab Island, in the north east of Brazil.

Crab Island seems a dangerous place, haunted by a murderous force at work. On April 30, 1986, a second tragedy plunged the Brazilian Northeast into mourning with an air of déjà vu. Again, four men - Verissimo (21), Juvêncio (22), Anselmo and Lazaro (both in their 40s) - were sailing on a boat similar to the *Maria Rosa*. They landed on the island on April 28, 1986. They came to cut wood and worked hard for two days, cutting nearly 300 poles. As they went along, they stored them on the shore, ready to load them later on board.

April 30, 1986, 6:00 pm. The day's work is finally over. Exhausted, the men take a well-deserved break. 8 p.m.: the lumberjacks decide to eat. Juvêncio then starts to prepare the supper. At this moment, Verissimo says that he feels bad. He asks for a clove of garlic to rub on his arms. This, he thinks, should make him feel better, but Juvêncio is dizzy. He lost consciousness and collapsed on the deck of the boat. Immediately afterwards, Anselmo and Lazaro fainted as well.

1er May 1986, noon: Lazaro comes out of his torpor. He realizes that he remained unconscious eighteen hours, then he discovers, horrified, that Verissimo is dead. No trace is visible on the corpse of the young woodcutter. The only detail: a little blood has flowed from his mouth.

1er May 1986, 2 p.m.: Anselmo wakes up.

1er May 1986, 17 h: Juvêncio regains his senses, almost twenty-four hours after having collapsed. He notices then that the right side of his head is "as burned and swollen".

The three men, sick and shaken by nausea, wonder about the causes of the death of their comrade. But for the moment, it is necessary to leave quickly. Anselmo and Lazaro try to load poles in the boat. Deprived of strength, after having embarked less than 30 pieces, they decide to give up. They quickly weighed anchor. The return trip to São Luís was difficult. The men are in bad shape. They constantly feel like vomiting.

Upon arrival, the three witnesses were questioned by the port authorities. They are unable to answer. They keep repeating the same thing: they have fainted and are therefore not aware of anything. The port officials take their testimony seriously. But this case is quite a headache. Looking for an explanation, the agents first ruled out the hypothesis of food poisoning. Indeed, the four loggers did not eat anything before losing consciousness. It is also unlikely that they were poisoned by toxic gases emanating from the nearby marshes. The witnesses did not smell anything suspicious.

To find out more, an autopsy should be performed on Verissimo's corpse. Alas, he was badly decomposed. A doctor decreed that "emotional shock" was surely the cause of death and then, for the administration, wrote a death certificate, this time stating: "Cause undetermined".

Note that something unusual happened on the island that night. Between 6 and 8 p.m., the men heard a huge noise, like a crash among the nearby vegetation. It happened very close to them, in the dark. They will say:

- It was as if a large tree had fallen.

However, after verification, no large tree fell on the Crab Island. For the Brazilian ufologists and a part of the citizens, the case is heard. It is surely a *chupa-chupa* that landed there, injuring these men and killing the youngest of them. A neighbor of Juvêncio confided to the investigator Bob Pratt that, one night in 1983, while he was sailing on a small river between Alcântara and Itauna, close to the Island of the Crabs, a big luminous object descended from the sky and stopped directing a big light on the boat. He and his companions dived overboard and hid in the bushes of the shore. He added that several people on other boats in the area that year had similar experiences.

Last disturbing coincidence: Juvêncio and Verissimo (the deceased young man and brother-in-law of Juvêncio), were related, either by blood or by marriage, to the four men involved in the first incident of the Crab Island.

Since the tragedy, Juvêncio and Lazaro refuse to get back on a boat. And the port authorities (who have a similar role to our coast guard) have forbidden anyone to go to the island to collect wood. Until now, the ban, theoretically in effect for a long time, was not enforced. After this second tragedy, the authorities informed all boat owners in the harbor that no leniency would be granted from now on.

Sources

MUFON UFO Journal n°232, August 1987, p. 18 - Bob Pratt, *UFO Danger*, Trajectory, 2010, pp. 214-216.

UFO. Are we in danger? The black book of ufology

Tragic confrontation in Colombia

Date: July 4, 1969.

Location: *hacienda* Tocarema, on the border between the villages of Anolaima and Cachipay, Colombia.

This is without a doubt the most famous ufological case in Colombia. It all begins on a July evening with the family. We are 65 kilometers from Bogotá, in a beautiful hacienda where they grow blackberries and raise dairy cows. Arcesio Bermúdez, 54 years old, welcomes family and friends for the vacations. There are six children: Mauricio Gnecco (13), Enrique Osorio (12), Andrés Franco (13), Marina Franco (11), Rosita N. (10) and German N. (14). As well as five adults: Arcesio Bermúdez, his sister Lucrecia, Rosa Ortiz, the butler Luis Carbajal and his wife Evelia.

20 h 30. The night has fallen. Mauricio and Enrique linger outside. They scan the sky for shooting stars. As there is no electricity yet, the visibility is perfect. And the show is grandiose. At this time, the sky attracts all the glances because the mission Apollo 11, thanks to which the man should reach the Moon, is about to begin.

Suddenly, in the distance, Mauricio sees a yellow-orange light moving from east to west. It seemed strange to him. After a moment of surprise, the two boys call the family:

- Come, Aunt Rosa, Daddy and Mommy Garza (that's how Arcesio and his sister Lucrecia are called), come and see!

At first, no one moves. As Mauricio insists, children and adults finally go to the terrace. Indeed, what they discover is amazing. Each one gives his opinion. A meteorite? No, more like a plane.

- This light grew, Mauricio remembers. We were looking for the sound of an engine but nothing, it was totally silent.

A spherical "thing"

Mauricio then points his flashlight on this phenomenon which hovers at 180 meters of distance and sends signals in Morse code. And there, surprise: a kind of contact is established. As if answering to the young man, the object - because the thing is visibly solid - gets closer at a lightning speed, stops at 50 meters from our stunned witnesses, before stopping between two walnut trees, at 12 meters from the ground. Panic-stricken, Rosa Ortiz starts to shout:

- This thing will fall on us. Mauricio, turn off your lamp!

The "thing" is spherical in shape and measures between 1.50 meters and 2 meters in height. "Of the size of a car", it is of amber color and surrounded by a kind of luminous arc. The witnesses distinguish, in its lower part, two blue tripods with green ends.

The object plunges gently down to the valley. Mauricio, Enrique, Marina and Andrés climb up to a promontory behind the farmhouse to get a better view. While Arcesio Bermúdez - the only one who is not afraid - grabs the children's flashlight and heads resolutely towards the intruder below. Soon, we see him running through the blackberry fields. He wants to know for sure.

Strange and not very reassuring: the cows start to bellow and the dogs to bark. The chickens also make quite a racket, waving and cackling in concert. Moreover, a small monkey tied to a chain, is also struggling like a beautiful devil, jumping in all directions, terrified and trying to flee.

A traumatic encounter

Now, Arcesio Bermúdez stands in front of the UFO that has almost landed and does not cast any shadow. At 11 meters from the object, he calls the butler:

- Come on, Luis! he shouts. Come and see this martian!

Mauricio remembers:

- We stayed for four minutes watching Arcesio in front of the object. Then the object rose vertically 30 meters above our heads and, as you see in a science fiction movie, in a flash it went "fiiiit" and disappeared. Nothing and no one ever came down from that ship.

A few moments later, Clemente Bolivar and Rosalba Prieto, who live 3 kilometers away from the *hacienda*, see a strange yellow-orange light passing in the sky and moving slowly in the direction of Bogota.

At the farm, everyone is perplexed and quite shaken by what has just happened. The observation lasted a total of fourteen minutes. An uneasiness settles in and starts the beautiful carefree vacation. The children set up their mattresses in the living room. Because of the fright they have just experienced, they prefer to sleep together. Once in bed, they can't sleep a wink. They all keep quiet and wait in silence for the morning to leave the *hacienda* as soon as possible and forget.

At dawn, Mauricio's parents' car arrives at the farm to take the children back to Bogotá. Everyone gathers their things and prepares. When it was time to leave, Rosa Ortiz and the cousins called Arcesio Bermúdez to greet him and thank him for his hospitality. It is Lucrecia, his sister, who answers: Arcesio is bedridden, sick. He says that he has shivers and feels very weak.

A tragic end

After his face to face with the UFO, Arcesio Bermúdez is not well. He does not leave his bed, complains of being deprived of strength and of being cold all the time. He is however a solid man and until then in full health. The villagers know him well as a very nice man with a big moustache and his eternal rubber boots. But now, nothing goes right. In a few days, his condition deteriorates. His temperature drops to 35°C. This hypothermia is accompanied by "black vomiting" and diarrhea with blood flow. He was taken to Bogotá.

There, on July 12, at 11:00 a.m., he was examined by Dr. Luis Borda. Then, at 7:30 pm, by Doctor Cesar Esmeral. His state does not stop getting worse. And Arcesio Bermúdez died the same evening, at quarter to midnight. The two doctors were not informed of his strange experience with a UFO.

Physician's reports

Regarding this July 12, Dr. Luis Borda noted the following:

> I was called by the family at 9 am. I arrived at 11 am and found Arcesio Bermúdez suffering from vomiting and diarrhea. His pulse was almost imperceptible. His face was pale. I administered 2 centigrams of emetine because his liver was inflamed. I also gave him a heart tonic (drops of a preparation containing digitalis extract). I returned in the evening at 6:00 p.m., and found her condition worsening. I could not find her pulse and her temperature was below normal. I suspected an attack of gastroenteritis.

For his part, Dr. Cesar Esmeral recorded these observations:

The victim's temperature dropped to 35°C. The cardiopulmonary system presented: pericarditis, asphyxia, cough, chest tightness, slow pulse. The digestive system was affected: bloody diarrhea, black vomit, dry mouth, painful abdomen, especially on the right side. Mental faculties and nervous system: normal. The skin was dry, pale, cold and dehydrated.

Equally confusing is the testimony of María Cristina, his niece:

When he was pricked, pure crystals sprang up from his skin and fell on the bed. His blood was like crystallized and frozen.

Gastroenteritis is the third leading cause of death in the country, so it is accepted as the final diagnosis. Arcesio can be buried.

The survey

July 16: John Simhon - investigator of the Colombian branch of APRO - went to the *hacienda*. He talks with the witnesses and asks the children to draw what they saw. At 8:00 p.m., he is joined by Dr. Luis E. Martinez Garcia, from the National University of Colombia, who subjected four of the children to a regressive hypnosis session, performed at the request of the children's relatives. Their separate stories fit together perfectly.

July 17: John Simhon is joined by Elías Nessim, second investigator of APRO. The two men searched the site of the sighting but did not find any suspicious traces. They question Luis Carbajal. This one declares that Arcesio Bermúdez called him to observe the UFO. Unfortunately, he saw the object only from far, when it moved away between the trees. Surprising detail: arrived at proximity, Arcesio would have confided that the object suddenly went out. He would then have seen a character inside. The upper half of the entity was human. But from the waist down, its anatomy resembled the letter "A" and was luminous.

The case is getting out of control

The Colombian press enters in game. For them, the object seen at the *hacienda* Tocarema came from another world! The daily *El Tiempo* headlines: "A strange

UFO. Are we in danger? The black book of ufology

object was seen in Anolaima, which looked like a flying saucer". *El Espectador* is more direct: "13 people saw flying saucers in Anolaima".

For the locals, however, it was the *gaucha*, a light emitted by the spirits, that killed the unfortunate man. It is said that the *hacienda* was built on a once sacred site, the temple of an indigenous chief. Under the house is said to be an altar made of human skulls... and a treasure.

The hypothesis of a gastroenteritis, considered more realistic than a UFO or hypothetical vengeful spirits, nevertheless raises questions. And does not convince the investigators of the APRO. Lucrecia Bermúdez is almost sure of it:

- It's probably this thing that landed on the farm that's responsible!" she says.

An autopsy is no longer possible because Arcesio was not embalmed before being buried. Dr. Luis Borda, who signed the death certificate, is also going back on his conclusions. He now regrets that he did not perform other tests while the patient was still alive. Or immediately after his death. He doubts, he says, because "Arcesio's medical records show that he was a perfectly healthy man and had never suffered from gastroenteritis before.

Many speculations arise as to the cause of Arcesio's death. His clothes and wristwatch were sent to the Colombian Institute of Nuclear Affairs (CINA). The experts found no trace of radiation. However, CINA informs the investigators, unofficially, that Arcesio's symptoms are similar to those caused by a lethal dose of gamma rays.

In order to obtain further professional advice, APRO contacted two specialists. The first was Dr. Horace C. Dudley, professor of radiation physics at the University of Illinois Medical Center in Chicago, who stated that "Mr. Bermúdez's illness and death may indeed have been caused by a radiation effect. But unfortunately we have no laboratory data to support such a conclusion... Without a complete autopsy and a serious pathological study, a doctor cannot advance such a precise cause of death."

The second is Dr. Benjamin Sawyer, APRO's consultant in medicine, who states:

> The symptoms of common enteritis are almost identical to any of the three forms of intestinal disturbance due to radiation exposure. It is therefore very difficult to differentiate between them. We have nothing specific in the medical report to indicate whether the death was related to enteritis or radiation.

Conclusion: The thorough investigation carried out by APRO has not been able to determine the exact cause of death of Arcesio Bermúdez.

The body is gone!

A final twist: six years later, the body of Arcesio Bermúdez must be exhumed so that his remains can be transferred to an ossuary. This is a common practice in Colombia. Some family members are present. When the coffin is opened, the surprise is great. It is empty. The body has disappeared! (This will be confirmed again in 2002 by Gustavo Bermúdez, his nephew).

At the central cemetery, no one can provide an explanation for this disappearance. Obviously, the craziest theories are circulating. For some, it was NASA that stole the body. For others, aliens came to retrieve the body... In short, nothing really factual.

The only lead the family could get? Some men would have given money to an old gravedigger to allow them to take the corpse and transport it to France! It is not known who these people were or how much credence to give to this rumor. Alan Murdie, from the British magazine *Fortean Times*, concluded: "Arcesio Bermúdez then inherited a new posthumous distinction. He in effect became the first abductee UFO witness after his death!"

And today...

Since that summer of 1969, many waters have flowed in the *rivers of* the country. Mauricio Gnecco is a 65 year old man. He sometimes returns to the *hacienda* Tocarema where they now cultivate aromatic plants. He admits that his youth was difficult. He was bullied by his teachers and colleagues who called him "the boy who sees UFOs". But after studying mechanical engineering, things finally calmed down. Now respected, he works as an expert in renewable energy.

Even today, for Mauricio, Arcesio's death can be explained by the waves and radiation emitted by the luminous object. And maybe such an exposure has awakened a sleeping evil. For him, these waves "that agitate every molecule of the body, can trigger unsuspected reactions."

- Of course, he admits, there are people who will never believe this story. They'll say it's impossible, that it's imagination, fantasy or whatever. But everyone has a right to their own bouts of skepticism. This event is unusual, I agree. But it was a UFO that we saw that day, not a plane. It was totally silent. And if it killed, it was by accident. As far as I am concerned, this object never intended to harm Arcesio.

Sources

El Espectador, July 17, 1969 - *El Tiempo*, July 18 and 20, 1969 - *The APRO Bulletin*, July-August 1969, pp. 1 and 4-5 - *The APRO Bulletin*, September-October 1969, pp. 4-5 - *UFO-NYT*, March-April 1970, pp. 61-64 - Jim and Coral E. Lorenzen, *Encounters With UFO Occupants*, Berkley, 1976 - *Lo inexplicado*, vol. VI, n°70, 1983, pp. 1379-1380 - Jacques Vallée, *Confrontations*, Robert Laffont, 1990, pp. 165-167 - Anne Canadeo, *UFOs The Fact or Fiction Files*, Walker & Company, 1990, pp. 59-61 - John A. Keel, *Operation Trojan Horse*, IllumiNet Press, 1996, p. 271 - Lynn Picknett, *The Mammoth Book Of UFOs*, Carroll & Graf, 2001, p. 98 - *Fortean Times* #160, August 2002, article *Spirit In The Sky*, p. 40 - Iker Jiménez, *La noche del miedo*, Edaf, 2004, pp. 95 and 96 - José Antonio Caravaca, *UFOs, las 50 majores evidencias*, Cydonia, 2017, evidence 27: *La muerte de Acersio Bermúdez*, pp. 190-194 - *El OUNI de Anolaima*, comic book by Julio César R.

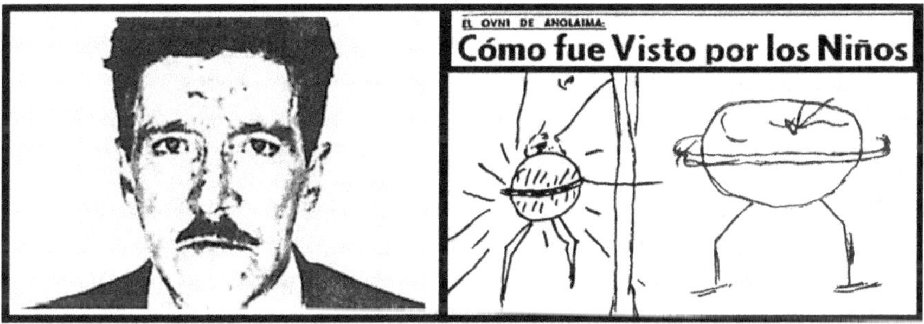

Arcesio Bermúdez (left). The UFO drawn by the children (right).

A green and fatal ray

Date: August 13, 1967.

Location: *fazenda* (farm) Santa Maria, between Crixas and Pilar de Goias, in the state of Goias, on the borders of Mato Grosso, Brazil.

Inácio de Souza, 41, is married to Maria and has five children. This simple, illiterate man has been employed for the past six years as an agricultural servant on the Santa Maria *fazenda*, a farm of several thousand hectares that includes a landing strip for the private plane of the owner, el senhor Ibiracy de Moraes. Important fact: Inácio de Souza has never heard of "flying saucers". However, it seems that he will have a tragic confrontation with one of them.

A buzz of bees

August 13, 1967, 4 pm. Returning on foot from a nearby village where they had done some shopping, Inácio and Maria returned home. Close to their home, they noticed "a strange object in the shape of a bowl with a downward opening", and even more surprisingly, between the object and the house, there were three strangers.

- Maria and I were returning from Crixas," says Inácio de Souza. The beings were already there. At first I thought they were people who had come to visit us. But, very quickly, I was frightened by the strange plane they had, which was sitting on the road. It looked like an overturned bowl, about 35 meters in diameter. The beings had the same appearance as us, except that they were completely bald. When we saw them, they were playing, frolicking like children but in silence. When they saw us, they pointed at me and started running in our direction. I shouted to my wife to run back to the house and take cover. I thought they wanted to attack us. I got scared and, since I had my .44 rifle, I shot the nearest one. Immediately a green ray of light shot out of the overturned bowl as if from a lantern, hitting me in the chest on the left side. I fell to the ground. Maria rushed to me and picked up the rifle. The beings returned to their craft, which rose vertically, then left at high speed, with a slight noise, similar to the buzzing of bees.

Three days later, Ibiracy de Moraes, a wealthy owner of the *fazenda* and former director of the Bank of Brazil, visited the de Souza couple.

- I arrived at the farm three days after the event," he says, "and I didn't know anything about what had happened. When I got off the plane, Inácio de Souza's wife was waiting for me and told me that her husband was sick. I was surprised, because her husband was a strong and healthy man, and this was the first time he had been in bed. I went to his bedside and asked him energetically, "What's wrong, boy?" He

---

said, "Boss, I killed a man!" Surprised, I asked him, "But how is that possible?" He then told me in detail what happened.

Trusting his tenant farmer, the owner leads his own investigation. First, he examined the landing site to see if there were any traces of the craft. He does not find anything. Inácio de Souza is convinced that the intruders are men from São Paulo who have come to kidnap his family. Ibiracy de Moraes, aware of stories of "flying saucers" in the country, avoids talking about it. Another disturbing detail is that Inácio de Souza claims to have "aimed at the intruder's head". It is unimaginable that the farmer, an excellent marksman, could have missed a target at a distance of 60 meters. However, no trace of blood is visible at the scene of the encounter. The mystery thickens.

The boss tries to find out more about these strange individuals. According to Inácio de Souza, they were naked; according to his wife, they were wearing "a kind of sticky shirt of a faded yellow". Impossible to distinguish their sexual organs, undoubtedly masked by their clothes.

Alarming symptoms

During the two days following the meeting, Inácio de Souza suffered from tremors, nausea, tingling and numbness of his whole body. The boss decided to take him to Goiânia, more than 300 kilometers away, to see a doctor. He advised him not to tell anyone about his unbelievable misadventure.

In Goiânia, the doctor noticed a burn on the left side of Inácio de Souza's trunk, almost at shoulder height. It is circular and measures about 15 centimeters in diameter. The doctor applied an ointment called "picrato de butambeno", a local anesthetic indicated in these cases. Regarding the other symptoms, the practitioner believes that they are the result of poisoning due to the consumption of toxic herbs. Given the complexity of the case and the misdiagnosis, the boss decides to reveal to the doctor what really happened that day at the *fazenda* Santa Maria. Inácio is then subjected to a battery of complete examinations (blood, urine, feces...).

After four days of observation, he was sent home and the verdict was in: he was lost! Indeed, Inácio de Souza suffers from a lightning leukemia. At the most, he has only two months to live. Inácio de Souza suggests not to reveal what happened to him. He has a name to preserve, he explains, and this would only cause unwanted panic. Between astonishment and skepticism, the doctor, overwhelmed by such a story, decides:

- I have heard nothing and I know nothing. I have a reputation, too, and in my eyes, his case is nothing more than leukemia!

A tragic end

According to his wife's account, Inácio de Souza's health deteriorated rapidly. He was in horrible pain. His body was covered with yellow and whitish spots, "the size of a fingernail". He lost an alarming amount of weight. At the time of his death, he had only skin on his bones.

Inácio de Souza died on October 11, 1967, 59 days after that fateful meeting. He had demanded that, after his death, his mattress, his bed and all his personal belongings be burned. His wishes were respected.

The GGIOANI (*Grupo Gaúcho de Investigaçao de Objetos Aéreos Nao Identificados*), a civil association of ufological research from Porto Alegre, has carried out a serious investigation on this most disturbing Brazilian case. Dr. Machado Carrión and Jader U. Pereira, president and secretary of GGIOANI, publicly revealed the strange aggression suffered by Inácio de Souza, as well as his tragic end. Unfortunately, despite its gravity, the case did not generate any official reaction.

Attempts to explain

According to Professor Felipe Machado Carrión:

> Inácio de Souza presented the classic symptoms of leukemia of radioactive origin. From the moment he was hit by a green light beam, his health was altered, and he began to present all the symptoms characteristic of exposure to deadly ionizing radiation... The part of the human body where the first physical signs of an irradiation dose appear is the skin, and there is an irritation similar to that caused by a burn. In the case of Inácio de Souza, a burn was clearly visible in the area affected by the light

UFO. Are we in danger? The black book of ufology

beam. According to the clinical picture defined by the *British Medical Research Council*, a state of nausea is one of the classic and acute symptoms of irradiation, and it is usual that this symptom disappears after two or three days, exactly as in Inácio de Souza's case. In those exposed to radiation, small hemorrhages of the skin can be observed, followed by the appearance of subcutaneous vesicles that produce very painful ulcerations. Other symptoms that can appear in those exposed to a beam of radiations, and that Inácio de Souza also presented, are a sensation of tingling and numbness of the irradiated regions, accompanied by tremors and cardiac dysrhythmia... So all the symptoms presented by Inácio de Souza were those of a leukemia caused by a strong dose of radiations.

Others believe that, although the clinical picture presented by Inácio may well be that of leukemia, it is likely that it had already been declared. He would have then lived a hallucinatory episode, provoked by his declining health. His boss of 6 years does not believe it. He describes Inácio de Souza as a "robust, healthy man, never bedridden". Moreover, the theory of a hallucination also seems to be contradicted by Maria's account, which is consistent with her husband's. Some have suggested that Maria did not see anything but, out of duty and loyalty, validated her husband's strange account. This hypothesis raises two questions. If the witness was indeed already suffering, could the process of his illness have been accelerated by a dose of radioactivity received on this occasion? And would such a sick man, on that day, have been able to go shopping on foot?

As usual, the most skeptical have postulated that this scenario was elaborated by the couple, looking for a hypothetical desire for publicity... or looking to be transported to the nearest hospital, located several hundred kilometers away. Again, the owner of the farm is very doubtful.

There remains the possibility that Inácio and Maria de Souza lived what they tell us, even if it is a serious challenge to reason. The only certainty is that no one knows what caused the sudden death of Inácio de Suza.

Similar facts

The de Souza case is related to three other tragic events. According to the Brazilian press and the *National Enquirer* tabloid of December 29, 1981, it took place in the vicinity of the small town of Parnarama, also in Brazil.

In the night of October 17, 1981, Ribamar Ferreira and Abel Boro, two hunters, see in the sky a kind of giant and luminous "tire of truck". This light is so intense that it "changes the night into day". This strange object that turns on itself focuses on Abel Boro and soon surrounds him with a glittering light. Ribamar Ferreira flees and warns at once the family of his friend. In delegation, and of return on the scene, they discover, horrified, that Abel died without apparent lesions. His body, as if bloodless, is completely white.

Two days later, on October 19, while hunting at night, Raimundo Souza and Anastacio Barbosa, are posted in Parnarama when they see a disc coming down from the sky. The object shines a light beam on them. Raimundo grabs his rifle and shoots the intruder. Anastacio, him, hides among the vegetation whereas the disc turns above their heads. He manages to flee and returns to his home. But, without news of his comrade, he decides to leave to seek him and ends up finding him, covered with purple spots, suffering from fractures and bruises. Raimundo dies a few hours later, without having regained consciousness.

In December, in the same township, Dionizio General was on top of a hill with a sidekick, Jose dos Santos. Suddenly, the two men see a strange craft hovering over them. Dionizio is then touched by a light beam, emitted by the disc, which he will describe as "a big ray of fire". According to Jose dos Santos, Dionizio General seems shocked and rolls down the hill. The three following days, the unhappy man remains as mad of terror... then dies.

The region around Parnarama is extremely wild and inhospitable. The local inhabitants live in precarious conditions, most of them without electricity. The few roads and paths that lead there are hardly passable and not paved. There are no modern means of access. This probably explains why the Brazilian authorities let two months pass before going to the site and investigating. Afterwards, they refused to reveal the results of their investigations.

Sources

Correio do Povo, Porto Alegre, December 22, 1968 - Report by Professor Felipe Machado Carrión, January 30, 1969 - *Phénomènes Spatiaux* n°19, March 1969, pp.

24-28 - *Flying Saucer Review*, vol. 15, n°2, March-April 1969, pp. 13-14 - *The APRO Bulletin*, March-April 1969, pp. 1 and 5 - *2001*, Argentine magazine, year 1, n°10, May 1969, pp. 22-24 - *Saucers, Space & Science* n°55, 1969, p. 16 - *Stendek* n°3, December 1970, pp. 25-26 - *Inforespace* n°12, 1973, pp. 38-41 - Jacques Lob et Robert Gigi, *OVNI, Dimension autre*, Dargaud, 1975, pp. 19-22 - *Historia*, Hors série n°46, 1976, pp. 77-78 - Jim and Coral E. Lorenzen, *Encounters with UFO Occupants*, Berkley, 1976, p. 169 - R. Jack Perrin, *Le mystère des OVNI*, J'ai Lu, 1978, pp. 112-121 - *Lo inexplicado*, vol. 6, n° 65, 1981, pp. 1279-1280 - Antonio Ribera, *Encuentros con humanoides*, Planeta, 1982, pp. 132-136 - *MUFON UFO Journal* n°299, March 1993, p. 5 - Lynn Picknett, *The Mammoth Book of UFOs*, Carroll and Graf, 2001, pp. 91-92 - *UFO* n°98, April 2004, Brazil, p. 29 - *TOP Secret* n°46, December 2009-January 2010, p. 19

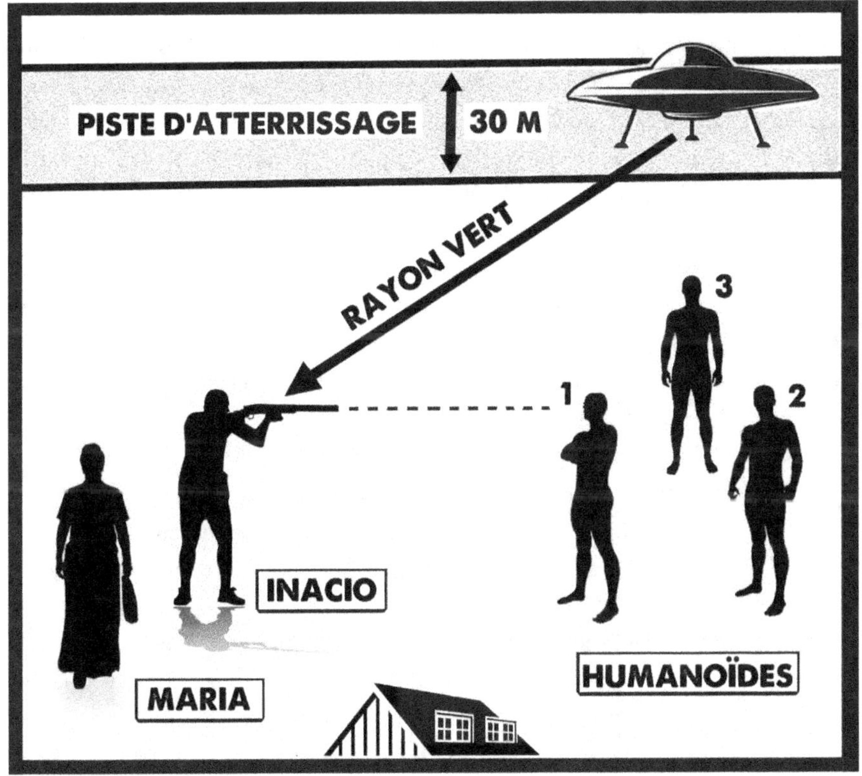

Reconstruction of the drama by the author

Atrocious death in Brazil

Date: March 4, 1946.

Location: Town of Araçariguama, about 70 kilometers from São Paulo, in southeastern Brazil.

João Prestes Filho is a 44 year old married man. He is both a farmer and a merchant. He is a healthy man with a robust constitution and is much loved by his family. Luiz Veronezzi Prestes, one of his nephews, remembers:

- Uncle João did not drink. He was an excellent person. I remember him walking in Santana de Parnaíba. He liked to wear a hat and boots, unlike uncle Lazinho who walked only barefoot.

In 1946, life in Araçariguama was rather harsh. There was no electricity, no telephone, no sewage system. The only luxury was a single transistor radio, around which, on certain evenings, the villagers gathered to watch the *Campeonato paulista de futebol* (the São Paulo soccer championship). The work in the fields is exhausting, especially since no one owns a plow. The land is still worked with a hoe. Moreover, the explosion of two atomic bombs in Hiroshima and Nagasaki had a lasting effect on everyone's morale. The fear of a nuclear apocalypse due to these weapons of a new kind hovers in every home, however humble and isolated.

On March 4, while waiting for the end of the world, it is Mardi Gras and Carnival day in the village. João Prestes Filho, who does not appreciate these festivities, decides to go fishing with his friend Salvador dos Santos, 39 years old. He tells his wife, Silvina Nunes Prestes, that he might be late.

- You, in the meantime, go to the Carnival with the children! he suggests.

Then he gathered his belongings, hitched up his cart and left the Água Podre neighborhood where he lived, to go to the banks of the Tietê River, about 2 kilometers away. At that time, the river was extremely full of fish. The hours glide slowly on the dull and quiet waters of the *river*. On the way back, the friends separated at a fork in the road, each going home. João Prestes Filho finds the house empty. He begins by putting away his cart and driving the horse into the corral. Then he decides to enter his house through the window that opens from the outside. At that very moment, a ray of light from the sky fell on him and enveloped him! In an instant, everything lights up. With his hands, João Prestes Filho tries to protect his eyes and head. But he collapses heavily, without losing consciousness. He feels his body burning, especially his face and the sparse hairs of his beard. Terrorized, succeeding as well as possible to get up, he leaves to seek help by running, barefoot, through the dirt roads. He covers 2 kilometers and ends up in Araçariguama. There, he goes to Maria, his sister. Haggard, finding with difficulty his words, he tries to tell her what he has just lived. Barely able to stand up, he ends up asking to go to bed.

As João, with an altered voice, begged: "Help me, help me!", the news quickly spread around the village. Several people crowded around him: his sister, neighbors Jonas de Souza, Guilherme da Silva (both merchants) and João Gennari (real estate agent). The municipal delegate João Malaquias was informed of the facts and rushed to the bedside of the unfortunate man.

- What happened?" he asks, worried.

- What attacked me is not of this world, informs it, for lack of better, João Prestes Filho. It is an invisible thing!

A terrifying spectre

We contact Araci Gomide who, that day, is in the village at Sebastião, one of his relatives. Araci is a friend of the Prestes family. He is the tax inspector of the municipality of São Roque and the treasurer of the municipality of Araçariguama, but he was a nurse in the armed forces. You never know, it might help.

Rushing to João's bedside, and seeing in what state the unfortunate man is, Araci asks him who dared to burn him with boiling water. João, perfectly lucid, answers:

- No one.

He claims that he was not burned and that he has no idea what happened.

Araci notices that his friend's hair, eyes and clothes (short-sleeved shirt unbuttoned on the chest, pants rolled up to the calves) are intact and do not show any abnormalities. What had happened to the patient, whose eyes dilated with fright and whose interrupted voice suggested the worst?

Araci bends down, sniffs the body of the recumbent. He doesn't perceive any smell of burning or fuel such as kerosene or alcohol. Then the scene turns to horror. João's flesh takes on a nightmarish appearance. They look like beef cooked for long hours in boiling water. Slowly, they start to detach from the bones. The sight is unbearable. They fall off in pieces "from the jaw, chest, arms, hands, fingers, lower legs, feet and toes. Some fragments still remain attached to the tendons. And the process of "decomposition" intensifies. The teeth and bones of the unfortunate man are exposed. People are stirring around him. We don't know what to do. They offered him water, which he refused energetically. What surprises the audience the most is that, while his body is falling apart, João does not feel any pain.

It's all so terrible that the relatives hardly dare to look. And then his nose and ears fall off and roll down the sheets to the floor. The unfortunate man is now a terrifying spectre that is falling apart. On his skinned face, we can only see his eyes wide with terror. He tries in vain to speak. His words are only guttural complaints, choked by a mouth that is distorted, disarticulated. To try one last time to communicate, he moves his head with extreme difficulty. At the end of his strength, he ends up standing still.

He was then taken to the hospital of the city of Santana de Parnaíba, the closest health unit. The unfortunate man was wrapped in his own sheets and loaded onto a cart. But the road was very bad, and they got stuck in the ruts, struggling to make progress. João Prestes Filho died on the way, before he could get help.

Undetermined cause

No explanation seems satisfactory to explain the ordeal and the horrible agony of the witness. The cause of death indicated on his death certificate is: "burns". Brazilian investigators were able to obtain a copy of the document, on January 13, 1998, through Luzia Anastácio da Silva, notary of Santana de Parnaíba. In the document, the death was certified by Dr. Luiz Caligiuri, who stated that João Prestes Filho died of "cardiac insufficiency and generalized burns to the 1er and 2ème degrees" (death certificate no. 2397, p. 79 of the death register C-014).

After visiting the scene, the technical police of São Paulo concluded that lightning was responsible for the death of João. Unlikely. Because, if this had been the case, the whole body should have been burned. However, we know from many witnesses that only the face and hands of the victim had reddened, as if fried. His hair and clothes were not damaged in any way. In addition, according to Professor Felipe Machado Carrion, who worked on this case, the weather on March 4, 1946, under a light and uniform mist, was not stormy but serene, therefore unsuitable for the formation of lightning.

In addition, the agents found that in the house, except for João Prestes Filho, nothing had been burned, not even the chair on which he had been sitting. They found an extinguished lamp filled with kerosene. Therefore, it was not the cause of the tragedy. The experts from Osasco, Barueri and Santana de Parnaíba did not find any trace or evidence indicating a crime or a domestic accident. João Prestes Filho was a peaceful and well-liked person. Nobody had a reason to kill him.

For their part, the investigators Fernando Grossmann and Luiz Jesus Braga Cavalcanti de Araújo concluded that the victim had not been burned by a flame from conventional fuels (kerosene, gasoline, firewood, fuel) nor by a very hot liquid (boiling water, spilled soups or other compounds thrown aggressively). In his last moments, João Prestes Filho, himself, kept repeating that no one should be accused or blamed because this thing was not of this world.

Funny objects, funny lights

In the country, for a long time, strange phenomena have been observed in the sky. These lights and singular objects terrorize the population. These phenomena are called *Boitatá, Mãe d'ouro* (the golden mother) or *Lagartão* (the lizard, because in many rural areas of Brazil, the expression refers to a light that stretches out, taking the shape of a lizard or a dragon).

João Prestes Filho had to deal with these phenomena. In his youth, still living with his father, he was a cowherd. One afternoon, while he was driving his herd on a high hill, he saw a luminous ball falling from the sky. The ball passed so close to him that it almost touched him, as he stood near the gate of a chapel where there was a cross. Then other balls appeared, in groups, up to twelve. These balls were reddish and the size of a full moon.

The brother of the witness, Emiliano Prestes, was also confronted with the *Boitatá* behind the cemetery of Ibaté. The entity manifested itself in the form of two "balls of fire" that went, came and collided. These fires approached Emiliano and began to surround him. Fear made him kneel down and pray.

In Araçariguama and in all the surroundings, a lot of people see these lights. We don't know where they come from or what they are. But, while being suspicious of them, they talk about them openly. Since it was 1946, the term "flying saucer" (which, as we all know, was born from the observation of an American civilian pilot, Kenneth Arnold, in July 1947) was still unknown. The term *"objecto" is* used instead to evoke the astonishing "objects" that we see dancing in the sky and that sometimes accompany these lights.

Born in 1927, Hermes da Fonseca, an expert in local history and folklore, recalls:

> On August 24, 1955, exactly one year after the suicide of President Getúlio Vargas, many people saw an unknown object. I know this because I was among them. They were working on the construction of the cable car of the Santa Rita cement factory, later property of *Votorantim*, located in Amador Bueno Street, near Itapevi. There were gondolas there transporting stones from the Araçariguama dam. It was a warm day and the sky was blue. Suddenly, at about 11:15, we saw a shiny aluminum dish-shaped object. It spun around and left behind a white circle of smoke. We all stopped working to look at it - even the foreman, who didn't like to see his employees standing still and scattered like that! Then, at about 12:10, five or six jets arrived, probably from the Brazilian Air Force. And in a few seconds, the thing just vanished into thin air. The next day, the newspapers reported the appearance, in Osasco, of a very strange object.

Nelsom de Oliveira, 53 years old, gravedigger of the Araçariguama cemetery since 1976, also testified:

> I have never seen a ghost. However, about 8 years ago, I saw an aluminum-colored object, shaped like a round hat. It was flying high above the cemetery. It was going in a straight line while swaying very slowly and reflecting the sunlight. It looked like a round hat, but with the brim up.

According to the informative bulletin of APEX (a Brazilian ufological association), published in 1975:

> If we let our imagination run wild, we could suppose a source of intense thermal energy, without flame, falling directly on the victim and lasting only a short time, since its effect was stopped, at least as far as we can evaluate it, by the clothes of the unfortunate person. The image of the atomic bomb

on the cities of Hiroshima and Nagasaki at the end of the Second World War immediately comes to mind. Outside the epicenter where everything is destroyed, the physical damage, i.e. the immediate, not the delayed damage, consists of burns caused by a terrible heat wave. This physical agent is however often stopped by a simple obstacle. It then burns everything that is located towards the epicenter and preserves what is on the other side. One can also think of a "burning light", which would limit its action to living cells, sparing the dead cells, in this case the clothes and hair of the victim, and which would not reach the living cells left in the shade. But all this is only speculation based on the report of a single witness... We are therefore left with only uncertainty as a certainty.

One last disturbing detail: according to a report published by the Brazilian newspaper *Notícias Populares* on October 23, 1972, the French government requested the skeleton of João Prestes Filho for analysis. Astonishing, isn't it?

Sources

Phénomènes Spatiaux n°30, December 1971, pp. 19-22 - *Stendek* n°13, June 1973, Barcelona, pp. 23-27 - Antonio Las Heras, *Informe sobre los visitantes extraterrestres y sus naves voladoras*, Rodolfo Alonso, 1974, Buenos Aires, pp. 115-123 - *Bulletin Informatif de l'APEX,* São Paulo, January-April 1975, year 1, n°2 and n°3, pp. 5-10. - *La Revue des soucoupes volantes* n°2, 1977, p. 33 - R. Jack Perrin, *Le Mystère des OVNI*, J'ai Lu, 1978, pp. 122-129 - Antonio Ribera, *Encuentros con humanoides*, Planeta, 1982, pp. 136-143 - Jacques Vallée, *Confrontations*, Robert Laffont, 1990, pp. 158-159 - *Reporte OVNI* n°41, February 1995, p. 22 - Cláudio Tsuyoshi Suenaga, *A Dialética do Real e do Imaginário: Uma Proposta de Interpretação do Fenômeno OVNI*, thesis presented in 1999 at the University of São Paulo, Faculty of Sciences and Letters, History Department, pp. 104-112 - Timothy Good, *Contacts Extraterrestres*, Presses du Châtelet, 1999, pp. 51-53 - José Antonio Caravaca, *UFOs, las 50 majores evidencias*, Cydonia, 2017, evidence 26 *"João Prestes, abrasado para un UFO"*, pp. 187-189.

IX. The Mothman
or the man-phalene

The report of the American Defense submitted in April 2022 to the magazine *The Sun*, evokes, among the phenomena related to UFOs, the occasional appearance of "entities" singular, as "resulting from our myths and legends". Here is an unavoidable example.

In 1966, the town of Point Pleasant in the United States was the scene of supernatural events that terrorized the population and had a tragic outcome. The inhabitants of the place saw in the sky many mysterious aerial objects. And a strange winged creature: the moth man.

This "monster" was said to be more than 2 meters long. It had disturbing red eyes and a pair of wings with a wingspan of 3 meters. This terrible event chilled America as it unfolded, day after day, the ingredients of a horror movie with a dark prophecy as its backdrop. Here is how, in spite of all logic, the intrusion of the fantastic and the paranormal made a small town with no history fall into both insanity and grief. And it is all the more impressive because it is 100% authentic...

The story that follows could have been conceived by Edgar Allan Poe or Stephen King. It contains enough chills and darkness to be one of those cruel tales that one likes to read at night. But that doesn't help you sleep.

Virginia's sky

West Virginia is a state located in the northeastern United States. This mountainous and rural territory is bordered by Pennsylvania, Kentucky and Ohio. It is one of the wildest areas in the eastern United States. The population maps of pre-Columbian America are clear: the native tribes were spread throughout the United States. Even the inhospitable deserts of the Far West were occupied. Strangely, only one place on these maps is marked "uninhabited": West Virginia. A few centuries later, many communities still live there in some isolation.

In 1966, the Virginia sky was the scene of strange apparitions. Balls of fire, luminous spheres, disc-shaped objects, and stars with erratic trajectories were regularly observed by local people. These witnesses are circumspect and, fearing ridicule, prefer to remain silent. They are unaware that an event to come, of a fortuitous excess, will soon untie tongues...

In a cemetery

It all seems to begin on November 12, 1966, in a small cemetery near the town of Clendenin. The day is ending and the evening falls coldly on the line of crosses and wreaths with faded flowers. Kenneth Duncan, head gravedigger, assisted by four of his employees, is digging a grave for his father-in-law, Homer Smith, who died the previous Sunday. While the five workers are at work, a strange brown creature, half man, half bird, emerges from a nearby clump of trees, dives at a dizzying pace over the workers and passes, without a flutter of its wings, over their heads, so close that Kenneth Duncan has time to observe it.

- It was scary," he said later. She just walked by, within shouting distance. I saw her for a good minute. Then it was gone. It wasn't a bird. It looked like a man with a pair of wings.

Source
Charleston Gazette, November 18, 1966.

Headstone of Homer Smith

In Salem, a dog goes missing

On November 14, 1966, the hills of Salem, West Virginia are dark. Newell Partridge is sitting quietly in his home. He is watching TV. And it is then that this creature, which one starts to speak about in the country, will appear. Here is the testimony of the person concerned, reported by the press at the time.

> It must have been 10:30 p.m. when suddenly the screen of my television set went black. A kind of shape, like fish bones, appeared on the screen. At the same second, the TV started to emit a shrill noise, very violent, which went very high in the treble before going down again, like a scale where one goes from the highest to the lowest. It repeated itself. It was like an electric generator... Suddenly, on the porch, Bandit, my dog, a large German shepherd, started to whimper. I grabbed my flashlight and went outside.

The dog was sitting at the end of the porch, howling toward the hay barn, which is way over there in the back. I shone my lamp in that direction and lit up two red circles - two eyes that looked like bicycle reflectors. There was something in those eyes that is hard to explain.

When I was a kid, I used to go hunting at night all the time. I know exactly what the eyes of animals look like in the dark: a badger, a cat or a dog in the dark. But these eyes were much bigger. There is almost the length of a soccer field between the house and the barn, 150 meters at least. And yet, at that distance, those eyes were huge!

As soon as the beam of my lamp lit up those eyes, Bandit snarled, his hair bristling. And he rushed at them. I was seized by a cold chill. I was seized by an absolute fright that prevented me from following my dog. I rushed home and locked my door. That night I slept with a loaded rifle beside my bed.

The next morning, I went looking for my dog. I went to the barn, looking for tracks. Here and there I could see Bandit's footprints. They were easy to see because he is a massive dog and the ground was muddy.

Where the eyes had stood, Bandit's tracks drew a circle, as if the dog had chased his tail, which he never did. There was nothing else. The tracks were not going in any other direction. They just went in a circle. You could clearly see the dog's footprints as he ran from the house to the barn. Then they stopped there, in that circle. And nothing else.

That night, I lost my dog. Bandit just vanished. I never saw him again. Yet, for the past three years, he never left the house for more than fifteen minutes. My son who is 6 years old is inconsolable.

The most difficult thing to express is the feeling you get. I've never felt anything like that before. It's like you know something is wrong, but you can't figure out what...

Source

Williamson Daily News, November 18, 1966.

Newell Partridge (left).
Bandit now has his effigy at ufological meetings (right).

Point Pleasant and the TNT Zone

A graveyard, a dog that disappears and a strange creature that doesn't match anything known: everything is there to lead to a thrill. But this is only a preamble. And this strange creature - an enigma for scientists, whether biologists or ornithologists - seems to have chosen to settle in a small, previously quiet town called Point Pleasant.

In 1966, Point Pleasant is a town of 5,000 inhabitants, located on the Ohio River. There are a lot of factories and a fairly qualified workforce. The population was mainly rural and very religious. There are 22 churches in Point Pleasant for 5,000 inhabitants. That's saying a lot. And not a single bar!

During World War II, explosives were manufactured in Point Pleasant. About ten miles outside of town, the military had set up an area that is still known today as the TNT Zone. Within this area, the military had dug miles of underground tunnels connecting buildings and manufacturing facilities during the war. It had also built more than a hundred "igloos" in the fields and woods: huge concrete domes with heavy steel doors. This is where the explosives were stored. After the war, the explosives were shipped elsewhere. The factories were dismantled, the "igloos" emptied and sealed with concrete blocks. The TNT area became a meeting place for walkers and motocross enthusiasts. The wooded areas, denser and bathed in shade, are now home to lovers.

It is there, in this TNT Zone, that most of the encounters with the winged creature are concentrated. Unpredictable, they will strike fear into the city, then the State, then the Union.

A disused igloo where explosives were once stored

A hypnotic encounter

The first face-off takes place on November 15, 1966 at 11:30 pm. Two young couples from Point Pleasant drive through the TNT Zone in their 1957 Chevrolet.

There is Roger Scarberry, 18, and his wife Linda. And Steve Mallette, 20, and his wife Mary. There aren't many distractions in Point Pleasant. So, to liven up their weekend, these newlyweds have found a new hobby: they "burn rubber" on the deserted and winding roads of the former military zone.

Exhausted by the speed, they finally decide, by mutual agreement, to make a stop. They park in front of the old abandoned power station. Everything is silent. The pale moon reflects in the half-glazed windows of the building. Suddenly Steve Mallette shouts:

- I saw eyes! Right there! And it was scary!

- Me too!" confirms Roger Scarberry. It was as if they were staring at me. As if they wanted to see inside me. Or through me.

He would later confide:

- I couldn't take my eyes off of them. It was as if they had a hypnotic power. They were of an unusual color: red and bright. They were about 5 centimeters in diameter and 15 centimeters apart.

Both worried and intrigued, the witnesses try to distinguish what's behind those fluorescent eyes. Not easy in the dark. And yet, here they are, moving, moving. And our walkers, mouths agape, discover that they belong to a monstrous biped.

The creature has the shape of a man, but bigger. It measures between 2.20 meters and 2.50 meters in height. It has two large wings attached to its back. And it seems to flee from the light.

Steve Mallette recalls:

- This thing was trying to run. It was waddling along with its wings pointing backwards. It staggered like a crippled chicken. It disappeared as it slid behind the building.

- Let's get out of here!" yells Steve in a panic.

The four hikers rush back to the Chevrolet and start off at full speed. Roger is at the wheel. He mashes the gas pedal and heads for Highway 62.

Phew, safe! At least that's what they think. But the nightmare begins again. The young people, stunned, see again, on the side of the road, this creature which seems to wait for them. As they pass by, it spreads its gigantic wings, the wings of a bat, and rises into the air.

- My God, she's following us!" screams Mary, prostrate in the back seat.

- We were doing 160 km/h," recalls Roger. And this strange bird stayed at our level. It didn't even flap its wings.

- I could hear the noise he was making," says Mary. It squeaked like a huge mouse.

This creature escorts our horrified witnesses to the city limits. A hellish chase. Then it disappears, as if it wanted to avoid the lights of Point Pleasant.

The witnesses then storm into the local police station. They stammer their story to the deputy sheriff, Millard Halstead.

- I've known these kids since they were born," the officer said later. They never caused any trouble. That night, they were really scared to death. I took their story very seriously.

The press relays the incident

The very next day, the sheriff organizes a press conference. The journalists of the area seize the case.

On November 16, 1966, *The Athens Messenger*, the local daily newspaper, reported that a "red-eyed, winged thing chased two Point Pleasant couples across the countryside." The paper triggered a cascade of articles.

Winged, Red-Eyed 'Thing' Chases Point Couples Across Countryside

By MARY HYRE
Point Pleasant Correspondent

POINT PLEASANT — What stands six feet tall, has wings, two big red eyes six inches apart and glides along behind an auto at 100 miles an hour?

Don't know? Well, neither do four Point Pleasant residents who were chased by a weird "man-like thing" Tuesday night.

Two young Mason County married couples today told of being chased by the "strange creature" around midnight Tuesday.

Mr. and Mrs. Steve Mallette, 3505 Jackson Ave., and Mr. and Mrs. Roger Scarberry, 809½ 30th St., described their hair-raising experiences, which began in the TNT area.

The two couples were riding in a car and as the auto crested a hill, an object loomed in front of them. The object was in the form of a man, about six feet tall with wings on its back.

Becoming frightened, the couples drove away. As they approached a traffic circle near

Meteor Shower Due In Skies Tonight

CAMBRIDGE, Mass. (AP) — A meteor shower after midnight tonight may produce one of the most spectacular sky shows in more than a century.

The Leonid meteors may flash through the skies about 2 a.m. (EST), toward the east and a little south. Weather, however, could obscure the show.

FIVE DAY FORECAST
Temperatures Thursday through Monday will average 4-8 degrees above normal. Representative normal highs and lows: Cleveland 47-31, Columbus 49-31, Cincinnati 51-35. Not much temperature change until weekend, when it should turn cooler. Precipitation will total .1 to .3 inch as rain or showers about end of week.

Route 62, they said the thing loomed in front of the car again.

Mallette, 20, said they drove toward Point Pleasant on Route 62 at 100 miles an hour, with the strange creature drifting along behind the car.

The couples said the thing seemed to avoid lights. When they turned into the C. C. Lewis farm, the creature was again in front of the car. What appeared to be a large dead dog was lying on the road.

Later, the couples and police returned to the farm, but the dog had vanished. Deputy Sheriff Millard Halstead searched the TNT area. The deputy said the "thing" was gone, but he found "a strange pile of dust."

Scarberry, 18, said, "Believe me if you ever saw it, you'd be a believer." The men said they might go looking for the thing tonight, but indicated they were afraid they might find it.

"The Athens Messenger, November 16, 1966

The newlyweds' misadventure later made the front page of the *Pacific Stars And Stripes*, a daily newspaper published for American soldiers serving overseas. The November 19, 1966 edition confirmed that a red-eyed creature had recently been spotted in West Virginia. And it's spreading terror.

The *Athens Messenger* of November 18, 1966 delivers the most detailed report of this mysterious encounter. It also publishes a photo of the witnesses. The paper is entitled: *"The Monster is no joke to those who see it."* We learn that Linda Scarberry, very shocked, had to be medically treated. That the creature that emerged from the darkness was terrifying. And that its spread wings reached 3 meters of amplitude.

Roger Scarberry then sketched a sketch of the winged creature. A sketch, which has become a classic of its kind, will be reproduced many times in books dealing with ufology or cryptozoology.

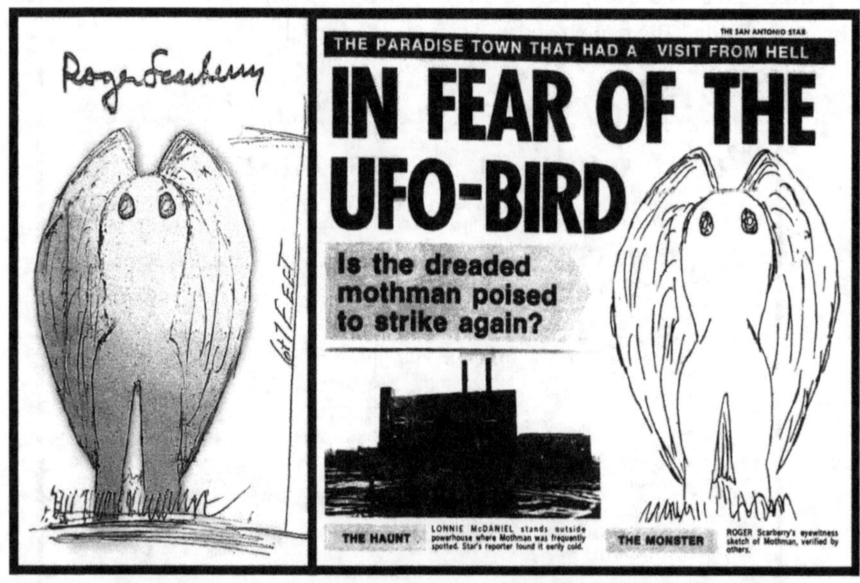

Original drawing by Roger Scarberry (left). San Antonio Express, February 16, 1975 (right)

   UFO. Are we in danger? The black book of ufology

A funny name

The following night, the citizens get organized. To try to find this monster, armed to the teeth, they organize a hunt in the TNT zone. Alas, without result.

Although the creature cannot be spotted in the military zone, it is now on the front pages of the country's newspapers. The press has named it Mothman, the man-phalen, after the superhero of the Batman comics. And this man-phalen is going to be talked about again...

A trying face-off

On Friday, November 16, at 9:00 p.m., Marcella Bennett drives into the TNT Zone with her brother, Raymond Wamsley, and sister-in-law, Cathy Wamsley. They had decided to visit a couple of friends, the Thomases, who reside in the former military zone, among the disused "igloos. Having heard about the strange Mothman the night before, the guests decide to play a little joke on the Thomases: they want to surprise and frighten them by knocking on the windows. Alas, that evening, the Thomas couple were absent. At home, there are only their three children: Rickie, Connie and Vickie. The visitors decided to go back to their car and turn around.

Marcella is walking slowly because she is holding her 2 year old daughter Tina in her arms. As she approaches the vehicle she freezes. Indeed, a huge black figure - "bigger than a man" - with red eyes has just appeared from the back of the car. It stands up in front of her. And slowly unfolding its large wings, this thing stares at Marcella who suffocates with horror.

It is a chilling apparition. Raymond and Cathy also see it and cannot believe their eyes. Giving in to panic, the trio runs to take refuge at the Thomas! But in her haste, Marcella stumbles, drops her daughter on the gravel driveway and falls heavily on her.

- I thought I had killed her," she said later.

Unable to get up, her knees and hands bleeding, Marcella remains on the ground, facing this nightmare creature. As if petrified, she is then deprived of will.

- She was as if in a trance, her brother confided to the investigators.

After the shock, Marcella Bennett gets up with difficulty, recovers her daughter who has started to cry and manages to take refuge in the house as best she can.

Inside, it is the panic! Everyone is terrified, especially as the frightening creature steps onto the porch and tries to push open the front door! Then it starts to scrutinize, with its fluorescent eyes, the interior of the room.

Raymond was very upset and managed to call the police. Fifteen minutes later, when the officers arrived, the "thing" was gone. It seemed to have vanished into thin air.

This trying face-to-face meeting will not be without damage for Marcella Bennett. Traumatized by this encounter, she will consult a doctor once a week for several months. Haunted by the Mothman, she will see him constantly in her dreams and will be convinced that he follows her, always on the lookout, and that he regularly turns around her house.

The mystery thickens

Marcella Bennett is not the only one in this case. Practically all the witnesses who were confronted with the Mothman kept terrible after-effects. Some hear strange sounds in their homes. Their telephone rings without there being anybody at the end. Or metallic voices, almost inhuman, spout endless lists of numbers. Others tell of paranormal experiences. Objects move or fall off their shelves by themselves. Not to mention the frequent visits of strange characters, dressed in black, driving in old Cadillacs, who threaten the witnesses if they tell what they have seen...

We see, in fact, the arrival in Point Pleasant of these famous *men in black* that we often find in the ufological press. These funny agents, often clumsy, with a robotic voice, would have visibly a goal: to prevent the general public from accessing knowledge concerning UFOs. Their repeated visits, rich in threats, will make the inhabitants of Point Pleasant say:

- Their presence frightened us so much that we locked our door, whereas before, we never locked it!

It must be said that most of the witnesses in Point Pleasant feel spied upon, oppressed, uneasy. They sense that something terrible is about to happen. It's an inexplicable feeling, one that seems unfounded, yet often grips them to the point of dizziness. For them, it is almost palpable: a dark threat hovers over the city.

                                          UFO. Are we in danger? The black book of ufology

The birth of a legend

If the citizens are doing badly, the Mothman is doing quite well. America, at the same time perplexed and subjugated, adopts him and makes him a star. He thus joins, in the pantheon of mysterious creatures, the Yeti, the Bigfoot, the Dogman and the Chupacabra. A brotherhood of frightening cryptids.

He is now listed, sketched and passes, in a few days, from anonymity to posterity. He inspires painters, graphic artists and illustrators. And the sculptors, competing of audacity, shape clay and bronze to breathe some life into him.

Mothman sculptures by Jean St. Jean, 2018 (left)
and Brad Painter (right)

The Mothman strikes again

In Point Pleasant, sightings are increasing.

- On November 18, 1966, Captains Paul Yoder and Benjamin Enochs, volunteer firemen, saw the red-eyed monster.

- On November 25, 1966, Thomas Ury, a 35-year-old shoe salesman, was driving his convertible on Route 62, near the old TNT factory. He saw a large gray human form on the side of the road.

- Suddenly," he says, "this shape spread a pair of wings and took off vertically, like a helicopter. It started flying over my convertible, circling, even when I was doing 120 km/h. It was incredible. I was too terrified to go to work that day. The being had a wingspan of at least 3 meters. It could have been a bird, but I have never seen one like it. I was afraid that it would come down on me! Nothing about it was normal. Something was wrong. I know this may not make sense, but it's the only way to put into words what I felt.

- On Sunday, November 27, Connie Carpenter, an 18-year-old college student, was driving home from church when she spotted a huge creature on the side of the road, spreading its wings, speeding toward her car, brushing against her windshield and making a sharp turn before disappearing. After this encounter, Connie suffers from conjunctivitis. For two weeks, her eyes are red, swollen and painful. The young woman is the only witness to have seen the Mothman's face clearly.

- It was horrible," she said. It looked like something out of a science fiction movie.

- On December 4, 1966, at 3:00 p.m., Everett Wedge, a well-respected pilot working at the Gallipolis airport, saw a huge bird flying across the sky with three friends. This strange creature was flying at over 110 km/h without flapping its wings. The witness stated:

- This thing was so big that it could have grabbed me and taken me away. And you with it. Yes, it was that big. I've spent a lot of time here, I've never seen a bird that big. Believe me, I've seen it. Now my eyesight has gone down, but back then I had perfect vision.

A stray bird?

The above is only a part of the testimonies noted at the time. Faced with the numerous sightings, experts are trying to provide a rational explanation for this frenzy that is shaking the country. They wish to answer the question that everyone is asking: what is this creature that we see in the TNT Zone?

Duane Pursley, a biologist at the University of Virginia, believes that the Mothman is a large sandhill crane (*Grus canadensis*) that may have strayed during its last migration. A second biologist, Dr. Robert L. Smith, shares this opinion. But the witnesses who were presented with photos of the bird in question are formal. The creature that haunts the TNT Zone looks nothing like this reassuring wader.

In 2002, Joe Nickell, an avowed skeptic, offered his analysis:

> A popular legend in the Point Pleasant area holds that the Mothman was the creation of a prankster. Supposedly, a local man dressed in a Halloween costume... But this local legend is not credible. Detailed reports show that the original Mothman sightings were no hoax. The reflective nature of the creature's eyes is telling. As birders know, the eyes of some birds glow bright red at night when caught in car headlights or illuminated by a flashlight. Because of the Mothman's squeaky call, "funny little head," and other characteristics, including its presence near barns and abandoned buildings, I identified it as an owl: the barn owl.

In other words, a small raptor of 35 centimeters which would fly without flapping its wings and would sometimes stand upright, on the lookout at the side of the roads, to chase cars? Everyone will judge.

Sources

The Herald Dispatch, November 22, 1966 - *Spokane Daily Chronicles*, November 24, 1966 - Joe Nickell, "Mothman Solved!", *in: Skeptical Inquirer*, vol. 26, no. 2, March-April 2002 - Joe Nickell, *"Mothman Revisited: Investigating on Site,"* in: *Skeptical Briefs*, vol. 12.4, December 2, 2002.

The investigation and UFOs

That's when a character from New York enters the scene. Journalist, fiction writer and ufologist, his name is John A. Keel. Intrigued by this story of a red-eyed monster, he decides to go without delay to Point Pleasant to investigate.

On the spot, he befriends Mary Hyre, one of the most influential journalists in the city. The two of them will do a lot of work by re-interviewing witnesses, making an inventory and verifying all the cases. Almost compulsive, John Keel spends his time filling in the pages of his notebooks. These can be consulted today and are a mine of information concerning the Mothman case. We learn in particular that, on November 1er, a national guard saw the creature perched in a tree. At first he thought it was a deer hunter on the prowl, but then he didn't tell anyone about it.

Untiring, assisted by Mary Hyre, John Keel tracks down the smallest detail. And having amassed a substantial amount of material, he ended up writing a book on the events of Point Pleasant entitled *The Mothman Prophecies* (French title: *La Prophétie des ombres*). This book is now considered a classic among the plethora of essays devoted to ufology. It inspired the film of the same name, directed in 2002 by Mark Pellington, with Richard Gere and Laura Linney in the main roles.

At the time John Keel was writing his book, he noted:

> On my first visit to Point Pleasant in December 1966, I was very surprised that no local newspaper reported any UFO sightings. However, it turns out that a lot of people have seen them. I was able to find this out in just a few hours and by meeting several witnesses with Mary Hyre.
> Following this, an article summarizing all these testimonies was published. Suddenly, a dam seemed to break: a multitude of witnesses came forward, from the simple farmer to the local notable.
> Clearly, a major wave of UFO sightings had hit the area and was ignored by the local press, as witnesses were afraid to speak out. But as soon as the door opened, UFO fever spread throughout the region. And since then, Mary Hyre has received up to 20 sightings a day.

John Keel holding a cast of the Mothman (source: Internet)

Ultraterrestrial omens

For John Keel, there is no doubt: this creature with night wings is an epiphenomenon linked to UFO sightings. His book develops the following thesis: UFOs and their curious ambassador, the Mothman, are semiophores, that is to say signs induced by an invisible reality that surrounds us. It is less a question of extraterrestrials than of "ultraterrestrials", a manipulative intelligence that has been with us for a long time. And which plays, for us, the role of an omen!

One might think that to make his book more appetizing, John Keel adds mystery to mystery. And yet...

He himself, who is often in Point Pleasant, who sees - with Mary Hyre - strange objects in the sky during nights of vigil... He himself, who frequents the witnesses and ends up sharing their worries, seems to be won over by a dull anguish.

On November 3, 1967, he sent a letter to Mary Hyre that leaves one wondering. A letter on yellow peel paper that says:

> Mary, I have good reason to suspect that a disaster is about to strike Point Pleasant. It won't be these mysterious UFOs that will be the direct cause. Rather, it will be a building, a facility on the riverfront that may explode or burn. Maybe even the Navy center that is located in town. There may be a large number of casualties. If this happens, let me know immediately. Report it to the press in the normal way. And don't say a word to anyone about what I just told you!

The river... the victims... Mary Hyre also has terrible nightmares. She dreams that wrapped gift packages float on the grey and icy waters of the river.

The drama

On December 15, 1967, thirteen months after the appearance of the Mothman, just over a month after this letter from John Keel, an unprecedented disaster struck the town of Point Pleasant.

It's 5:05 p.m. The Silver Bridge, a suspension bridge built in 1928 to connect Point Pleasant, West Virginia, to Gallipolis, Ohio, is jammed with traffic. It's rush hour. Citizens are hurrying. Many are on their way to do their Christmas shopping. Suddenly, the bridge collapses. A truck driver who narrowly escaped tells us:

- The bridge didn't fall into the river right away. It began to undulate like a snake. Then it buckled. And lots of cars, sliding down its sides, plunged into the river.

In total, 31 vehicles were thrown into the icy waters. And 46 people drowned.

This tragedy shakes America to its core. And soon, the idea circulated that the presence of the Mothman in Point Pleasant was a harbinger of this tragedy. Strangely enough, after the bridge collapsed, no one in Virginia saw the disturbing creature again. And the paranormal phenomena will abruptly cease.

Sources

Point Pleasant Register, December 16, 1967 - *Charleston Daily Mail,* December 16, 1967.

UFO. Are we in danger? The black book of ufology

An unprecedented tragedy: the collapse of the Silver Bridge (period sources)

The Mothman today

Since then, the Mothman seems to have become more relaxed. The consumerist appetite of our societies has declined into various goods: toys for children or refreshing beer for adults.

In 2003, the town of Point Pleasant celebrated him by erecting a huge statue of 3.50 meters made by the sculptor Bob Roach. A museum is dedicated to him. And the municipality organizes every year the Mothman Festival.

Despite this late recognition, the mystery remains. Who was he really? Where did he come from? What did he want? Was he the "Angel of the Weird" dear to Edgar Allan Poe? An ordinary bird of prey? Or was he a dark messenger, bearing a lightning message, weaving dark omens into a shroud for a city?

Sources

The APRO Bulletin, November-December 1966, p. 10 - *Flying Saucer Review,* vol. 14, no. 4, July-August 1968, pp. 7-14 - *Saga,* vol. 37, no. 1, October 1968, pp. 34-37 and 67 - Gray Barker, *The Silver Bridge,* Clarksburg, 1970 (the first reference book) - *UFOLOGEN* no. 12, November-December 1973, pp. 2-6 - *High Times,* no. 57, May 1980, pp. 42-45 and 75 (mothman illustrates cover) - *Awareness,* vol. 13, n°4, season 1984-1985, pp. 20-22 - Jerome Clark, *Unexplained!,* Visible Ink Press, 1999, pp. 474-481 - John Keel, *The Prophecy of Shadows,* J'ai Lu, 2002 (indispensable!) - *Fortean Times* n°156, March 2002, pp. 26-48 (the mothman illustrates the cover) - Donnie Sergent Jr. and Jeff Wamsley, *Mothman: The Facts Behind The Legend,* Mark

S. Phillips 2002 - Jeff Wamsley, *Mothman: Behind the Red Eyes*, Mothman Press, 2005 - Q. L. Pearce, *Mysterious Encounters: Mothman*, Kidhaven Press, 2010 - Ken Gerhard, *Encounters With Flying Humanoids*, Lllewellyn Publications, 2013, pp. 101-134 - Loren Coleman, *Mothman, Evil Incarnate*, Cosimo, 2019.

Left: Motman statue erected in Point Pleasant. Right: Mothman beer

X. Oanis, these UFOs that get wet!

To conclude, sticking to the current events, let us consider the recent about-face of the US Navy concerning the reality of UFOs.

On May 17, 2022, the U.S. Navy declared it had unresolved files on "400 unidentified aerial phenomena"! Scott Bray - Deputy Director of Intelligence for the U.S. Navy - stated that an "ever-increasing number" of mysterious objects have been reported at sea "since the early 2000s.

Certainly troubling confidences, evoking in particular a file that ufologists and amateurs of mysteries of the sky know for a long time: that of the Oanis or Unidentified Aquatic Objects.

What is an oani?

In the introduction to his superb book, *Dans le sillage des monstres marins*, Bernard Heuvelmans wrote *:*

> I have denounced the imperfection and the fragmentary character of our knowledge of the continents, on which, however, it seems that men can circulate without too much difficulty. Our ignorance of the marine world is even greater. It is such that, I do not hesitate to affirm it, EVERYTHING is still possible in the ocean.

And how! Some sailors tell of having seen "a wheel of light", like a spitting sun, dancing on the waves. Others, from the shores of a lake or from a pier, claim to have seen, in a geyser of foam, an "object" spouting from the lace of the waves.

When we thought we had a grasp of the UFO phenomenon, we realize that we are missing the essential. Many objects enter and leave lakes, swamps or oceans. They seem to be able to go underwater and to move with great ease. They are usually seen by a contingent of people sailing on the water (fishermen, sailors, boaters), moving underwater (submariners) or flying over the water (pilots). Some are also detected by sonar.

They are commonly called oanis or osnis (Unidentified Submersible Objects). Many ufologists believe that UFOs and UFOs refer to the same phenomenon: "objects" capable of flying at unprecedented speeds while possessing intriguing amphibious properties. This sounds like science fiction. However, the oceans cover 71% of the surface of our planet. They have an average depth of 3800 meters. 5% of their liquid immensity is known to humans. No doubt about it: water - this ubiquitous chemical compound - still holds many mysteries.

The oani of Christopher Columbus

Going back in time is a source of wonder and surprise. But not without risks: is the chronicle of yesteryear safe? Men have always interpreted reality according to their codes, their knowledge and their culture. In the past, the capricious nature revealed itself between prodigies and diableries. And the epic style of the writers of then does not arrange anything to our business.

However, it is tempting to think that one of the first oani sightings may have been on October 11, 1492. On that day, aboard the *Santa María*, at 10 p.m., Admiral Cristóbal Colón, standing on the deck, saw a strange light emerging from the water.

According to his logbook (partially transcribed by Columbus' second son and by the Dominican priest Bartolomé de las Casas), this kind of light "like a wax chain, rises and falls." It looks like the flame of a large candle. Fearing that he was being deceived by an illusion of his senses, Columbus immediately summoned Pedro Gutierrez, gentleman of the King's chamber. He confirmed the presence of a light that seemed to rise from the surface of the water and then strangely rise into the sky. Is it an unexplained maritime phenomenon? Or is it an indication of human activity, since we are getting closer to land?

Four hours later, the three ships (*the Niña*, the *Pinta* and the *Santa María*) anchored on the coast of Guanahani Island, in the Bahamas. History would have it that Christopher Columbus had just "discovered" America. The term is rather abusive. Can one only "discover" a land already populated?

UFO. Are we in danger? The black book of ufology

Sources

Don M. F. De Navarrete, *Relations des quatre voyages entrepris par Christophe Colomb*, t. 2, Treuttel et Würtz 1828, pp. 38-39 - Michel Bougard, *La Chronique des OVNI*, Jean-Pierre Delarge, 1977, p. 77

The oanis of Charles Fort

Charles Fort (1874-1932) is the first researcher to have studied the oanis. Surveyor of mysteries, tireless seller of miracles, he spent his life tracking down all the strange events rejected or mocked by science. He drew up meticulous inventories of them. Thus, in the *Book of the Damned* (1919), he listed a large number of "cursed" facts, inexplicable for the experts of the time. Among them, two singular observations of oanis. He writes:

> On June 18, 1845, on board the brigantine *Victoria*, 1300 kilometers from Adalie, in Asia Minor, at 36° 40' 56" N. lat. by 13° 44' 36" long. E., three luminous bodies were seen coming out of the ocean at 40 meters from the ship and remaining visible for ten minutes. Professor Baden-Powell published a letter from a correspondent in Mount Lebanon which described the same wonder but only mentioned two luminous bodies five times larger than the moon, and with appendages "in the form of sails" resembling large flags inflated by the breeze.

To the scientists concluding that it was most probably a meteor, Charles Fort pointed out that "a meteor is only visible for a few seconds, rarely more, although some have reached half a minute", certainly not ten minutes! Second case of oani reported by Charles Fort:

> I will borrow my first data from *Science*, a Puritan publication, which has provided us with little material: Puritans rarely go wild. According to a report to the Washington Hydrographic Office (California branch), at midnight on February 24, 1885, at 37° N. lat. and 170° long. E., somewhere between Yokohama and Victoria, the captain of the *Innerwich* was awakened by his mate, who had seen something unusual in the sky. In the time it takes to wake up (it can take a long time), the captain went to the deck of the ship and saw the sky on fire. "Suddenly a large flaming mass appeared above the ship, completely blinding the spectators," and fell into the sea. Its size can

be estimated from the volume of water it raised, which rushed over the ship with a deafening noise, submerging it "under a white and roaring foam". The captain, an old and experienced sailor, declared that the horror of the spectacle defied description.

Sources

Science, vol. 5, n°11, March 20, 1885, pp. 242 and 243 - Charles Fort, *Le Livre des Damnés,* Éric Losfeld, 1967, pp. 212-213.

A fireball comes out of the sea

Masses of fire swirling, plunging or emerging from the sea? It seems inconceivable. However, it is not the first time that sailors describe this kind of apparition. By searching the chronicle, we discover that on November 12, 1887, at midnight, sailors of the English *steamer Siberian* (which was cruising off Cape Race, near Newfoundland) saw a huge ball of fire rise from the sea and approach the ship while moving against the wind. It rose to an altitude of about 15 meters and finally moved away and disappeared after five minutes.

A month later, the very serious magazine *Science* reported this observation. This case of "aquatic strangeness" obviously raises questions. What was the nature of the glowing phenomenon? How can a fireball emerge from the water? And can flames move against the wind? The acronym oani - Unidentified Aquatic Object - fits perfectly to this observation.

Sources

Science, vol. 10, no. 256, December 30, 1887, p. 324 - *Amazing Stories,* November 1947, 4ème cover.

An oani covered with scales

Beginning of the xxe century. Men of science dare to take a more pragmatic look at the blue of the oceans. But, in front of the marine singularities, the explanations are still tinged with old superstitions. The thousand-year-old terrors of divers and sailors of the past still surface. The Kraken is never far away, unleashing its tentacles.

UFO. Are we in danger? The black book of ufology

And the great Sea Serpent, with a sinuous grace, shakes its long mane of brown seaweed. As Andrew H. Rayner, first officer of the ship *Fort Salisbury,* testifies...

Date: October 28, 1902.

Location: South Atlantic, in the Gulf of Guinea. Maritime coordinates: latitude 5°31' South; longitude 4°42' West.

On this autumn day, *Fort Salisbury is* sailing peacefully on the waters of the South Atlantic. The sea was calm, the sky starry and the view clear. At 3:05 a.m., the watchman spotted a large, dark "object" on the starboard side of the ship, moving across the water. He immediately called his supervisor. Andrew H. Rayner climbed on deck and saw "a large object between 150 and 180 meters long. It has two distinct lights at the front, as bright as those of a boat. And it seems to be propelled by a mechanism, a kind of fin that agitates the water.

According to Andrew H. Rayner, as the object moves forward, it leaves a long trail of foam behind it. The eddies it causes are clearly audible. The water around the object took a phosphorescent tint. Rayner notices that the back of the object presents an irregular surface: it seems covered with scales! Then, slowly the oani dives and disappears in the depths of the ocean. Questioned by investigators, the captain of *Fort Salisbury* confides:

- All I can say is that Mr. Rayner is extremely serious. He did see, as well as the watchman and the helmsman, something in the water that was large as he could describe it.

Obviously, this meeting in the heart of the ocean fascinates the public. And the biologists of the time tried to pierce the mystery of this aquatic monster. For some, it was only a ship that was capsizing. But, after verification, no vessel of this size, and in this precise zone, was missing. We think of a cetacean, sperm whale or whale... but with two position lights? Unlikely! Some more daring cryptozoologists affirm that it must have been the frolicking of the mythical sea serpent. Only certainty: this "monster" has, with a skilful dive, carried its secret towards the black abyss.

Sources

Southland Times, NZ, issue 18038, January 7, 1903, p. 3 - *The Bunbury Herald,* January 12, 1903 - Jacques Vallée, *Anatomy Of A Phenomenom: UFO's In Space,*

Ballantine Books 1974, p. 17 - *Lumières dans la Nuit* n°100, June 1969, p. 6 - in *Un siècle d'atterrissages* by Jacques Vallée, case n°32.

THE SEA SERPENT.

Mr A. H. Rayner, second officer of the steamship Fort Salisbury (Bucknall line), which arrived recently at Plymouth from the Cape, sends the following to the *Daily Mail* :—

" Extract from the log of the second officer of the steamship Fort Salisbury : Oct. 28, 3.5 a.m.—Dark object, with long luminous trailing wake, thrown in relief by a phosphorescent sea, seen ahead, a little on starboard bow. Look-out reported two masthead lights ahead. These two lights, almost as bright as a steamer's lights, appeared to shine from two points in line on the upper surface of the dark mass Concluded dark mass was a whale and lights phosphorescent. On drawing nearer, dark mass and lights sank below the surface. Prepared to examine the wake in passing with binoculars.

The Bunbury Herald.

" Passed about forty to fifty yards on port side of wake, and discovered it was the scaled back of some huge monster slowly disappearing below the surface. The breadth of the body showing above water tapered from about 30ft. close abaft where the dark mass had appeared to about 5ft. at the extreme end visible. Length roughly about 500ft. to 600ft.

" Concluded that the dark mass first seen must have been the creature's head The swirl caused by the monster's progress could be distinctly heard, and a strong odour like that of a low-tide beach on a summer day pervaded the air. Twice along its length the disturbance of the water and a broadening of the surrounding belt of phosphorous indicated the presence of huge fins in motion below the surface."

The Bunbury Herald, January 12, 1903

Wheels of light

As early as the 1920s, some scientists dared to express themselves on "unexplained marine phenomena". In particular in the very serious *Marine Observer*, a British scholarly journal dedicated since 1924 to the observation of meteorological phenomena. A number of testimonies were accumulated in our seas and oceans reporting the observation of "luminous bars", "beams of projectors", "underwater projectors flashing by periods", "luminous wheels", "pulsating phosphorescent spots", "spinning rays" reported by seasoned sailors.

UFO. Are we in danger? The black book of ufology

For example, it is mentioned that on December 19, 1927, at 2:00 p.m., the ship *Arracan*, which had just left Rangoon and was sailing towards the west coast of Australia, found itself in an area "where spots of phosphorescent light were scattered on the surface of the sea. Strange, because these spots were organized in bands that rotated rapidly in an anti-clockwise direction. The sailors described it as a fireworks "sun" with the center about 200 meters from the ship.

At 2:05 a.m., the rays of this sun began to turn in the opposite direction. And the phenomenon stopped at 2:15 am.

It seems that some of these phenomena are of natural origin. They could be caused by the luminescence of planktonic organisms called noctiluca *scintillans*. For Richard Turner, a specialist in marine biology, it would be the intervention of a group of pressure waves of seismic origin that would give birth to these wheels of light. Earthquakes and phytoplankton, in a liquid vortex, would create these superb aquatic rounds. But algae and plankton do not explain everything. In some cases, neither of them can spring from the bottom of the ocean and propel themselves, in silent flights, towards the sky. They cannot emerge from seas of ice leaving a circular hole, proof then of a solidity hardly contestable.

Sources

Marine Observer, vol. 5, 1928, p. 245 - *Space Phenomena* #32, June 1972, pp. 15-19 - *Flying Saucer Review,* vol. 13, no. 5, September-October 1967, pp. 7-9 - *Lights in the Night* no. 406, March 2012, p. 25.

The Aleutian Islands oani

Date: summer 1945 (some ufologists place this observation more precisely in March).
Location: The Aleutian Islands, an archipelago of 300 volcanic islands located southwest of Alaska.

A surprising encounter for the crew of the military transport ship USAT *Delarof,* loaded with ammunition and equipment for Alaska! In *The Invisibles Under the Sea,* Ivan T. Sanderson recalls this spectacular episode during which 14 crew members saw a dark spherical object rise from the water:

The *Delarof* incident occurred in the summer of 1945 while Robert S. Crawford was serving on board as a military radio. Returning to Seattle, the ship was off Adak. The sun was about to set, and Crawford was standing on the port side, near the radio booth, when he heard crewmen shouting. He turned and saw a large round object that had just risen from the sea (several crewmen actually saw the oani appear under the sea, about a nautical mile from the *Delarof*). The unfamiliar craft, silhouetted darkly against the setting sun, climbed almost vertically for a few moments. Then it bent its flight to come horizontally and began to describe circles around the boat. All observers were convinced that it was a very large object. Comparing it to the width of a finger held at arm's length, Crawford estimated that it was between 45 and 75 meters in diameter. As it circled around the *Delarof*, the object was within range of its guns. But the sailors did not open fire, remaining alert for any sign of hostility. The oani circled the ship two or three times, in a regular and totally silent flight. All witnesses believed that it was self-propelled; otherwise the strong wind would have affected its movements. After several minutes, the flying object disappeared to the south or southwest. The crew then saw three flashes of light coming from the spot where it had disappeared.

Once ashore in Seattle, the 14 crew members who witnessed the incident wrote and signed a report. The main witness, Robert S. Crawford, who served as a radio operator on the *Delarof*, later became a consulting geologist at the Indiana Soil Testing Laboratory in Griffith. He then reported his observation to Professor N. N. Kohanowski of the Geological Survey, who was an advisor to NICAP (*National Investigations Committee on Aerial Phenomena), a* private U.S. UFO research association, which handled the case.

Sources

UFO Investigator, vol. IV, n°5, March 1968, p. 4 - *Lumières dans la Nuit* n°100, June 1969, p. 8 - case n°54 in *Un siècle d'atterrissages* by Jacques Vallée - *Beyond Reality* n°23, November-December 1976, p. 46 - Ivan T. Sanderson, *Invisible Residents*, Tandem, 1974, pp. 43-44 - French version : *Les Invisibles sous les Mers,* trans. France-Marie Watkins, Albin Michel, 1979 - Mack Maloney, *UFOs in Wartime: What They Didn't Want You To Know,* Mass Market Paperback, 2011 - *The UFO Musketeers Gazette* #58, June 28, 2018, p. 7.

UFO. Are we in danger? The black book of ufology

An oani on the screens

Date: 1947.

Location: Alaska.

American pilots have been talking about these oanis since the 1940s. One of the first documentaries to tackle the phenomenon head-on in earnest was entitled *Flying Saucers Are Real*. It was directed by Ed Hunt. Particularly interesting is the testimony of former Lieutenant Colonel Wendelle Stevens, then retired and since then passionate about ufology.

This veteran aviator was transferred in 1947 to Alaska. There, he collected testimonies of in-flight encounters of B-29 pilots with unknown circular objects. After 23 years of active service in the U.S. Air Force, this specialist in technical intelligence and aerial innovation *design* confides, on camera:

> My first memory is of the day one of the pilot teams came back and said:
> - We saw a bogey!
> That's how they referred to UFOs. This one was very high and flying at a high speed. The pilots tried to describe it, but it was going too fast, much faster than the planes we had.
> On average, I collected UFO sightings twice a month. Pilots were observing these circular flying objects from near or far, alone or in groups. I remember one team of pilots describing a UFO landing on the ice floe. Landing a plane on that ice was an exercise we were unable to perform. Other pilots told me that they saw a UFO moving underwater. Then it broke through the surface and flew away, heading straight up into the sky. None of our machines were capable, in 1947, of performing such feats.

Source

Flying Saucers Are Real, documentary by Ed Hunt, November 1979, produced by Marianne Chase for "A Group 1 Film".

Lt. Col. Wendelle Stevens on duty (left).
The same in 1979 (right).

A British oani

Date: 1er September 1957.

Location: Porthcawl coastline, County Glamorgan, Wales, United Kingdom.

Here is a case where respectable English policemen were confronted with an unexplained maritime phenomenon. It is midnight. Two officers are patrolling along the coast. The night is quiet until they see a luminous, blood-red object, separated by a darker median line, rising from the sea. The police officers reported it to their superiors. And they did not hesitate to talk to local ufologists. Chief Inspector Reginald Jones, a member of the D Division of the Glamorgan Security Force, confirmed to the British magazine *Flying Saucer Review* that two of his men patrolling the seashore saw a strange phenomenon. At first, they thought they saw a burning ship on the skyline around Ilfracombe. But then a strange object rose from the waves and rose into the air like a "bloody sun". According to the two police officers, the object was much larger than the full moon.

Our two witnesses observed this phenomenon, speechless. The object remained motionless for a moment on the surface of the water. Then it took off and disappeared at a dizzying speed towards the open sea, in the direction of the Atlantic.

Inspector Jones said that a detailed report was prepared and sent to the highest authorities. A spokesman for the airborne military forces speculated that the two police officers were probably misled by a planet they mistook for a UFO.

- At certain times of the year, he said, Venus can fool many people. This is due to the particular weather conditions at the time.

The investigators of the *Flying Saucer Review* consulted the ephemeris and found that Venus, this evening of September 1[er] 1957, had disappeared behind the horizon one hour after sunset. The sun having set at 19:48, Venus disappeared at 20:48. The agents having observed the phenomenon at midnight, we can, in a formal way, discard the hypothesis of a mistake with this planet.

Since the witnesses were highly credible, the case was taken seriously. Especially since, disturbingly, many sightings of unidentified flying objects were reported at that time in the nearby town of Port Talbot.

Source

Flying Saucer Review, vol. 3, no. 6, November-December 1957, p. 9.

An oani scalps a palm tree!

Date: October 31, 1963.
Location: Iguape, southeast of Santos, São Paulo State, Brazil.

Rute de Souza is 8 years old. On this beautiful October day, like all the little girls of her age, she is busy playing near her house. Suddenly, she hears a humming noise coming from the sky and gradually gaining in intensity. Intrigued, she looks up and sees a plate-shaped object that is losing altitude and heading towards the Peropava, the nearby river. But surprise: after flying over the house, the UFO hits the top of a palm tree! It starts to wobble, to turn on itself, to swing in an alarming way. The little girl, stunned, sees this strange craft finish its race in the river, plunging not far from the opposite bank.

Rute rushes at once towards the house. She sees Elidia, her mother, who, alerted by the noise, runs towards the Peropava. Elidia is accompanied by uncle Raúl de Souza who was working 100 meters away and heard the sound of a collision.

Arriving at the river's edge, our three witnesses could not believe their eyes. At the place where the object crashed, the water boiled "as when one plunges a piece of incandescent iron in cold water" and a real eruption of mud and then of sludge sprang up from the depths.

Rute was not the only one to see this oani. On the opposite bank, several fishermen observed the object until it plunged into the water. Among them, a witness of Japanese origin, Tetsuo Ioshigawa. The man declared to the official investigators and to the journalists:

- This object had the shape of a basin. It measured between 7 and 8 meters in diameter. It had the appearance of polished aluminum. And it was flying 6 meters above the ground when it hit the palm tree.

All believe that the object was damaged as a result of its collision. This is also the feeling of the authorities. Professional divers have searched, with and without tanks, the muddy bottom of the river, which at this point reaches a depth of 5 meters. But they found nothing. Later, engineers combed the area with metal detectors. Also without success.

Sources

The APRO Bulletin, January 1964, pp. 1 and 2 - *Spacelink,* vol. 3, n°2, summer 1966, pp. 11-12 - *Inexplicado* n°56, 1982, p. 1104 - *The Australian UFO Bulletin,* September 1990, p. 14.

A Russian oani

Date: 1965.

Location: Atlantic Ocean.

Many unidentified submersible objects have been observed in the waters of the former Soviet Union. It is known that the files of the Russian Navy contain a lot of information concerning these oanis. Thanks to the ufologist Paul Stonehill, who has been conducting incessant research on the subject, some cases, previously kept secret, have been revealed to the public. The investigator reports in particular the disturbing testimony of a team of Soviet sailors on board a nuclear submarine. This case is extracted from the personal archives of Colonel Kolchin.

One evening in 1965, a Russian submarine cruises in the waters of the Atlantic. Its mission: to reach a ship in the open sea. As it arrived at the rendezvous with half an hour in advance, the submarine surfaced. And the captain allowed the soldiers to go up on deck to relax. No ship was in sight, the sky was clear and very starry.

Suddenly, the man on watch saw a cigar-shaped object at altitude, moving without a sound. As the submarine was in international waters, the Soviet sailors thought it was an American plane. The alarm was given. The submarine was about to dive. But the onboard radar did not pick up anything, so the captain suddenly changed his mind and kept the submarine on the surface. It was then that the UFO emitted three rays of light. The submariners could examine it in detail. Surprise: the strange airship has neither nacelle, nor rudder, nor aileron. With an estimated length of between 200 and 250 meters, it is therefore immense, and very different from the smaller American airships.

Then the UFO loses altitude. And, lights still on, dives in the ocean to disappear under the surface of waters. Whereas the oani gains the depths, the sonar of the submarine perceives a brief and piercing whistle, which stops abruptly.

All the sailors who witnessed this strange apparition were ordered to write a report with a sketch which they immediately gave to the Department of Naval Intelligence. It is not known what happened next.

Source

Paul Stonehill and Philip Mantle, *The Russian Roswell, Revelations on the Ufological Mysteries of the Soviet Union*, Present Time, 2015, pp. 322-323.

A Brazilian submersible

Date: July 30, 1967.

Location: open sea off the coast of Brazil, where the bottom is higher than 1000 meters. Maritime coordinates: L = 28° 48′ S and G = 46° 44′ W.

It is 6:15 pm. The Argentine liner *Naviero was* cruising peacefully 220 kilometers east of Cape Santa Marta Grande. Suddenly, the first officer Jorge Montoya saw something unusual on the port side. He immediately alerted Captain Julián Lucas Ardanza, who was having dinner. Gathered on the deck, the two men noticed that a submerged object, sailing between 3 and 5 meters deep, was following the boat.

This cigar-shaped object is about 30 meters long and 4 to 5 meters wide. It is completely silent. Its glare is white-yellowish. Its surface, completely smooth, does not present neither periscope, nor kiosk, nor footbridge, contrary to a conventional submarine. The oani will follow the *Naviero* during fifteen minutes, according to a parallel trajectory, standing at only 15 meters of distance from the ship. Sailing at a speed of about 25 knots (46 km/h), it produces no eddies or waves, which is unusual.

Suddenly, the craft accelerated, made a turn to port, dived and slid under the ship. It reappeared on the starboard side, at the level of hold 2, then plunged at high speed towards the shallow waters where the crew saw it disappear, leaving an intense light in its wake.

This oani will be described by the witnesses as "luminous", but in a singular way. Indeed, the emitted glow did not seem to be produced by position lights or projectors located on its hull. It seemed to come from "the whole surface"! In a telegram sent from the high seas to the Argentine National Maritime Prefecture, Captain Julián Lucas Ardanza specified that he should not have spoken of an "illuminated" object (*iluminado*) but rather of a luminous object (*luminoso*).

Concerning the general shape of the submersible, the logbook noted that its silhouette (*silueta*) was clear. When it turned 90° to pass under the cargo ship, no deformation of its rectilinear structure appeared. This excludes that it is a species of marine animal.

This sighting was widely reported by the Hispanic and South American press at the time. Captain Julián Lucas Ardanza gave several interviews where he affirmed that it could not be "neither a whale nor a submarine". For him, this oani "sailed", that is to say that its displacement was guided and intentional. For his part, the second captain Carlos Lasca described the object as "a submersible UFO equipped with its own lights".

Important detail: it was specified that the oani was detected by the onboard radar. After investigation, this case was classified by the Argentinean maritime authorities as "Unidentified Submersible Objects".

Sources

The APRO Bulletin, July-August 1967, p. 1 - *La Vanguardia*, Barcelona, 1er October 1967 - *La Voz del interior*, Buenos Aires, 3 August 1967 - *Flying Saucer Review*, vol. 14, n°2, March-April 1968, p. 22 - *Phénomènes Spatiaux*, GEPA, n°16, June 1968, pp. 13-14 - *Australian Flying Saucer* n°10, December 1969, p. 40 - which quotes *La Razón*, August 2, 1967 - *Phénomènes spatiaux*, GEPA, n°23, March 1970, p. 18 - *UFOs, un desafío a la ciencia* n°6, March-April 1975, p. 7 - *The Australian UFO Bulletin*, September 1990, pp. 12-13 - *Pix-People*, Sydney, 25 May 1985.

The oani of Cape Juby

Date: 1968.

Location: off the coast of North Africa, at the height of Cape Juby, near the volcanic island of Lanzarote, one of the seven main islands of the Canaries.

Our witness is named Auréliano Négrin Armas. He lives in Lanzarote, a Spanish island 80 kilometers long, nicknamed "the black pearl". And this is what he says:

I was fishing, about 10 kilometers from the coast, off La Caleta. It was a beautiful day, the water was calm, the morning looked excellent. Suddenly, at only about 50 meters above me, I saw a very fast flying object appearing, as if out of nowhere. It spun around, throwing long sparks of bright and changing colors. The object continued to lose altitude and, about 1.5 kilometers from where I was standing, it hit the sea at an angle and sank steeply. Not without emitting a dazzling flash. Its contact with the sea did not provoke any bubbling or steam emission - which would tend to indicate that the object, in spite of its great speed, was not hot. It did not emit any notable noise either.

I immediately started my small engine and, abandoning my fishing, I headed for the spot where the object had disappeared. I found absolutely nothing there, no wreckage, no foam, no trace of gasoline floating on the water, as would have been the case if an airplane had crashed into the water. I cruised around for over an hour, checking to see if any wreckage was coming to the surface - as is often the case when a boat or plane sinks in deep water. We can also see air bubbles coming up. But there, nothing! I then headed for the port of Arrecife where I reported my observation to the port captain. I never believed in flying saucers until now, but now I am shaken. I am even convinced that I witnessed the sinking of one of them...

The witness was described as "a middle-aged commercial sailor with a pilot's license who had traveled the world and was a good observer. His testimony puzzled local maritime authorities, who took it very seriously.

After his observation, Aureliano Negrin Armas contacted the Canary Islands Air Region and the civil airports of the archipelago. He was told that at that precise time no aircraft with a registered flight plan had flown over the area of Lanzarote. And that the radars have not detected any aircraft, even unidentified.

Sources

Phénomènes Spatiaux, GEPA, n°16, June 1968, pp. 14-15 - which quotes *La Flandre Libérale* of January 11, 1968.

A Vietnamese oani

Date: 1969.

Location: Pacific Ocean.

It is the middle of the Vietnam War. Ensign Will Miller is on duty on the *destroyer* USS *Leary* (DD-879). The ship is in the Gulf of Tonkin on a coastal bombing mission. Indeed, a *destroyer*, as its name suggests, is designed for naval gunfire.

As it approaches rural fishing areas, the crew on board must maneuver to avoid hitting the wooden boats of Vietnamese fishermen. The bows of these junks are equipped with lights that attract fish at night. And these boats drag long nets behind them.

Suddenly the lookout calls out:

- There, a light!

Will Miller rushes in. He sees a light gliding along the surface, diving under the waves and then heading rapidly towards the *destroyer*, 45 degrees from its bow. Miller can't believe his eyes when he sees it pass under the hull of the ship!

Alerted, the sailors rushed to the other side to see if this luminous object reappeared. But it had completely disappeared. The sonar, the surface radar and the ECM (electronic countermeasure detection system) did not detect or record anything.

- I don't know what it was, Miller will say, but it sure as hell wasn't a submarine.

The crew did not feel it necessary to wake the captain. But Miller reported the observation in the bridge log, which is customary on a warship when an unusual incident is witnessed. And the accounts in these logs are then compiled into an official report.

- Years later," Miller says, "I was given access to the archives of the U.S. Naval Historical Center. Strangely, on the date of our sighting, nothing was reported in the official record.

Source

Timothy Good, *Need To Know, UFOs, The Military and Intelligence,* Pan Books, 2007, pp. 284-285.

An Argentinean oani

Date: May 31, 1971.
Location: The coastline of Pinamar, in the province of Buenos Aires, Argentina.

In Latin America, the national press, unlike here, is never afraid to report sightings of UFOs or oanis. Here is a case treated by the daily newspaper *La Nación*. And which evokes a strange object emerging from the sea.

Zulema Bruno, a renowned psychologist, was driving along the coast of Pinamar when she saw a huge object swirling on its axis from the Atlantic. The object, which sprang from the waves, emitted powerful orange rays of light. Relatively flat, it had the shape of a plate.

Amazed, Zulema noticed that the object had started to follow her. It escorted her for 300 meters. Then, negotiating an acrobatic turn, it rose at a dizzying speed before disappearing in the sky.

Sources

La Nación, August 8, 1971, p. 9 - *Ovnis, un desafío a la ciencia,* March-April 1975, p. 8 - *The MUFON UFO Journal* n°130, September 1979, p. 5.

Argentinian illustration of the observation of Zulema Bruno

Norwegian Oanis

Date: November 1972.
Location: Sogne Fjord, Norway.

Closer to the pole, while searching the archives of Northern Europe, a large number of unknown submerged objects have been spotted swimming in the waters of Sweden and Norway. Here is a typical case.

During the autumn of 1972, and for nearly two weeks, the Norwegian Navy tracked down an oani in the Sogne Fjord, the largest fjord in the country, which is 205 kilometers long and 1,300 metres deep.

It all started between November 12 and 21, when several witnesses saw a shiny object moving in the fjord. As the presence of a Russian spy submarine was suspected, the Navy immediately dispatched 30 vessels to explore the water. No results were found.

On November 20, at 1:00 a.m., the submersible object was spotted on the north shore of the fjord, near the village of Kyrkjebo. 15 minutes later, five police officers spotted it on Kvamsoy, a small island located 50 kilometers from Kyrkjebo. A frigate launched a mine on the oani. Still without result.

The next day, during the night of November 21, in Hermansverk, four witnesses saw four "projectiles" emerging from the water, similar to silent red balls of light. In the afternoon, in order to get rid of the intruder, the army decided to fire an anti-submarine missile at this location. The blast was so powerful that it could send small boats 10 kilometers to the shore. Any conventional submarine would have been damaged or even destroyed. The Norwegian submersible object, however, vanished without a trace.

Sources

http://www.ufoevidence.org/documents/doc1713.htm%20/,

http://www.waterufo.net/item.php?id=430

A transalpine oani

Date: May 18, 1973.

Location: Lido dell'Aeronautica of Miliscola, in Bacoli, in the metropolitan city of Naples.

The Lido is a military beach frequented by thousands of visitors. But reminds the bathers that the rules issued by the armed forces are in force there. The main witness is named Carmine Arcucci. And here is his testimony, collected by the Italian magazine *Notiziario UFO* :

> After a walk, my partner Giovangiuseppe Lenci and I stopped by car near the Lido dell'Aeronautica of Miliscola (Naples) to admire, along the coast, the fireworks that were part of the night festivities. Suddenly, something very bright caught the attention of my friend, who turned his gaze towards the sea. We saw, at a distance of about 50 meters, at the height of the shore, a luminous object in the shape of a plate, topped by a dome. Both of us had the clear impression that the object had emerged from the waves near the beach. We are almost certain of it.

The oani rises then to 3 meters above the surface of water. Then, inclined of about 30° with respect to the horizon, it goes slowly towards the two witnesses. Giving way to the panic, Giovangiuseppe tries, several times, to make start the car.

Alas, without success. During these attempts, neither the lights of the dashboard nor the headlights light up. The two men, paralyzed with terror, can only look at this thing that is inexorably approaching them. Carmine Arcucci continues:

> The dome of the object emitted a white, intense and dazzling light, similar to that of a neon light. The underside of the oani, shaped like a tray, was metallic in color and luminescent. As he approached, we noticed a red light circling around the base of the dome, making the effect of a light band. Throughout this observation, my partner and I perceived an intense rhythmic noise, similar to that produced by a small fishing boat.

The oani takes nearly four minutes to cross the 50 meters that separate it from the car. Once close, hovering at 3 or 4 meters above the ground, the two men can estimate its diameter: between 8 and 10 meters. The object is then positioned above the vehicle. It lasted a few seconds but for the witnesses, "it seemed like an eternity". Then the light emitted by the object fades and the noise decreases. Carmine and Giovangiuseppe deduce that the intruder rose quickly, vertically, and disappeared. At that moment, they try to start the engine again. This time, the car starts without difficulty, and the witnesses can leave the place. Carmine will later confide:

> When the oani was very close, our hair stood up almost painfully, either because of the terror we felt or for some unknown reason. The hair on our legs, in part, broke through the fabric of our pants.
> The next day, my friend and I felt an unexplainable physical weakness. We attributed it to the emotion we had felt the day before. As for me, this violent emotion made my hair turn partially white overnight. The day before, it was quite black.

The investigation will note that the evening of the observation, the weather conditions were excellent. The sky was clear and starry. There was no wind, and the sea was calm.

Source
Notiziario UFO, vol. 2, n°2, February 1979, pp. 13-14.

An oani from Marseille

Date: November 15, 1975.

Location: Couronne lighthouse, near Marseille.

After the sardine, it is a local oani that has temporarily blocked the port of Massilia. Because the French coastline also has its share of amphibious UFOs!

16 h. In the company of sixteen technicians, including the lighthouse keeper, a lighthouse and beacon engineer takes a coffee break on the rocks. The weather is radiant, the sea is calm and the sky is of this incomparable Mediterranean blue, without the shadow of a cloud. It's time to relax and have fun. The jokes are flying and follow one another.

A few meters behind the men is a workshop-wagon in which a 100 W radio-light transmitting antenna is installed for some tests.

Suddenly, 200 meters from the shore, the water starts to bubble. The men looked on without understanding. It was then that, coming from the depths, a "silver disc of a rather impressive diameter" broke the surface then rose into the sky in large spirals, up to an altitude of 20 meters.

- The device was more or less 10 meters in diameter, explains the witness. The duration of the ascent of the disc was perhaps 5 seconds.

The oani remains stationary for 1 minute and a half. It oscillates slightly on itself. Then it suddenly takes the direction of the south, towards the open sea.

- It was difficult to estimate its speed when it moved away. But it was going faster than a jet plane. There was no flame, no noise, except the sound of water. It was AMAZING!"

Stunned, still unable to believe what they saw, the sixteen technicians gave their testimony to the official investigators. And our witness concluded:

- My tolerant presumptions were simply transformed into conviction, the day when (...) I had the honor and the pleasure of witnessing the particularly splashy takeoff of a flying saucer, apparently underwater.

Sources

Lumières dans la Nuit n°159, November 1976, p. 17 - Henri Julien and Michel Figuet, *OVNI en Provence,* Éditions de Haute Provence, 1993, pp. 147-148.

Oanis de Colares

In 1977, the island of Colares - located in the northeast of Brazil, in the delta of the Amazon River - was the scene of an invasion of UFOs that stalked and injured the inhabitants with light beams. As we have seen before, the Brazilian army went there. Between October 1977 and January 1978, intelligence agents and Air Force experts conducted an extremely thorough investigation under the name "Operation Prato" (plate or saucer). These men took nearly 500 photographs, mostly at night. They also shot several rolls of film in which one can see objects diving or rising from the sea.

The astrophysicist and investigator Jacques Vallée went there to conduct his own investigation. In his book *Confrontations*, he reports:

> It was in the islands around Belém, where the waters of the Tarantins and the Amazon meet majestically before they meet the ocean, one degree south of the Equator, that the Brazilian wave of 1977 reached a climax. (...) The UFOs appeared every night from the north. In some cases they came down from the sky, in others they emerged from the ocean. I saw a photo of one of these objects that had a white ring and that came out of the tumultuous waters, at nightfall.

Jacques Vallée does not seem at all surprised by the existence of such amphibious UFOs. In the same work, he specifies:

> It is important to note that such observations of submerged objects, although rare, are not inexistent in the ufological literature. For example, on September 27, 1978, at 6:40 p.m., two fishermen from Falcone (Piombino) in Italy saw, less than 50 meters from where they were, a luminous bell-shaped object that emerged from the sea with a metallic sound and flew away.

However, Jacques Vallée seems to have been impressed by these Brazilian submersibles. In 2006, he published a novel entitled *Stratagème*, a *thriller* in which two Brazilian oanis lead a strange sabbath.

Sources

Jacques Vallée, *Confrontations,* Robert Laffont, 1990, pp. 79-80 and 280 - Jacques Vallée, *Stratagème,* L'Archipel, 2006.

Russian Oanis

In January 1990, the same Jacques Vallée went to the Soviet Union, accompanied by the journalist Martine Castello, to meet with scientists, soldiers and witnesses. This in order to study the phenomenon behind the Iron Curtain. The two investigators published in 1992 a book (unfortunately not translated into French) entitled *UFO Chronicles of the Soviet Union: a Cosmic Samizdat.*

During their research, the two authors met Dr. Vladimir Azhazha, a Russian naval officer specializing in hydroacoustics and ship noise. In 1977, Vladimir Azhazha had been sent by Vice Admiral Y. V. Yvanov, head of the Naval Intelligence Bureau, to conduct research on "the hydrospheric aspects of the UFO phenomenon". For more than 10 years, he worked on this thorny problem. According to him:

> Too many incidents with UFOs have been reported. Their reality cannot be denied. Our real interest began when we tried to discover the exact nature of certain submerged objects that followed our submarines. Sometimes these UFOs even anticipated our maneuvers!
>
> At first we thought they were American submersibles. One day, one of these objects surfaced in a spectacular way. One of our icebreaking ships was making its way through the frozen Arctic Ocean when a very bright spherical object, rising from the depths, suddenly broke through the ice cap and rose vertically into the sky, literally dusting the ship with ice fragments. All the officers and sailors on deck could see it. It was impossible to deny its reality, given the large hole it left behind on the ice cap.

Source

Jacques Vallée and Martine Castello, *UFO Chronicles of the Soviet Union: a Cosmic Samizdat,* Ballantine, 1992, p. 28.

A Canadian oani

Date: October 4, 1967.

Location: Shag Harbour, a small fishing port on the south coast of Nova Scotia, Canada.

Inevitably quoted when the file of the unidentified submersibles is approached, here is without question the most famous oani of contemporary ufology.

Chris Styles, a 12-year-old boy, lives with his parents in a house on a hill in Dartmouth. From up there, the view of Halifax Harbour is breathtaking.

22 h. The evening is calm. In his room, Chris is practicing, stringing together a few chords on his guitar as best he can. Suddenly, while throwing an eye by the window, he sees in the sky a suspicious light. It was in fact "an orange luminous object, the color of metal heated at the forge". For Chris, it is a shock. He will say:

- I knew right away that this was not ordinary. It was something that was both familiar and foreign to me.

To get a better look at the phenomenon, Chris ran down the stairs and left the house, his grandfather's binoculars in hand. He ran across Prince Albert Road, past St. James Church and then Canal Street. There, he saw the object dive into the harbor. The strange craft remained on the surface for a while, drifting noiselessly on the water.

- It was an opaque sphere, devoid of visible external structures. Until then, I hadn't realized how huge it was. It must have measured between 15 and 20 meters in diameter!

Chris doesn't know yet how much this observation will change his life.

At the same time, Laurie Wickens, 18 years old, is driving on the National 3. Suddenly, he saw an object in the sky with four pulsating lights perfectly aligned. As it gradually loses altitude, Laurie attracts the attention of his passengers. The girls who accompanied him also saw this strange craft descending towards the port "at a moderate speed". Sometimes, it seems to slow down, glide, and then descend again. Laurie can't take her eyes off it. The waters of the harbor are 30 meters away from him on the left. He does his best not to leave the road that winds through this sleepy fishing village.

In the car, it is both anxiety and excitement. The young people are convinced that it is a plane in trouble. For them, the situation is serious. All the more so as this machine was heading straight for the port. A curtain of trees momentarily hid the object from the view of the witnesses, who then distinctly heard a whistling sound and then an explosion.

Once they reached a promontory where they had a clear view, they saw the object hit the surface of the ocean, 200 to 300 meters offshore. The object, very dark, sways on the water and then drifts, emitting a pale yellow light. Laurie thought that some of the passengers would need help. From a roadside pay phone, he reached the Royal Canadian Mounted Police office in Barrington Passage.

At first, Corporal Victor Werbicki is more than doubtful. The kids must have partied and had one too many drinks, he thinks. But he is soon inundated with calls reporting a plane crash in the harbor. They were all positive: an object about 20 meters long had crossed the sky in an easterly direction and then descended into the sea at high speed. The object finished its course in the waters of the harbour, producing a flash of light and a loud explosion.

The Royal Police immediately went to the scene. Indeed, a device was "floating" on the waters of the port. Assisted by local fishermen, the police tried in vain to reach it before it sank. To do so, they crossed a layer of floating foam, shiny and yellow, which gave off the smell of sulfur. Bubbles emerge from the depths and surround the boats. Unfortunately, the object has disappeared.

The search continued until 3:00 a.m., with no results. Later, the Department of National Defence dispatched a team of seven sailors to probe the seabed, again without success. Witnesses who thought they had seen a plane in distress crash into the waters of the harbour were taken aback. The hypothesis of an oani emerged, because the object that had dived seemed to have quietly drifted away into the depths without suffering any damage. The number and the quality of the witnesses (police officers, coast guards...) exclude the hypothesis of a hoax or an affabulation.

This night of October 4, 1967 will remain engraved in the memory of Shag Harbour for a long time. The young Chris Styles became a ufologist and devoted his time to tracking down these mysterious flying objects. He co-wrote two reference books on this particular case: *Dark Object* and *Impact To Contact*.

The authorities took the matter seriously. In 1978, the Canadian government declassified its private archives concerning UFOs. On October 29, 2007, 9500 federal documents were made public and posted on the web. These documents come from the Department of National Defence, the Department of Transport, the National Research Council and the Royal Canadian Mounted Police. Among the numerous UFO sightings reported, the "Shag Harbour case" remains the most emblematic. It is referred to as the "Canadian Roswell"!

Since then, the Shag Harbour UFO has become a national attraction. In 2008, the office of Canadian Heritage Minister Josée Verner stated, "This is a well-documented historical fact." On October 1er 2019, the country released a rectangular, fine silver, photoluminescent $20 coin. On one of its color sides, three fishermen aboard a boat stare at a ghostly image of a flying saucer crashing into the ocean. When a small ultraviolet lamp (supplied with the coin) is shone, the spaceship disappears but four orange lights remain in the sky. What corresponds to the testimonies of then. This coin, printed at 4000 copies, was sold out in a few hours.

Sources

The Chronicle-Herald, Halifax, October 7, 1967 - *Saucers, Space & Science* No. 49, Fall 1967, p. 11 - which quotes *The Cape Breton Post* of October 6, 7 and 9, 1967 and the *Toronto Daily Star* of October 12, 1967 - *The APRO Bulletin,* September-October 1967, p. 7 - *UFO Investigator,* Vol. IV, No. 5, March 1968, pp. 4-5 - Kevin D. Randle, *The Randle Report, UFOs In The '90s,* Evans and Company, 1997, pp. 1-10 - Don Ledger and Chris Styles, *Dark Object,* Dell, 2001 - *Province,* Vancouver, July 29, 2001 - *UFO Review* No. 5, October 2004, pp. 13-26 - *UFO* No. 128, Brazil, January 2008 - case illustrates cover - Chris Styles and Graham Simms, *Impact to Contact, The Shag Harbour Incident,* Arcadia House, 2013.

Vintage press (left). Detail of the commemorative coin (right)

An Iranian oani

Date: September 3, 1989.

Location: Sari, capital of Mazanderan province, located on the southern coast of the Caspian Sea, Iran.

A well-known chemist, who informed the British magazine *Flying Saucer Review,* reports that one of his employees was walking with some friends on one of the beaches of Sari. At 6:30 p.m., the group saw, 250 meters from the shore, a bright orange luminous object rising from the depths of the Caspian Sea. This object measured between 8 and 12 meters in diameter. The beach was until then very busy. The oani sowed such a panic there that the places emptied in a flash!

Terrified, the witness took refuge behind a tree. Thus hidden, he had time to observe this strange object for two minutes, before the object disappeared at a dizzying speed towards the northwest.

About fifty people who had come to bathe witnessed this amazing spectacle. The witness was then able to speak with some of them.

Sources

Flying Saucer Review, vol. 36, no. 4, 1991, p. 13 - Carl. W. Feindt, *UFOs and Water,* Xlibris, 2010, p. 16.

A Taiwanese oani

Date: January 27, 2012.
Location: Taiwan, an island located southeast of mainland China.

Here's what it says on *Taiwan News as of* February 1er 2012:

> The Taiwanese Navy said Monday that the unidentified object seen underwater near its base was neither a Chinese submarine nor a marine mammal.
>
> Let's review the facts: a newspaper reported that on January 27, during a military maneuver exercise, a helicopter spotted an illegal submarine in Taiwanese territorial waters near the Tsoying naval base. The Navy

immediately went to the scene and asked the submarine to identify itself. Without responding, the submarine fled the area. The press immediately assumed that the vessel was of Chinese origin, but the Taiwanese navy rejected this hypothesis, saying that their sonar had located an object that could in no way be a submersible.

On Monday, Lee Tung-Fang, commander of the 168ème Fleet, said the submarine did not dive quickly to escape detection. It merely quietly maintained its course at a speed of 2 miles per hour (3.7 km/h). The data also indicated to the Navy that this could not be a submarine, whale or dolphin, the commander revealed.

The 168ème Fleet was conducting a patrol off the eastern coast of Taiwan when it was called to the vicinity of Tsoying Base in Kaohsiung to participate in the submarine detection exercise. The Taiwan Strait area is a difficult terrain to spot submarines, the senior officer told reporters. He added that his unit has had several such experiences in detecting submerged objects that turn out not to be military submersibles.

Source

https://www.taiwannews.com.tw/en/news/1169954

OANI: an acronym in apnea

The above is a very partial inventory, compared to the numerous sightings of oanis around the world. No ocean, delta, sea, lake, river, estuary is spared. But what is the intrinsic nature of these amphibious "objects"? And what causes, what intelligences may be at work behind this apnea acronym?

In 1989, James Cameron's film *Abyss* proposed a *bankable* hypothesis: that of extraterrestrial vessels sheltering in the depths of the sea. If this supposition is telegenic, it is nonetheless hypothetical. From then on, everyone has their own hypothesis. Some people try to link the real world to the current data of science. Is this a mistake? Others imagine that they can perceive, in wonder, the presence of an elsewhere in a few sprays of water. This is not so bad.

The number of sightings of these phenomena acts as an alarm and prompts us to study. Even if we are groping, let us gather the clues and collect the facts. Let us continue to question our skies and oceans. It is a safe bet that the impossible of today will be the obvious of tomorrow. And that the solution is not always where we look for it. But where we often refuse to see it.

To go further

Ivan T. Sanderson, *Les Invisibles sous les mers*, Albin Michel, 1979 (a must read)

Carl W. Feindt, *UFOs and Water*, Xlibris 2010

Paul Stonehill and Philip Mantle, *The Russian Roswell, Revelations about the Ufological Mysteries of the Soviet Union*, Present Time, 2015

Sylvain Matisse, *OANI / OVNI, Enquête, méthode, réflexion*, Éditions Saint Martin, 2016

Paul Stonehill & Philip Mantle, *OANIS in Russia. Unidentified Aquatic Objects in Russian and International Waters*, Flying Disk France, 2020

Acknowledgements

A special thanks to Jacques Vallée for his listening and his benevolence. And Paola Harris for her friendship and trust.

Many thanks to Chloe, Richard, Colette and James. To Armande Altaï for being what she is, extremely precious. To Virginie, Nour and Fayçal Anseur. To Jean-Claude Moireau for his help, his infinite patience. To Yves Bacou, Hortense Dufour, Carlos Sottomayor, Audrey, Alain-Pierre, Elly, Kaiser-Sioux and Kalie.

Thanks also to Robert Dulbecco, always. To the Venant, Harfouche and Janoyer families. To Frank Istasse, Geneviève and Camille de Valensole, Ghislain and Loren, Seb Raoult, Jean Librero, Patrice Seray... as well as all those I forget but who count so much.

Thank you to my Didie, in spite of this indocile fog where we love each other by groping.

And, of course, infinite gratitude to Bob Bellanca and Jean-Charles Gérard.